1986

Boethian Apocalypse

STUDIES *in* MIDDLE ENGLISH VISION POETRY

By MICHAEL D. CHERNISS

PILGRIM BOOKS
NORMAN, OKLAHOMA

Library of Congress Cataloging-in-Publication Data

Cherniss, Michael D.
  Boethian apocalypse.

  Bibliography: p.
  Includes index.
    1. English poetry—Middle English, 1100–1500—History
and criticism.   2. Visions in literature.   3. Boethius,
d. 524—Influence.   4. Boethius, d. 524. De
consolatione philosophiae.   5. Apocalyptic literature—
History and criticism.   I. Title.
PR317.V58C4   1986   821'.1'09   86-17085
ISBN: 0-937664-71-5

To my parents, and to my other friends

CONTENTS

Boethian Apocalypse

PREFACE

T he initial idea for this book—that many of the best-known fourteenth- and fifteenth-century English vision poems belong to a definable genre which had been ultimately modeled upon Boethius's *Consolation of Philosophy*, and that our understanding of these poems could benefit from systematic study of them as related members of that genre—grew out of an investigation into Chaucer's *Book of the Duchess* which I undertook over a decade ago. At that time there were no extended studies which resembled, in generic point of view or in the nature of their subject matter, the one that I had in rather leisurely fashion decided to initiate. Progress has been slower and more intermittent than I had originally anticipated, however, and over the intervening years a few longer studies and a number of shorter ones that touch in a variety of ways upon either my major premises or my views about particular works have found their way into print. I have tried in my text and in footnotes to acknowledge my debts and major points of agreement and disagreements with these recent studies, as well as with earlier studies from which my work has benefited. If I have overlooked the contributions of some of my colleagues in the field of medieval literary study, I offer my embarrassed apologies here in advance.

I wish to thank collectively my colleagues and friends at the University of Kansas who over the years have supported and encouraged my efforts to bring this long project to its conclusion. I am grateful also to the University of Kansas Research Fund for several summer grants which enabled me to work upon portions of this book unencumbered by other duties. Finally, special thanks are due to Pam LeRow, whose word-processing skills and conscientiousness have made the final preparation of an often untidy manuscript virtually painless.

Boethian Apocalypse

If a few portions of this book seem vaguely familiar to some of my readers, that is either because I have tried out a few of my ideas upon them in person at various scholarly meetings, or else because a few sections have appeared elsewhere in print in different form. Articles on the *Roman de la Rose* that appeared in *Modern Language Quarterly*, volume 36 (1975), and in *Romance Notes*, volume 16 (1975), are incorporated into chapter 5. A large section of chapter 6 appeared as an article on the *Confessio Amantis* in *Res Publica Litterarum*, volume 1 (1978). Two articles on the *Book of the Duchess* from the *Journal of English and Germanic Philology*, volume 68 (1969), and *Papers on Language and Literature*, volume 8 (1972), now form parts of chapter 9.

Lawrence, Kansas   MICHAEL D. CHERNISS

Boethian Apocalypse

Part One   Boethian Apocalypse

1

INTRODUCTION

This book presents a series of interrelated studies of eight late-medieval visionary works which are profoundly, though not always obviously, influenced by Boethius's *Consolation of Philosophy*. The question of the influence of one literary work upon another is not always a simple one; some of the authors of the works dealt with here have certainly had direct contact with Boethius's great book, but others may have absorbed Boethian influences at one or more removes from their original source. Where one finds strong verbal or ideological echoes of the *Consolation* in one of these visions, he can be reasonably confident that the influence is direct from Boethius's Latin text or from some vernacular version of it. However, the primary criterion for determining the Boethian nature of the visions to be treated here is not one of specific content but rather one of formal structure, and the structural relationships among these various works are often highly complex and not immediately apparent. We shall be dealing with a formal model, an essentially poetic structural framework, which from a relatively simple, straightforward beginning grows intermittently more complex as it passes through the hands of some very sophisticated poets over the course of nearly a thousand years. I hope to demonstrate that this structural core, despite the innovations and devices which accrue about it and at times even obscure it, remains always central to the Boethian visionary tradition and distinguishes it from other, non-Boethian sorts of medieval vision.

The works to be considered here deal with sometimes complex, often interrelated philosophical ideas. These ideas are presented, defined, and explored by means of the dramatic portrayal of the interplay between a visionary-narrator who is the protagonist of the work and the figures—usually personified abstractions—and symbols which populate his visionary experience. I have grouped these works according to their apparent primary concerns as "Visions of Love and Nature" (chapters 4–7) and "Visions of Love, Loss, and Fortune" (chapters 8–11), but these groupings are partly a matter of logical convenience and should not be thought of as rigid categories. Various ideological concerns overlap these groupings, as do some concepts and concerns which are not reflected in the above titles, such as Philosophy (or Reason), Venus, and Cupid. As should become apparent, it is not the particular ideological content that characterizes the Boethian type of vision, but rather it is the way in which that content is presented to the reader.

The approach employed here can best be characterized as that of practical criticism. Each of the principal works receives a close critical analysis, which treats it as a coherent, unified literary artifact, capable of yielding meaning when placed within its historical context. I treat each work in essentially the same way, as the sequential record of the vision of a particular human narrator, in which a process of education or enlightenment unfolds itself. The readers, I think, are expected to observe the mind of the narrator as he traverses the course of his visionary experience, focusing upon what the narrator sees, hears, does, and understands, and at times upon the distances between the reader and narrator, together with whatever ironies such distances may generate. Practical questions concerning the reader—how he or she might be expected to respond to or understand the various narrators and their experiences—are often central to the analyses of the works both as individual artistic entities and as members of a definable generic tradition.

This book devotes only minimal attention to matters of literary theory. Its framework is that of genre study, but only in the limited sense that the form or structure, the "kind" of a given work, if recognized should alert a knowledgeable reader to the general nature of the work, the sort of conventions he may expect to find in it, and its general approach to its subject matter. The discussion of genre theory which concludes this introductory chapter is therefore necessarily brief and basic. By the same token, the discussion of allegory in chapter 3 is intended to be practical rather than theoretical; it is limited to the use of personification and symbolism and does not attempt to discuss in

Introduction

detail the various theories of allegorical reading and writing for which there is evidence in the late-classical and medieval periods.

Thus the purpose of this book is twofold. First, it attempts to define a medieval literary genre in dynamic terms, as it develops and at times is transformed over about a millennium. Second, it attempts to analyze the poetic strategies and in so doing shed light upon the intellectual and emotional content of some late-medieval works which employ the conventions and assumptions inherent in this genre. Much valuable scholarly and critical discussion has emerged and continues to emerge about these works, but attempts to ascertain the relationships among them, to gain an overview of them as members of a once vital literary tradition, have been largely inadequate. A sense that writers are consciously influenced by the works of their contemporaries, and consciously participate in literary traditions which they recognize and understand, doubtless exists, but this sense is often dissipated by the perfunctory and simplistic practices of lumping their works together as, in the case at hand, dream visions or love visions, or pointing out possible borrowings of isolated figures, incidents, and details. My purpose here is to show that this group of works — *The Book of the Duchess*, *Confessio Amantis*, and *The Kingis Quair* among them — coheres through its generic heritage and that the particular genre to which these works belong, a genre which I have christened "Boethian Apocalypse," can be defined with some degree of precision as to purpose and basic structure. The purposes and meanings of these works ought not to be sought for them in isolation from each other; if one views them in relationship to one another, he will be in a much better position to interpret them and to appreciate their individual accomplishments and shortcomings as works of art.

Genre study is scarcely a novel approach to literature, although its particular advantages may not always be apparent, especially when it degenerates into mere cataloging of features common to a number of works. René Wellek and Austin Warren years ago offered a still useful discussion of this approach to literature;[1] I need here only review a few basic principles. First, they suggest that genre may be conceived of "as a grouping of literary works based, theoretically, upon both outer form (specific meter or structure) and also upon inner form (attitude, tone, purpose — more crudely, subject and audience)." One or the other of these "forms" may be the basis of the genre, but the critic must discover both "to complete the diagram."[2] I shall follow these guidelines here: the "outer form," a basic structure which goes through various mutations while nevertheless remaining identifiable, will pro-

7

vide an initial, more or less objective criterion for identifying members of the genre. The "inner form," especially the apparent purpose of the work, will lead into considerations of the relation of structure and meaning, and ultimately to critical evaluation of the work.

It should be noted here that this sort of modern genre analysis differs in one essential respect from that practiced by the rhetoricians of late antiquity. As Francis Cairns explains in his study of generic composition in Classical poetry, ancient genres "are not classifications of literature in terms of form as are epic, lyric, elegy or epistle, but classifications in terms of content." For example, a *propemtikon*, the farewell to the departing traveler, whether an entire poem in itself or simply a passage in some larger work like an epic, would contain the specific "primary elements" of "someone departing, another person bidding him farewell, and a relationship of affection between the two, plus an appropriate setting. . . . it is only by recognizing these primary elements that an ancient audience could know to which genre a poem or speech belonged."[3] Thus, in our modern terms, the "inner form" was significant in determining genre; the "outer form" was not.

Wellek and Warren a bit later offer these cautionary remarks:

> Modern genre theory is, clearly, descriptive. It doesn't limit the number of possible kinds and doesn't prescribe rules to authors. . . . Instead of emphasizing the distinction between kind and kind, it is interested . . . in finding the common denominator of a kind, its shared literary devices and literary purpose.[4]

To this I must add that once one finds the "common denominator," once he understands how the "literary devices" should serve the "literary purpose," how, in short, the genre at its best works to convey meaning, then he can move from description to interpretation and evaluation. He will be able to decide whether any particular representative of the genre uses its basic form and conventions effectively, and whether it contributes anything to its tradition. This connection between description and evaluation is at least implicit in what follows:

> Men's pleasure in a literary work is compounded of the sense of novelty and the sense of recognition. . . . The totally familiar and repetitive pattern is boring; the totally novel form will be unintelligible — is indeed unthinkable. The genre represents, so to speak, a sum of aesthetic devices at hand, available to the writer and already intelligible to the reader. The good writer partly conforms to the genre as it exists, partly stretches it. By and large, great writers are rarely inventors of genres: Shakespeare and

Introduction

Racine, Molière and Jonson, Dickens and Dostoevsky enter into other men's labours.[5]

Finally, Wellek and Warren offer a partial justification, on historical grounds, for genre studies like the present one and suggest a starting point for it:

> One of the obvious values of genre study is precisely the fact that it calls attention to the internal development of literature, to what Henry Wells (in *New Poets from Old*, 1940) has called "literary genetics." Whatever the relations of literature to other realms of value, books are influenced by books; books imitate, parody, transform other books—not merely those which follow them in strict chronological succession. For the definition of modern genres one probably does best to start with a specific highly influential book or author, and look for the reverberations.[6]

If one strikes the word "modern" in the last sentence quoted, and I think this is obviously justifiable, the first step in this study should be evident: it requires a single work upon which to focus discussion, a generic touchstone which presents the genre in its basic form. That book is Boethius's *Consolation of Philosophy*.

That readers and writers of the Middle Ages greatly respected, and were influenced by, the *Consolation of Philosophy* scarcely needs demonstration in the wake of modern scholarship.[7] Its ideological "reverberations" are widespread and have been frequently recognized, although Boethian ideas become almost commonplace in the later Middle Ages, and therefore it is not always clear whether these "reverberations" in a given work come directly from the *Consolation* or from an intermediary of some sort. Its generic "reverberations," the influence of its form and purpose upon later medieval writers, have received very little attention—are indeed largely overlooked—and again this influence when it appears may be at one or more removes from its primary source, the *Consolation* itself. Nevertheless, as I hope to show, the *Consolation* is the most likely progenitor of the genre to which the later works under consideration belong, not only because of its enormous popularity and authority but also because of its often unique literary qualities. The *Consolation* is not the first example of a totally new literary genre; its form depends upon those of earlier works, from various generic traditions, which it combines in a new way. Thus it makes little difference here whether one considers the Boethian genre a new one, or rather a milestone in the development of an older one. If the latter, it realizes brilliantly the potentialities inherent in the earlier genre (or genres) Boethius knew, and in either case it contains the seeds of most later developments in its tradition.[8]

I am calling the genre of the *Consolation of Philosophy* "Boethian Apocalypse" to indicate its relationship to prior literary tradition, to suggest its unique position in that tradition, and, when applying the term to later works, to emphasize its central position in the tradition that descends from it. The importance of a number of earlier works, Judaeo-Christian as well as pagan, collectively known as apocalypses, in determining and identifying the genre of the *Consolation* has been clearly recognized since the appearance of Fredericus Klingner's important study of the work in 1921.[9] This particular class of literary works includes, in addition to the New Testament Revelation of John, the apocryphal Hebrew 4 Esdras (chaps. 3–14 of 2 Esdras in the official Apocrypha, 4 Ezra in the Vulgate), the Hermetic *Poimandres*, the Christian *Pastor* of Hermas, and the *Visio Sancti Pauli*, of which the *Poimandres* seems closest to the *Consolation* in its general type. As a generic term, however, "apocalypse" lacks the precision and clarity of, for example, "pastoral eclogue," or even that of "epic." The word is derived from the Greek *apocalypsis*, "uncovering," "revelation," and is in itself far too vague to suggest a particular literary genre, although it will do well enough as a descriptive term for the earlier works mentioned above. The real problem is that from very early in the Christian era it seems to have been associated specifically with the canonical Book of Revelation[10] and so has come in modern times to carry connotations of prophecy — especially of future eschatological events, of the end of the temporal world and the Christian Judgment — and of the use of a kind of symbolism hidden from all but the faithful. Thus the adjective "apocalyptic" and the noun "apocalypticism" refer not necessarily to visions or revelations but to an attitude toward historical events, an expectation or prediction of the end of the world.

The question whether apocalypse ought to be called a genre is arguable. The works mentioned most frequently as early apocalypses differ considerably among themselves in structure and content but resemble one another in their visionary nature, didactic purpose, use of frequently esoteric or obscure symbolism, and eschatological orientation. For scholars who deal with late Classical and Early Christian literature, the term certainly suggests a specific sort of work, if not exactly a genre. Robert Joly, in the introduction to his edition of the *Pastor* of Hermas, treats apocalypse as a genre and offers a useful list of its primary features:

> Apocalypse in that era had been for a long while a fairly well established literary genre, and not a specifically Christian one.

Introduction

One finds here the most typical conventions of this traditional genre, and this explains the secondary relationship which one can find between the *Pastor* and, for example, the hermetic texts: use of symbol and of vision, first-person narrative, a highly disproportionate dialogue between a loquacious instructor and a very unassuming student; the imposing or frightening appearance of the instructor, avowal of ignorance, insistence upon obtaining new revelations, remonstrances on the part of the instructor, and the charge to the student of an apostolic mission.[11]

The legitimacy of "apocalypse" as a generic term need not concern us here, since in any event "apocalypse" by itself is inadequate to describe the *Consolation*, which differs from earlier apocalypses in ways significant enough to put it into a class by itself. It partakes of features of a number of other kinds of literature, combining them in a new and unique way. F. J. E. Raby, largely for this reason, considers it a new type of literary work; he first quotes the words of E. K. Rand:[12]

> . . . "The work is an apocalypse of the general type of the Poemandres, but an apocalypse combined with Menippean satire, Stoic diatribe, and Platonic dialogue, with such a skill that like all great works of art it transcends the categories, and itself stands forth almost as a new literary type." [Rand] The type is new indeed, because the elements of which it is composed, derived as they are from the Hellenistic-Roman past, had never been combined before in such a fashion, and the apocalypse is the revelation of reason, and not of esoteric teaching given under a feigned seal of secrecy.[13]

Because the *Consolation* differs so significantly from its predecessors, I would argue that it, rather than any of the earlier apocalypses known to the later Middle Ages, provides the basic model for later works I would categorize as Boethian Apocalypses. It has a clear and definite, though relatively simple, dramatic structure (similar to the *Poimandres*); its purpose is essentially practical and secular; its concerns are therefore more attuned to life in this world than life in the next world (unlike any of the earlier apocalypses); and its method of presenting its argument is rational, straightforward, and systematic (as opposed to apocalypses that depend upon esoteric symbolism presented in mystical visions). In the following discussion of the *Consolation*, I will briefly review its primary philosophical ideas, and then examine its literary qualities, to provide a firm foundation upon which to base subsequent consideration of its Continental and English progeny. I must then return briefly to its generic antecedents to bring its uniqueness as well as its debts into proper focus.

11

2

THE CONSOLATION OF PHILOSOPHY

The philosophical content of Boethius's *Consolation* is familiar to every serious reader of medieval literature. The sources of his ideas have received extensive treatment elsewhere and are of little moment here.[1] The overriding concern of the work is the problem of reconciling humanity to life in a world which appears capricious and unjust. From this major problem spring the discussions which occupy Boethius and his consoler-guide, Philosophy. Boethius's personal misfortune, his fall from a position of public eminence and trust into imperial disfavor, exile, and imprisonment, triggers his awareness of this existential dilemma; the *Consolation* is the record of one man's struggle to come to terms by means of philosophy with the greatest calamity ever to befall him. If this problem were only personal, however, the *Consolation* would lay little claim upon the interest of succeeding generations. Boethius's problem is that of all human beings whose mundane lives are subject to the vicissitudes of events beyond their control: How can one best endure life in this temporal world? The answer comes to Boethius through the agency of rational analysis of his present situation and of his life in general. Boethius gains a new, profound insight into himself, an insight to which he has had access before but has been unable to pursue by himself, and which comprises a clearer perception of his relationship to the imperfect world and, ultimately, to the cosmos.

After an initial exposition of Boethius's misfortunes and of the existential questions about justice which these misfortunes raise, Philosophy analyzes his mental condition and leads him to reaffirm his belief in the government of the world not by chance but by God the Creator, from whom all things come (bk. 1). This is the first principle, upon which the (not necessarily Christian) philosophical discussion will be predicated. Philosophy then begins her analysis of human existence by considering the nature of Fortune and her gifts, that is, of the rewards one can receive in the temporal world. Fortune's primary characteristic is mutability; her gifts are the source of false happiness, for they are transitory and must be surrendered at death, if not before. The human soul, which is immortal, cannot benefit from such gifts, but, if it is virtuous, after death it is freed from this earthly prison and goes to Heaven, where it finds true happiness in its separation from earthly things (2, pr. 7).[2] Thus, by setting these worldly goods in a cosmic perspective, Boethius discovers that they are of no permanent value to him.

The devaluation of Fortune's gifts raises the question of the nature of the Supreme Good, which is defined as containing in itself all lesser goods, and the possession of which must therefore constitute true happiness. Discussion of the partial goods which men pursue, but which are insufficient for true happiness, leads to the conclusion that God, who is perfect and the source of human ideas of perfection, must be the Supreme Good and so also the source of perfect happiness. Men become happy by acquiring (or partaking in) divinity. God is absolutely good, and must therefore dispose everything according to the good; this leads to the corollary conclusion that evil does not really exist, since God, who can do all things, cannot do evil (bk. 3). Here, then, is the basic solution to Boethius's problem: a life of virtue (never clearly or completely defined, but apparently associated with the practice of wisdom and rectitude in public service; 1, pr. 4), which partakes of the divine essence, does not seek after the partial goods and fleeting happiness of the temporal world, and so brings one closer to the source of true happiness. Such a life is not subject to Fortune's fickleness because it seeks more lasting rewards. A few related problems remain to be solved, however.

Philosophy next considers the problem of apparent injustice in the world, asserting the existence of a just and beneficent Providence, which is present in the divine mind and governs all things. Providence is largely hidden from men, whose minds cannot understand the workings of the divine mind, but because it is conceived by God, it must be ultimately and perfectly just. Fate, the unfolding of Providence in the temporal world, may appear unjust, but this injustice is only apparent, not real, in its cosmic perspective. Thus, all fortune is ultimately good (bk. 4). Boethius's personal sense of victimization should give way to a sense of his misfortunes as part of a higher good, and, indeed, the *Consolation* is itself evidence of this phenomenon: his temporal suffering has resulted in his heightened understanding of the workings of the cosmos.

Finally, Philosophy considers the interrelated questions of the existence of chance, free will, foreknowledge, and necessity. These concepts bear directly upon the problem of whether one can in any real sense control the conduct of his life. Again, the resolution of a very complex set of existential problems is achieved through philosophical analysis, which attempts (although its success may be open to question) to set things in their cosmic perspective. Chance cannot exist in a universe governed by divine Providence. Man's free will to choose virtue or vice coexists with God's foreknowledge of future events, which imposes no necessity upon the course of those events. The apparent contradiction here is explained as the result of human inability to understand the simplicity of the divine mind, which exists outside of time, in an eternal present, and comprehends all events in time. With these last problems solved to Boethius's satisfaction, the *Consolation* ends with Philosophy's resounding affirmation of the existence of freedom and justice in the universe and her exhortation that men should live according to virtue, in expectation of rewards from the supreme Judge (bk. 5).

The purpose of the *Consolation* is essentially practical; it attempts to resolve philosophical problems pertaining to life in this world. The little theological material present — discussions of the nature of God and his Providence — is limited to that which provides a necessary foundation for inquiry into Boethius's existential problems, and it is discovered by a rational, philosophical methodology. While the work contains references to eternal rewards and punishments, Boethius refuses to discuss their precise nature. He offers consolation for the sufferings of temporal existence; he does not enter into the realm of eschatology. Throughout his admirable study of Boethius's life and thought, Henry Chadwick demonstrates the disjunction of faith and reason in Boethius's works. Chadwick argues convincingly that, "although he is a Christian, he wants to argue for providence exclusively on grounds of natural reason, deliberately setting aside any appeal to religious authority either in Christ or in the text of Scripture" in the *Consolation*:

> . . . in this profoundly religious book there is an evidently conscious refusal to say anything distinctly Christian. The book is a

15

work of natural, not of revealed, theology, and strives after a universal appeal to every man. Boethius' subject is the consolation not of theology but of philosophy. Throughout his life philosophy, and especially dialectic, has been the ruling passion of his mind. Now at the supreme crisis he asks what it may have to say to him, especially concerning providence and evil.[3]

For this reason the *Consolation* offers answers to its existential questions which are only provisional, not final. Life has not been outwardly transformed, and final answers are only hinted at. A medieval reader would have to supply from his Christian education not only guidelines for a specifically Christian life of virtue but also knowledge of divine revelation, which finally completes the *Consolation* by confirming its rational inferences and extending them into specifically Christian views concerning the afterlife. But nevertheless, Boethius treats problems central to human life, and his arguments were widely accepted in the Middle Ages. Thus it is almost inconceivable that essentially philosophical literary works like those with which we shall be dealing could not or would not be influenced by Boethius's great work.

Boethius's *Consolation* is presented as a dialogue; its structure is effectively dramatic. Rand calls it a "metaphysical drama."[4] To appreciate this dimension of the work, one must first consider its characters, the most important of whom is the narrator himself. This first-person narrator, who, because of the autobiographical information he supplies, must be recognized as the historical Boethius, functions as the consolee or, as Joly calls such a figure, the "privilégié" of the apocalypse. He is at once a "real" person, whose misfortunes engage the sympathy of the reader and whose occasional recalcitrance and obtuseness may amuse him, and by extension a kind of Everyman, a surrogate for all who suffer in similar circumstances or comparable mental states. He receives the philosophical instruction Boethius wishes to share with the rest of suffering humanity. He is the victim not only of unjust physical and political treatment but, in a more universally applicable way, of a philosophical dilemma which reduces him to a state of psychological confusion and impotence. He needs help to reconcile himself to the physical facts of his condition and to the nature of life in general. He must gain a valid perspective upon himself in relationship to the world around him.

In this process of reconciliation he appears as an active participant; the dramatic quality of the *Consolation* emerges from the interplay between Boethius and his consoler-instructress, Philosophy. He complains, prays, asks and answers questions; she badgers and rebukes, praises, prompts, asks and answers questions in turn. His restoration to psychic "health" appears as a process in which he progresses in marked stages from impotent despair over outward conditions to a positive, optimistic understanding of the whole of human life. Hence this process is in a profound sense educational; more accurately, it is a process of reeducation. Boethius already knows his consoler; she is his long-time "nurse" (1, pr. 3). He must already know the things she will again teach him. But clearly at the beginning of the book he is unable, because of the emotional impact of his misfortunes, to make practical use of the abstract, rational knowledge she had earlier taught him. He must with her guidance reassemble and reassess this knowledge in the new light of his personal experience. At the same time, it is his concrete experience which gives real, immediate meaning to this abstract knowledge. In this process of recovery and readjustment, Boethius is the central figure, the focus through whose mind the reader shares the experience of recovery and the accumulation of wisdom.

Boethius's consoler, the primary authority figure (Joly's "Révé-lateur") who guides him, is Lady Philosophy. Unlike the consolee-narrator, who must be a human being to engage the sympathy of, and function as surrogate for, the reader, she is the personification of an idea. This holds true no matter whether one interprets her as a force external to the narrator (e.g., the embodiment of true philosophical enquiry in general), or as an internal aspect of the consolee-narrator himself (e.g., his own rationally developed philosophy). Either way — and one can make a case for both positions — she in no way can be interpreted as a real person. She is, as Courcelle observes, perfect human wisdom, the highest achievement of human reason,[5] and as such she appears as a static character. Her personality does not change or develop in the course of the dialogue because she is throughout the perfect, ideal exemplar of what she represents.

Boethius properly subordinates all aspects of his presentation of Philosophy to her abstract identity. Her physical appearance, dress, and personality are emblematic of, and consistent with, her total meaning. She drives away the poetic Muses because they inhibit the rational activity she herself embodies (1, pr. 1). Her seemingly human anger and impatience with Boethius early in their dialogue reflect the initial disharmony between his self-indulgent frame of mind and her devotion to clear, dispassionate rationality. Also, her abstract identity limits her; she refers to the rewards and punishments of the afterlife but declines to discuss them (4, pr. 4), for the obvious reason that eschatology is beyond (or at least outside of) her carefully circumscribed area of competence. To have the embodiment of the fruits of human reason discourse upon matters appropriate to divine revelation would create an inconsistency that Boethius scrupulously avoids. Moreover, while her name tells us what to expect from her, it is her complete portrayal, from beginning to end, her limitations and omissions as well as the doctrine she presents, that truly defines Philosophy. She emerges as a self-defining figure, the sum total of all she says and does, no more and no less. For Boethius, philosophy successfully directed toward its highest task, the consolation and instruction of distressed humanity, *is* Lady Philosophy.

The Muses who inspire Boethius's complaint at the beginning of the *Consolation*, and whom Philosophy drives away (1, m. 1–pr. 1), are scarcely characters at all. Indeed, they appear to be a metaphor made momentarily concrete.[6] As characters, they do not speak in their own voices (except, perhaps, through the narrator), but they do make characteristically human gestures of shame as they leave Boethius's prison. They cannot represent all poetry, for Philosophy herself employs verse throughout the dialogue and even refers very early to her own personal Muses (1, pr. 1). Rather, as is clear from what Philosophy says of them, these Muses represent poetry of a particular kind, which she associates with emotional self-indulgence, and they are therefore inimical to the exercise of reason, and so to Philosophy herself.[7] They appear as something presently congenial to Boethius which she must supplant. In one of the few bits of symbolic action in the work, the primary personification drives away other personifications which oppose her, as a first step in gaining ascendancy over the human central figure. Their importance for us here lies in the fact that they are figures from Classical mythology who are employed with fairly specific symbolic meaning in a particular, limited context, a literary device we shall encounter in other works of this kind.

The goddess Fortuna is never quite present physically in the *Consolation*, yet as the personification of an extremely powerful force operative in the temporal world her influence assumes major proportions in Boethius's argument; Courcelle rightly calls her "the principal personage of books 2 and 3."[8] Philosophy impersonates Fortuna as a figure who speaks and acts; this portrayal is a rhetorical stratagem ("the sweet persuasion of rhetoric"; 2, pr. 1) used to convey in concrete form an important idea. Fortuna is thus a personification presented by a personification. Like Philosophy, she is static, incapable of development in a dramatic sense, and she has clearly defined limitations of thought and activity (in the administration of her gifts), and is self-defining. Her governing quality is mutability. Since Philosophy mediates between Fortuna and Boethius, however, her nature is illuminated by Philosophy's superior analytic abilities to a degree one could not expect were Fortuna presenting herself directly to the reader. Philosophy, the superior figure in Boethius's system of values, places Fortuna and her gifts in perspective for the consolee. By contrast, no figure in the *Consolation* is capable of performing such a critique upon, or defining the limits of, Philosophy herself.

Fortuna, like the Muses earlier, functions as a negative authority figure. She embodies an abstract idea which the consolee must learn either to ignore or to overcome. She does not lie about herself (she is not "false" in that sense), and so all the consolee requires is an accurate description of her nature and activities, a clear perception of her sphere of influence, in order to be safe from her. Recognition means victory over her power. Ultimately there is no point in objecting to her existence or activities; indeed, Boethius finally learns that her actions can be beneficial, when they are adverse (2, pr. 8). She exists as part of the cosmic order of things, and should be viewed in cosmic perspective, where her claims upon men are clearly subordinate to the higher claims of Philosophy and virtue. As a negative figure who in a sense educates the consolee just as does the positive authority figure, she opens the way for similarly negative figures in later works. Her role in the drama is therefore comparable in function to that of the Muses, whose influence Philosophy likewise helps Boethius overcome.

The "outer form" of the *Consolation*, its metrical form and its structure, calls somewhat less attention to itself than does the "inner form," the theme and purpose, contained within it. The "outer form" is, nevertheless, an integral part of the generic model and in large measure contributes to the effective presentation of its intellectual content. Boethius's use of the alternating prose and verse passages of Menippean satire has little if any influence upon the vernacular works which appear indebted generically to the *Consolation*, although this form does reappear in later Latin works influenced by either the *Consolation* or its probable formal model, Martianus Capella's *De nuptiis Philologiae et Mercurii*, or both. Boethius's prose carries forward the argument of the work; his verse passages, as Rand observes, "have something of the effect of the choruses in a Greek tragedy or the meditative passages in Lucretius. They give the reader an outlook, and a downwards look from the height to which he has climbed by the steep path of the argument."[9] The meters supply generalized summary and commentary upon the specific actions and observations of the prose sections; they have no real structural parallels in most later vernacular works. But Boethius's metrical form, specifically the presence of verse in the *Consolation*, may have been taken as a precedent of sorts for writing works of the same kind in verse. I see no way of confirming this admittedly speculative suggestion, but it is interesting to notice that the *Consolation* is probably the earliest of its particular type of apocalypse to use verse at all, and it certainly uses verse more extensively than any other early apocalypse. Whatever the influence (or lack of it) of Boethius's metrical form, his structure is extremely important to later works. Through the reappearance of this basic structure, and variations upon it, one can confirm the persistence of the Boethian genre, its conscious imitation by later writers.

Boethius begins the *Consolation* with a first-person metrical passage which he himself describes as a "complaint" (*querimoniam*; 1, pr. 1). While this twenty-two-line complaint says virtually nothing about the narrator's specific circumstances, it vividly and directly expresses his mental condition at the beginning of the drama (1, m. 1). By lamenting his grief and denouncing Fortune's treatment of him, he forces the reader to recognize that he is in a state of confusion, despair, and impotence and in severe need of help. The opening complaint will become one of the most stable elements of the Boethian Apocalypse; it engages the attention and sympathy of the reader for the as yet unexplained plight of the narrator, and in so doing it becomes a kind of signal to the medieval audience of the generic nature of the work it introduces. Its structural function, then, resembles that of the opening invocation of the epic; it raises a specific set of expectations about content and purpose for the work it introduces.

Almost immediately the authority figure, Philosophy, appears before the disconsolate narrator (1, pr. 1). His complaint has clearly precipitated her appearance, although he has not actually invoked any sort of aid. Indeed, his mental condition makes it unlikely that he could think clearly enough to know what sort of aid he needs at this juncture. No explicit reason is given for Philosophy's arrival at this moment of crisis. Since Boethius has not specifically invoked Philosophy, and since she does not suggest that she has been sent to him by some higher power, we can assume that her arrival at her own volition is meant to suggest that Boethius has been accustomed to turn to philosophy to solve his problems and to comfort him in distress. Boethius's experience is not presented, as are most such experiences, as a dream, but the references to his bed, where first the Muses and then Philosophy sit, suggest that he has been sleeping, as does Philosophy's diagnosis of his "illness" as a lethargy (*lethargum patitur*; 1, pr. 2), "a pathological urge to sleep."[10] Whether dream or waking vision, Philos-

She then begins to discuss the false felicity conferred by Fortune's gifts. Even public service, if directed toward the wrong goals, is of no lasting value (2, pr. 7). Only misfortune is truly beneficial to men (2, pr. 8).

Book 2 ends with Philosophy's song in praise of the love that sustains harmony in the universe ("Quod mundus stabili fide"; m. 8). This song recapitulates Philosophy's conclusions about good and bad fortune and looks forward to book 3; it also serves to elevate Boethius's spirits to a higher level at the beginning of book 3. He is eager to hear more:

> After a while I said, "You are the perfect comforter for weak spirits. I feel greatly refreshed by the strength of your ideas and the sweetness of your music; in fact, I think I may now be equal to the attacks for Fortune. And those remedies you spoke of earlier as being rather harsh—I not only do not fear them, I am quite eager to hear them."
>
> Philosophy answered, "I knew it when I saw you so engrossed, so attentive to what I was saying. I waited for you to achieve this state of mind, or, to put it more truly, I led you to it." [3, pr. 1]

Throughout book 3 Boethius takes a more active part in the dialogue than he had earlier. As his psychic health improves, he begins not only to pose but to answer questions himself and, generally speaking, to use his rational faculties again. It is he who, after the two of them have explored the nature of true happiness, suggests the most famous prayer in the *Consolation*, as a preliminary to seeking the source of such happiness:

> "But since, as Plato says in his *Timaeus*, we ought to implore divine help even in small things, what do you think is called for now if we are to gain access to the throne of the highest good?"
>
> "We must invoke the Father of all things without whose aid no beginning can be properly made."
>
> "You are right," said Philosophy, and she began to sing this song:
>
> "Oh God, Maker of heaven and earth, Who govern the world with eternal reason." [3, pr. 9–m. 9]

A bit later Philosophy returns to the question that had caused Boethius difficulty at the end of book 1 (1, pr. 6), but now Boethius is apparently capable of answering it, even though Philosophy, in accordance with her role as instructress, in fact answers it herself:

25

Boethian Apocalypse

Philosophy replied, "If you consider carefully the conclusions you have so far granted, you will quickly remember something else which you said a while ago that you did not know."

"What is that?"

"The way the world is governed," she said.

"I do remember confessing my ignorance about that," I answered, "and, even though I can now anticipate your answer, I want to hear it plainly from you." [3, pr. 12]

At the beginning of book 4 Boethius suggests that he is still afflicted by his former grief, but, as his question to Philosophy reveals, his primary concern is no longer his personal misfortunes but rather the paradoxical nature of earthly life, to which his consciousness of misfortune has led him: ". . . since there is a good governor of all things, how can there be evil, and how can it go unpunished" (4, pr. 1). That he can now formulate the question in this unemotional, rational manner indicates that he has attained a higher level of consciousness, at which self-awareness has replaced self-indulgence, and more general concerns have replaced merely personal ones. Philosophy recognizes the merit of his question and promises to lead him in thought to his heavenly home, where the resolution to the paradox is to be found (4, pr. 1–m. 1). She remarks that his health has improved enough that he can accompany her on this higher flight of their mental journey: "Your deduction is correct and indicates to your physician an improving state of health and resistance. But since I see that you are so quick to understand, I will condense my demonstration" (4, pr. 2). A bit later, in reply to further questions, she comments upon the difficulty of the answers she is about to advance:

Then she smiled a little and said, "You are asking about the greatest of all mysteries, one which can hardly be fully explained. . . . Among the many questions raised by this problem are these: the simplicity of Providence, the course of Fate, unforeseeable chance, divine knowledge and predestination, and free will. You yourself know how difficult these questions are, but since it is part of your medicine to know these things, I shall try to say something about them even though our time is short." [4, pr. 6]

From this point to the end of the *Consolation*, Philosophy's discourse elevates Boethius's mind to the contemplation of the divine mind, insofar as such contemplation can be achieved through the exercise of human reason unaided by suprarational revelation. In book 5

26

the human mind comes to perceive its direct relationship with the divine and in so doing attains the upper limit of its (and its in-structress's) capacity to comprehend ultimate truth:

"When the human mind knew the mind of God, did it know the whole and all its parts? Now the mind is shrouded in the clouds of the body, but it has not wholly forgotten itself; and, although it has lost its grasp of particulars, it still holds fast to the general truth. Therefore, whoever seeks the truth knows something: he is neither completely informed nor completely ignorant. He works with what he remembers of the highest truth, using what he saw on high in order to fill in the forgotten parts." [5, m. 3, lines 20–31]

The final meter of the *Consolation* again expresses the human capacity to discover divine truth, the capacity to which Boethius has finally been restored:

"The human race alone lifts its head to heaven and stands erect, despising the earth. Man's figure teaches, unless folly has bound you to the earth, that you who look upward with your head held high should also raise your soul to sublime things, lest while your body is raised above the earth, your mind should sink to the ground under its burden." [5, m. 5, lines 10–15]

The movement of the *Consolation* from relatively simple to highly complex ideas reflects Boethius's progress from confusion to mental clarity. He moves from his concrete personal experience through a general view of human experience in this world, to arrive finally at transcendental ideas and values which resolve rationally the problems and paradoxes encountered along the way. As Chadwick explains it, this movement is from diagnosis (1) through Stoic moralism (2–3, m. 9) to Platonic transcendence (3, m. 9–5).[12] At the end of the book he has reached the limits of Philosophy's powers; there is no leap into the realms of theology or eschatology. Boethius, the consolee, has been reconciled to human life; he can see himself in relationship to the cosmos and its creator, and this new view of himself should enable him to live out his temporal life. He knows how to live, even though nothing in the external circumstances of his life has changed. He must return from his mental journey to the life he left—this return is implicit in Philosophy's final exhortation—where he can write down the account of his journey for the benefit of other men who, like him, suffer the injustices of this world. The ending is affirmative but provisional; he has found reason for hope, but he has no guarantee that his temporal situation will ever be alleviated. He has received instruction for living, not a pardon.

Boethius's philosophical sources have received much more extensive attention than have his literary models. Klingner's brief discussion of the genre of the *Consolation* convincingly identifies it as an apocalypse, which has been ingeniously combined with several other literary genres,[13] a view accepted with little elaboration by Courcelle. Insofar as genre is concerned, then, the *Consolation* reveals both its continuity with literary tradition (in its use of the apocalypse form) and its originality (in combining this form with elements from other kinds of literary works). Since I am here trying to establish the position of the *Consolation* as the key work, the generic foundation, upon which a group of later works is constructed, it will be useful to consider briefly some of the antecedent apocalypses to place Boethius's work in its historical context and to further suggest ways in which it distinguishes itself from its predecessors.

Courcelle acknowledges Boethius's probable debt to Martianus Capella for the Menippean alternating verse and prose form of the *Consolation*. Chadwick agrees while also suggesting a very general conceptual affinity between the *Consolation* and the *De nuptiis Philologiae et Mercurii*, which "also describes a kind of intellectual pilgrimage ending in heaven." Likewise rejecting the Classical consolation as Boethius's immediate literary model, Courcelle follows Klingner in pointing out that by the end of the second century apocalypse had become an established genre, in favor with both Christians and pagans. He cites the hermetic *Poimandres* and the Christian *Pastor* of Hermas as examples of the genre in some ways similar to the *Consolation*. Finally, he points out what he considers to be striking similarities between the opening passages of the *Consolation* and the first book of the perhaps contemporary *Mythologiae* of Fulgentius, although he does not argue for direct borrowing upon either side.[14]

One cannot quarrel with the introduction of the *Poimandres* and the *Pastor* into a discussion of the literary sources of the *Consolation*. These works, as well as a few other early apocalypses, share similarities in structure and detail with Boethius's work; the *Poimandres* seems especially close to the *Consolation* in its basic structure, its unified quality and comprehensive scope, and its dramatic elements. But in spite of the similarities the *Consolation* differs profoundly from these apocalypses in that they make extensive use of esoteric, symbolic visionary materials, sometimes explicated in their texts and sometimes not, while the *Consolation* is composed almost exclusively of rational,

The Consolation of Philosophy

inherently practical dialogue. Any or all of the earlier apocalypses might conceivably have influenced Boethius, and he no doubt knew some of them, but no one of them could by itself have served as an immediate model for the *Consolation*.

Among the possible sources of inspiration for the *Consolation* certain works by Augustine have been suggested; two of these suggestions, by Edmund T. Silk and by Anna Crabbe, merit our attention here, if only to enforce a distinction which I wish to make between "inspiration" or "influence" on the one hand and formal or generic model on the other. Chadwick, throughout his book on Boethius, argues that, although Boethius sees a far greater disjunction between reason and faith than does Augustine, nevertheless there exists a harmonious relationship between both the Christianity and the Neoplatonic philosophy of the two men. Chadwick describes the *Consolation* as a work whose Platonic themes are accepted or anticipated in both early and mature works of Augustine.[15] Chadwick, however, is speaking of the ideological content of the *Consolation*; nowhere does he suggest that any particular work of Augustine provides a formal model or analogue for Boethius's work.

In 1939, Edmund T. Silk argued that in some respects the *Consolation* is a "sequel" to Augustine's *Dialogues* and *Soliloquia*,[16] but here we are dealing, in Silk's own words, more with "sources of inspiration" than with formal models.[17] The *Dialogues* share with the *Consolation* "the concept of Philosophy as the physician and guide of choice spirits in their quest of the *summum bonum*."[18] Silk concludes, however, that the "parallel extends no farther" than several concepts and narrative details which appear in both works.[19] The *Dialogues* are literary revisions of actual conversations and lack the formal unity of the *Consolation*, which, in Silk's view, "is, in effect, a sequel to the Dialogues.... the Dialogues suggested the [philosophical] project; Boethius executed it."[20] Silk goes on to suggest that the *Soliloquia* suggested to Boethius "a form for the sequel to take,"[21] that is, a dialogue between the protagonist and his Reason in which "Augustinus is a patient and . . . Ratio is his physician."[22] Silk may well be right concerning the general inspiration or the particular details which he discusses, but neither the *Dialogues* nor the *Soliloquia* offers an analogue for the *Consolation* in terms of formal structure or dramatic development.

More recently Anna Crabbe has addressed the "literary design" of the *Consolation* in light of Augustine's works.[23] Crabbe stipulates at the outset of her essay that the *Consolation* "parallels no genre precisely"[24] and then goes on to discuss certain aspects of its "main constituents, Greek philosophy, Roman philosophy and Latin poetry."[25] In the latter portion of her essay she argues that Boethius is in the *Consolation* both using and reacting against Augustine's view of the relation of poetry and philosophy in the *Dialogues* and his account of his conversion to continence in the *Confessions*. Finally, Crabbe suggests a general relationship between the *Consolation* and the *Confessions*. It is unnecessary to go into her argument in detail here. It should suffice to note that she begins by placing the two works together as the only Latin examples of early autobiography concerned more with spiritual than with temporal matters and then goes on to "suggest in what follows that Boethius was well aware that his *Consolatio* must inevitably challenge the *Confessions*, that he intended it to do so and that the similarities and contrasts between the two works give a clear insight into the very different mentalities of their respective authors, particularly with regard to their view of the appropriate relationship between man and God."[26] Crabbe's view of the *Consolation* as a sort of response to the *Confessions* is most provocative and deserves serious consideration, but clearly we are once again in the realm of "literary inspiration" rather than that of a formal structural or dramatic model.

The most elaborate and provocative recent attempt to place the *Consolation* securely within a single preexisting generic tradition is offered by F. Anne Payne in *Chaucer and Menippean Satire*.[27] Payne begins with a chapter in which she elaborates in considerable detail upon the description of the Menippean genre given by Northrop Frye, who places it among the forms of prose fiction and rechristens it "anatomy."[28] This genre or form, as Frye calls it, "deals less with people as such than with mental attitudes..., differs from the novel in its characterization, which is stylized rather than naturalistic, and presents people as mouthpieces of the ideas they represent."[29] Frye includes in this genre not only the satires of Lucian, Petronius, and Apuleius but also *Gulliver's Travels*, *Candide*, *Brave New World*, *Tristram Shandy*, and the *Consolation*, while Payne adds as examples *Gargantua and Pantagruel* and *Portnoy's Complaint*. The distinguishing mark of the genre, as Payne describes it, is that it "questions...not deviations from an ideal standard, but the possibility of ideal standards."[30] Its various conventions can appear in other sorts of works, but all Menippean satires display "the profound belief that no idea is capable of being validated," which "allows a consequent intellectual freedom of the highest order. The will is treated as free, and choice is the dominant factor, not only in human thought, but also in human action."[31]

Payne supplements Frye's description of Menippean satire with a list of fourteen "salient traits" of this genre provided by Mikhail Bakhtin in *Problems of Dostoevsky's Poetics*, to which she adds seven additional important traits of her own. Among these latter seven are a dialogue between "a know-it-all who is free of the restrictions and responsibilities faced by ordinary human beings" and a human interlocutor, an "endless quest" involving one of the characters, the embodiment of "the knowledge that man's unsuspendable freedom to think is his most elating gift and his most terrifying burden," and the absence of any "God" or unquestionable authority. All such traits are "related to the dominant concern of the satire, the satirization of the possibility of an acceptable norm."[32] In the dialogue structure "both characters are submitted to comic and ironic attack; . . . neither is allowed to have the final view of matters."[33] Within the main text selected traditional texts are treated in a parodic manner. The Menippean tradition makes frequent use of the journey and the symposium to establish a dialogical milieu, and from Martianus's *De nuptiis* onward it may include encyclopedic compendiums.

Even on the basis of this abbreviated summary, certain questions concerning the treatment of Menippean satire as a genre suggest themselves. First of all, one may wonder whether thinking of the sort of writing Payne (and Frye) describes as a "genre" or "form" is really very useful in practical critical terms. Its multifaceted quality and inclusive scope might lead a skeptic to think of it as a literary catchall in which to place any number of works which do not seem to belong in other categories. The prospect of being able to place most of the works with which we will be dealing here, at least some of the apocalypses mentioned earlier, many of the cosmological poems of the Middle Ages, and *Tristram Shandy*, into the same literary pigeonhole has its attractions, but perhaps the hole needs to be subdivided before it can tell us much of importance about the works it contains. The problem is one of categorization: terms like "poem" or "novel" or "apocalypse" are of limited usefulness as descriptive epithets; in sorting out genres one would like more precise and restrictive terms, which make clear what sorts of subjects, conventions, and so forth he might reasonably expect or not expect, terms like "pastoral eclogue," "picaresque novel" or, as I am arguing in this book, "Boethian Apocalypse."

Not only is the category Menippean satire an extremely broad one, it is, after all, also a very modern generic perception as described by Payne, constructed to encompass ancient, medieval, and modern works. One might justifiably balk at the notion that Chaucer, for example, would actually have perceived his own *Troilus*, *Knight's Tale* and *Nun's Priest's Tale* as being the same kind of works as the *Consola-*

tion, the *De nuptiis*, and Apuleius' *Golden Ass*, as does Payne, or that Chaucer's audience could readily identify these Chaucerian works with this specific generic tradition. In the last analysis, as Payne herself repeatedly points out, it is only an attitude, that of skepticism toward the ideas and ideals formulated by the human mind, that binds together all the disparate works which she calls Menippean satires. What Wellek and Warren call the "outer form," specific meter or structure, may or may not be shared by members of this genre. If one detects, or believes that he detects, this Menippean attitude in a given work, that is all that is necessary to label it a member of the genre, whether its apparent outer form be vision, romance, lyric, or whatever.

Even if we should grant Payne's premise that Menippean satire is an identifiable literary genre, there are, I think, very serious problems in the way of accepting her reading of the *Consolation* as a member of this genre. Earlier scholars have been content to call the *Consolation* a Menippean satire (among other things) on the basis of its "outer," prosimetric form alone, but Payne must make a much more elaborate case since her criteria are more elaborate. She presents the *Consolation* as a sort of bridge between the Greek Menippean satires of Lucian and the works of Chaucer which are the main subject of her study. The *Consolation* is for Chaucer a "privileged text" which "provides the world that the events of the poem call into question, intruding itself especially in the *Knight's Tale*, *Troilus and Criseyde*, and the *Nun's Priest's Tale*." But it has even greater kinship with these three works because it, like them, is a Menippean satire.[34] Apparently it is not absolutely necessary to Payne's reading of Chaucer's poems that the *Consolation* actually be a satirical work; it could just as easily provide from a nonsatirical context the orthodox medieval views which Chaucer's poems parody, but Payne believes otherwise. She admits that there are "startling superficial differences between the extant Menippean satires and the *Consolation*" but insists that these merely mask "underlying similarities" of "form."[35]

According to Payne, the mental journey of the *Consolation* is filled with irrelevant material, follows no inevitable sequence, and reaches no final goal.[36] Philosophy continually shifts her philosophical perspective, and the problems of Boethius's life in the temporal world are never resolved.[37] Boethius remains time-bound and unenlightened by Philosophy's discourses, while she is to be assessed ironically as a self-contradictory figure, "indifferent to mere temporal demands of logical consistency."[38] In short, since both Boethius and Philosophy are objects of irony, the *Consolation* satirizes the human desire to discover a utopian mode of life, to formulate adequate theories by which to live.

For the medieval writer, then, the *Consolation* "provided a brilliant, provisionally nonheretical model for containing, without necessarily espousing, the perception of the essential chaos of all matters in the universe."[39] In the dialogue Boethius "embodies the human awareness of the inescapability of chaos," while Philosophy embodies "the capacity to ignore it and concentrate on theoretical ways of thought which support the existence and possibility of escape, of a resting place where in freedom and light the power of superior thought transcends pedantry and tyranny (not, of course, chaos)."[40] Boethius achieves his lifetime task of reconciling Plato and Aristotle in the *Consolation* "through the imagining of an intellectual space large enough to contain whatever systems are put into it. What is listed under *A* does not invalidate or even disturb what is listed under *B*. It is the imagined world of the encyclopedist, not of a school, that we encounter in the resolution."[41]

Payne's is a most unusual reading of the *Consolation*, almost diametrically opposed as it is to virtually all previous commentaries, medieval as well as modern. Although she claims to deal with the "form" of the work, by that term she means "Menippean form," which is for her a matter of content, an ironic attitude which emerges from the clash of contradictory, irreconcilable ideas and arguments. Since this ironic attitude alone defines the genre of Menippean satire, it is not surprising to discover that she has found it in a work which she wishes to locate within that genre. But as my earlier discussions of the *Consolation* might suggest, I think that she is overzealous in discovering ironies and contradictions everywhere in the work. The ironies surrounding the figure of Boethius grow out of his confused mental state at the beginning of the visionary process and fade away as he absorbs Philosophy's medicine. Philosophy, it is true, is a limited figure, but not in the way Payne suggests; as pure rational thought, she is unable to provide certain kinds of transcendent, theological answers to Boethius's earthly problems, an inability that is consistent with her character. If one takes her seriously as the essence of pure rational philosophy, as, for example, do Courcelle and Chadwick, or as something like divine wisdom, as do many of the medieval commentators discussed by Courcelle,[42] then it is difficult to dismiss her arguments as incoherent and irrelevant or to argue that her course of instruction fails to reach its goal, not of resolution but of transcendence of the visionary's temporal problems. It is not possible here to take up Payne's discussion of the *Consolation*'s argument, its "form" as she calls it, point by point. Chadwick in a way does precisely that by demonstrating that the *Consolation* marks the culmination, not, as Payne seems to suggest, the rejection, of Boethius's lifelong devotion to rational philosophical study as it was pursued in his time. On the subjects of Neoplatonic ideals of mental ascent to a heavenly home, of transcendence of the temporal and corporeal, of cosmic harmony, and of the harmonizing of Stoic, Platonic, Aristotelian, and Augustinian ideas, Chadwick answers virtually all the questions raised by Payne concerning the coherence and seriousness of the *Consolation*'s argument and principal figures. That the *Consolation* shares with Menippean satire certain prominent traits is demonstrably true, but that it partakes of the ironic spirit that Payne demands of the genre appears highly doubtful.[43]

In all the discussions of Boethius's literary antecedents and analogues, one work, in itself quite popular and influential in the Middle Ages, Cicero's *Somnium Scipionis*, has been almost entirely overlooked.[44] This omission seems curious since the *Somnium* is closer to the *Consolation* in its structure, content, and purpose than has been hitherto noticed, and since Courcelle himself argues convincingly that Boethius had a copy of the *Somnium*, along with Macrobius's *Commentary*, before him when he was writing at least part of the *Consolation*.[45]

E. K. Rand calls attention to the common interests and attitudes which, as Romans, Boethius and Cicero share, observing that Boethius, "the last of the Romans," in various ways "declares himself the successor of Cicero."[46] In its purpose and general character, the *Consolation* closely resembles the quintessentially Roman *Somnium*, which one of its editors describes as "practical in character... an inspiration to humanity," a work intended "to instruct and inspire the young, to encourage citizens in the performance of their public duties, and to give comfort and solace to the aged and distressed."[47] Insofar as its purpose is public and, indeed, civic, and its character practical, the *Consolation*'s affinities are closer to this Ciceronian work than to the private, otherworldly visions of hermetic or Judeo-Christian apocalypses.

Boethius spent his mature life in the service of secular Rome, and, as Rand's description of him as "the first of the scholastics"[48] suggests, his intellect was more congenial to rational inquiry than to suprarational visionary experience. In the breadth and depth of its ideas the *Consolation* is surely a greater philosophical work than the *Somnium* (which is only a fragment), but nevertheless the two address similar questions and arrive at similar conclusions, and, as Courcelle has shown, Boethius adapted the central argument of the *Somnium* to his own larger argument.[49] Implicit in the *Somnium* is the question of how one should live his life in the temporal world, and Cicero's answer, like that of Boethius, emerges from a dialogue in which earthly values are placed in the perspective of eternity. Like Boethius, Cicero argues that the highest kind of life is lived in the pursuit of virtue, although his explicit characterization of the virtuous life as one of service to the state is at once more precise and more limited than Boethius's vague suggestions. Interestingly, the pagan *Somnium* offers more eschatological detail than the *Consolation* of the Christian Boethius, but Cicero's achievement is much the same: he employs a vision of cosmic truth to develop practical guidelines for living nobly and morally in this world.

The *Somnium* is an apocalypse and, although the otherworld is actually revealed to Scipio, it shares with the *Consolation* an essentially secular, philosophical character and a corresponding absence of overtly esoteric and symbolic elements. Structurally it resembles the *Consolation* at least as closely as the *Poimandres*, and more closely than any of the various well-known Judeo-Christian apocalypses. In its first-person narrative Scipio plays an active role in the dramatized story of his education by an authority figure, Africanus, who by virtue of his superior, otherworldly view of human life possesses knowledge otherwise unavailable to his pupil. Scipio in his vision gains through physical travel what Boethius gains through mental flight: a reliable perspective from which to view the vicissitudes of earthly existence. That Scipio's vision is explicitly a dream seems a minor difference; apocalyptic visions occur as dreams, waking visions, and mystical trances of an undefined sort. The setting of and apparent reason behind Scipio's vision are not quite as clearly related to the circumstances of the narrator as are those of the *Consolation*, but some suggestions of those relationships appear in the introduction Scipio supplies: he is in Africa in the service of Rome and is, as his deceased ancestor observes by predicting his illustrious future, at a crucial point in his public career, when he perhaps needs to be reminded of his duties and assured of the rewards that continued pursuit of the highest goals will bring him. Furthermore, Scipio himself accounts for his dream psychologically, in a way similar to what Boethius suggests about his vision of Philosophy: his long talk with Masinissa about the words and deeds of Africanus may have precipitated his dream of him (chap. 1).[50]

While not as pronounced as in the *Consolation*, the intellectual progress of the narrator functions in the (much shorter) *Somnium* as a structural and dramatic device; in this connection Cicero devotes some attention to Scipio's emotional reactions at various points in the narrative. Scipio at first apparently fails to recognize his guide, and upon recognition his reaction is one of fear, for which he is reproved. Such details in the *Somnium* contribute to an air of verisimilitude; when they reappear in the *Consolation*, they carry more complex suggestions concerning Boethius's psychological condition. Scipio's brief reunion with his father, Paulus, elicits his wish for immediate and permanent entry into the heavenly spheres, and he is reproved in much the same way and for essentially the same reason that Philosophy often reproves Boethius: his emotional response ignores larger considerations of the divine will and purpose (chap. 3). Africanus's main concern in the ensuing dialogue is to redirect Scipio's gaze, and thus his inner preoccupations, from the earth below to the heavens (chaps. 4–7). Like Boethius, Scipio has temporal values that inhibit his capacity to see life in terms of eternal values; conversion is finally achieved when Scipio affirms his desire to strive for heavenly rewards (chap. 8). The *Somnium* ends like the *Consolation* with the authority figure's final exhortation to the narrator to exercise his soul in the noblest achievements on earth, in hope of heavenly reward (chap. 9). Thus the *Somnium* depicts within a dramatic framework the process through which its central character is weaned away from false earthly concerns so that, given new insight into the workings of the cosmos, he can reformulate (or at least reaffirm) the goals of his temporal life.

I would suggest, then, that, while other apocalypses may have influenced Boethius's conception of the *Consolation* in various details, the *Somnium Scipionis* seems the most likely source of inspiration for the work as a whole—as a secular apocalypse which unites visionary experience, philosophical dialogue, and dramatic development of the central character. Boethius takes what are at times little more than suggestions in the *Somnium* and develops them into prominent features of a work of greater philosophical magnitude and greater dramatic and emotional impact. His literary originality consists largely in his having recognized and exploited the possibilities inherent in the apocalyptic vision for creating a philosophical work capable of conveying a secular, rational argument in genuinely dramatic, emotionally engaging form.

Boethius presents his philosophy within a fictional narrative framework and employs personifications rather than human authority figures like Africanus; he could find justification for such artistic liberties (if he felt that he needed it) not only in the practice of earlier writers of apocalypse and allegory but also in the theory offered by Macrobius's *Commentary* on the *Somnium*. In his introductory remarks Macrobius defends Cicero's use of a fictitious dream to convey philosophical truth (bk. 1, chap. 2). He argues that the *narratio fabulosa* is approved by philosophers of the stature of Plato and Cicero for presenting "a decent and dignified conception of holy truths, with respectable events and characters, . . . beneath a modest veil of allegory." Such fiction is appropriate for dealing with the (Neoplatonic) Soul, or the spirits of the upper and lower air, or gods in general, but not for "the Highest and Supreme of all gods," the Good and First Cause, or for the *nous*. Such divinities pass the bounds of speech and human comprehension, and can be treated only by the use of similies and analogies.[51] Boethius, to apply this theory to his own writing, might have had to reconcile Macrobius's Neoplatonic categories with his own Christianity, but this would hardly have been an obstacle to the greatest Christian Neoplatonist, especially since the *Consolation* is essentially a Neoplatonic work anyway. One could, I think, make a case for the *Consolation*'s adherence to Macrobius's strictures, although this would hardly be appropriate here.

Finally, it should be instructive to glance briefly at one other apocalypse, one which may be contemporary with the *Consolation*, Fulgentius's *Mythologiae*. I have argued that Boethius seizes upon a type of apocalypse as a potentially congenial form for his purposes and transforms it into a genre which later writers will find useful and appropriate for similar literary purposes. Fulgentius appropriates the same sort of apocalypse as his form for the *Mythologiae* and does virtually nothing with it. The *Mythologiae* appears to be a debased, mechanical derivative of the type of apocalyptic dialogue best represented by the *Poimandres*; the similarities pointed out by Courcelle between its opening and that of the *Consolation*[52] are superficial and suggest only that Boethius and Fulgentius knew earlier apocalypses in which nonhuman authority figures appear. More important, however, is that, unlike Boethius, Fulgentius fails to use his visionary framework for any organic literary purpose; the framework merely introduces, in a clumsy manner, the myths and interpretations which are his primary interest.

The prologue to book 1 of the *Mythologiae*, in which the narrator-author invokes the aid of the Muses and is subsequently confronted by the authority figure, Calliope, might have some sort of hidden allegorical meaning to relate it to what follows, but if it does, that meaning seems to me entirely obscure. The narrator appears troubled, but not by anything clearly related to his vision of Calliope or to the subject matter of his book. Calliope, as an authority figure, is initially "heavyhearted"[53] and seems fond of rebuking her pupil, but her motives for such behavior are never clear. The obvious explanation, I think, is that Fulgentius is familiar enough with the conventions of earlier apocalypses to copy the behavior of their visionary-narrators and guides as a decoration for his treatise but either cannot or does not care to justify in fictional terms the use of the machinery of apocalypse in his work. As Leslie Whitbread observes, the irony of having Calliope, who is ostensibly dictating the principal matter of the *Mythologiae*, explain away pagan myths seems lost upon Fulgentius.[54] Indeed, once Calliope has established herself, in the somewhat chaotic introductory section, as the author's source of inspiration and information, she disappears entirely from the narrative, and the visionary framework itself is forgotten. The dramatic possibilities of the apocalypse structure, exploited so successfully by Boethius, are totally unrealized here; the narrator and the authority figure play no part whatever in Fulgentius's presentation of his mythology.

Both the *Consolation* and the *Mythologiae* appear to derive their form from literary apocalypse; in the former Boethius brilliantly integrates form and content; in the latter form and content have little to do with one another and are in consequence entirely separable. The *Consolation* is a highly successful work of art; the *Mythologiae* is merely a compilation of stories, with commentary, masquerading as a single, unified literary production.

3

A NOTE ON ALLEGORY

oethian Apocalypse does not as a genre in any way demand the employment of allegory as a vehicle for communicating meaning, and I have avoided referring collectively to the works which compose the genre as "allegories" because I think the term as it is commonly used is often misleading, for reasons which should become apparent shortly. Nonetheless, medieval literature in general is filled with allegory of various kinds, and so it is perhaps inevitable that we should find the influence of this extremely popular mode of expression in at least some particular examples of the genre. Therefore, in discussing any given work in the Boethian genre, one must consider the possibility that it contains allegorical meaning or implications and deal with this possibility on the basis of the individual work.

Definitions and discussions of allegory, and its literary cousin, symbolism, in modern criticism are numerous, complex, and controversial; this is not the place to try to sort them out.[1] Even if one limits himself to a consideration of allegory as it was understood and practiced in the Middle Ages, the obstacles in the way of formulating clear, concise, and dependable critical principles for defining and dealing with it are formidable. Ideally, an understanding of what medieval allegory is and how it works should emerge from a thorough study of its theory and practice as it developed throughout the period.[2] The best we can do here, however, is to formulate a few provisional principles which will define our problems and guide us either through or, failing that, around them. What follows, then, makes no pretense to being an original contribution to the theory of medieval allegory; rather it is a distillation of insights from earlier critics, selected and modified for practical purposes.

For the sake of simplicity, we can start with Isidore of Seville's accepted medieval, rhetorical definition of *allegoria*: "Allegoria est alieniloquium. Aliud enim sonat, et aliud intellegitur."[3] This basic definition is still accepted by a recent theoretician of this "protean device," Angus Fletcher: "In the simplest terms, allegory says one thing and means another."[4] The obvious problem with this definition is that it is so simple and serviceable that it tends to be all-inclusive. It can apply to simple personification of abstract ideas, to metaphorical use of language, or to what we usually think of as symbolism, and it does not distinguish between entire works which mean something other than what they literally say and isolated passages in works where the literal action and statement dominate. Finally, it says nothing about polysemous meaning of the kind which medieval exegetes often discover in passages of Scripture—as, for example, the four "levels" enumerated in the Latin distich "Littera gesta docet, quid credas allegoria, / Moralis quid agas, quo tendas anagogia" ("The letter tells of the deeds, the allegory what one should believe, the moral level what one should do, the anagogical where one tends").[5] If we are to use the term "allegory" at all, and it seems virtually impossible to avoid it, we had best take care to use it as clearly and precisely as possible in any given context.

The approach suggested by Robert W. Frank should prove useful for the works which we will be considering. Frank argues that, when reading medieval allegory, one should distinguish between what he calls "personification-allegory" and "symbol-allegory." In symbol allegory, like the *Divine Comedy*, "characters and significant details are concrete and have a second meaning, that is, are *symbols*," while in personification allegory, like *Piers Plowman*, "characters and significant details are abstractions and have only one meaning, that is, are *personifications*."[6] Medieval writers often use both these kinds of allegory in the same piece of writing, but in practice it is easy enough for a reader to distinguish a personification from a symbol, and usually the problems which arise in properly interpreting symbols are solved in the text itself. Personification allegories use abstractions as though they were concrete substances and are thus closer to the literal than symbol allegories. In personification allegory characters are never allegorical, since they literally mean what their names say they mean; the actions in which they engage, however, may be allegorical. Frank states his method of reading the two kinds of allegory as follows:

A Note on Allegory

In symbol-allegory, the reader must make two interpretations before he can understand the "other" meaning of the narrative. He must interpret, first, the symbols, and, second, their pattern of relationship and activity. . . . In personification-allegory, on the other hand, the reader must make at most *one* translation to understand the allegory. He does not have to find a second meaning for the personifications in the allegory, for they have none. Their names . . . express their one and only meaning. What the reader must sometimes do is to find the second meaning for the pattern of relationship and activity in which the personifications are placed.[7]

In *The Consolation of Philosophy* one must first take up the larger question, whether it is as a whole "an allegory." If it is, according to the medieval definition with which we began, then it must mean something other than, or in addition to, what it literally says, and the reader must attempt to determine what its action and dialogue, taken as a whole, really represent. Of what, in short, is it an allegory? One faces immediate difficulties here because, as Northrop Frye points out, "all commentary is allegorical interpretation, an attaching of ideas to the structure of poetic imagery. The instant that any critic permits himself to make a genuine comment about a poem . . . he has begun to allegorize. Commentary thus looks at literature as, in its formal phase, a potential allegory of events and ideas."[8] Commentary by its very nature can turn a literary work into allegory simply by generalizing from what the work literally says. By suggesting that Boethius intends his personal experience as an example for other men in similar kinds of physical or mental distress, we turn him into an allegorical figure, an Everyman. But even though our suggestion may be right, we cannot, I think, assume that the possibility of discovering some sort of general meaning, beyond what is literally stated in a given text, is by itself sufficient justification for calling the text "allegory," especially when the discovery of this meaning must depend to some extent not upon what the text actually says but upon general implications which the commentator believes he can see behind it.

To quote Frye again:

> We have actual allegory when a poet explicitly indicates the relationship of his images to examples and precepts, and so tries to indicate how a commentary on him should proceed. A writer is being allegorical whenever it is clear that he is saying "by this I *also* (*allos*) mean that." If this seems to be done continuously, we may say, cautiously, that what he is writing "is" an allegory.[9]

41

Boethian Apocalypse

The practical question to be asked at the outset, then, of Boethius and of other writers whom we will consider is whether some "other" meaning is continuously intended and pointed toward by the writer in the work at hand, and the answer for the *Consolation*, I am convinced, is that it is not. Boethius means the *Consolation* to be read as a literal account of the process by which a particular human being, about whom specific biographical details are supplied, overcame his existential despair and learned to understand and accept his condition through the agency of philosophy. The literal level of the drama is of primary importance.

One can, with absolute justification, I believe, argue that Boethius intends that his reader apply the experience presented in the *Consolation* to himself and to others and that therefore "Boethius"-the-narrator *is* Everyman and that the work is in some way an "allegory" of the consolation available to all men through the proper application of their rational faculties. However accurate such conclusions may be, and however important this application of the literal text to humanity in general may be, so long as the literal level of the work as a whole holds a position of primacy for the reader in the act of reading, the work cannot properly be called an allegory. The act of generalizing ideas from a fictional (or nonfictional) narrative, or from "real life" for that matter, the act of interpretation, whatever the validity of the conclusions reached, cannot turn literal action and statement which is not intended as allegory into allegory; it can only allegorize it.

The *Consolation* does, however, contain isolated allegorical elements of the transparent kind which Frank calls personification allegory. Lady Philosophy, as we have observed, stands for an abstract idea — perfect, ideal philosophical inquiry. When this personification drives away the Muses, Boethius is resorting to allegorical action to communicate his meaning, and the reader must find the second meaning; he must interpret the literal statement in figurative terms to understand it properly. The reader does not have to interpret Philosophy, however. The meaning of the action depends only upon his understanding of the abstract ideas represented by the figures of Philosophy and the Muses, and their names tell us what they are. Some momentary confusion may arise from the slightly ambiguous nature of the Muses; they seem to be more symbolic figures than is Philosophy, but their meaning, and therefore the meaning of the episode, is clear enough from what Boethius and Philosophy say about them in the text itself. Fortuna is likewise a personification allegory; she stands for a particular abstract idea, and only her actions require interpretation. That both Philosophy and Fortuna interact with "real" human beings

A Note on Allegory

like Boethius, and that Philosophy interacts with more or less symbolic figures like the Muses, need not disturb us since, as Frank observes, personification allegory (and, we should add, symbol allegory as well) is an elastic form: "...all the characters in a personification-allegory need not be abstractions.... Personification of states of mind and of categories of objective reality, moral types, specific individuals—the reader must accept them all as characters and try to relate them to the theme which the writer is developing."[10]

While, as I have tried to show, the *Consolation* is probably not intended by Boethius to be read as an allegory—a work whose hidden, figurative meaning is as important as its literal, surface meaning and is necessary to the reader's understanding of the work as a whole—nevertheless, interpreters and adapters of the later Middle Ages often imposed explicitly Christian meanings upon Boethius's philosophical statements and in so doing resorted to allegorization. Lady Philosophy, for example, was commonly interpreted as Sophia, the divine wisdom of scriptural revelation. Courcelle's work on Boethius's interpreters amply demonstrates that Christian interpretations and allegorizations of the work made even the doctrinally questionable passages acceptable to most orthodox readers and, from Alcuin on, assured its success.[11]

In this regard we may consider for a moment a passage of general commentary which D. W. Robertson calls "perhaps the best introduction [aside from unpublished commentaries] to the work as it was understood in the later Middle Ages," Jean de Meun's Preface to his thirteenth-century French translation of the *Consolation*.[12] As Peter Dronke observes:

> Jean shows a new conception of the practical function of Boethius' work.... all things tend to their good, only mankind must choose their goods, must learn an intelligible good by way of sensible ones; yet many people lack the mind and judgment to achieve this—it is they who can be helped by Boethius' book. The emphasis is social rather than individual...for "Boethius loved the common profit very much."[13]

The didactic material, according to Meun, is presented allegorically:

> However, one who is elevated by intelligible goods endures fortune well and wisely and by such goods passes into blessed life. Therefore this man is divided into two parts, that is, into a man tormented and controlled by sensual passions and into a man divinely elevated by intelligible goods. And because philosophy

43

alone elevates us by the gift of God to intelligible goods, Boethius presents himself in the role of a man troubled, tormented and controlled by sensual passions and presents philosophy in the role of a man elevated and pursuing intelligible goods. Thus in the role of himself he reveals his sorrows and the causes which precipitate them, and in the role of philosophy he introduces the things which remove his sorrows and shows the consolation which rids him of them. And so this book is called The Book of the Consolation of Philosophy. So two persons are signified here, that is, the patient and the physician, because sorrow and infirmity of the heart on account of temporal goods are found in a man of weak and frail thought, but a man of noble and perfect understanding possesses the ability to console and strengthen himself against such sorrows. [14]

Meun has thus, in the course of offering explanatory comments on the *Consolation*, to a degree allegorized it. His interpretation of "Boethius" and "Philosophy" as two aspects of the historical Boethius is perhaps justified by the text itself, but when he goes on to suggest that they stand for "li malades et li mires" in general, he has imposed a "second meaning" (in Frank's phrase) upon figures which do not require such interpretation to be understood, and which do not by the manner of their presentation suggest clearly that they are what Meun says they are. Meun is, I think, guilty of creating what Rosamond Tuve calls "imposed allegory," of discovering meaning which is not justified by the images of the work as the author wrote it. Tuve offers two principles as safeguards against such misreading of allegory: (1) "if large portions of a work have to be covered with blotting paper while we read our meaning in what is left, we are abusing instead of using the images," and (2) "the principal drift *governs* the meanings attributable to the incidents borne upon the stream; the latter cannot take their own moral direction as they choose."[15] Meun's interpretation does not seem a very serious distortion of Boethius's text, but he does, I think, abuse the image of "Boethius" insofar as he ignores the development of the figure in the course of the work; Boethius could represent "li malades" at the beginning of the *Consolation*, but he could not do so at the end. And to interpret Philosophy as simply the positive aspect of a human being, the part of man raised up to seek intelligible goods, or as the spiritually "healthy" human being in general, is to ignore both her ideal nature and her limitations. Meun's brief allegorization in a way oversimplifies the figures in the *Consolation*.

Whatever the validity, or lack of it, of Meun's interpretation and

A Note on Allegory

amplification of the meaning of the *Consolation*, his Preface is important for our purposes here. His assumption of Boethius's desire to serve
"le commun profit," which we have likewise assumed earlier in our
discussion, is one which can be made for virtually all of the works in the
genre; the "malades" and "mires" in these philosophical works are
doubtless intended to reflect generally applicable truths for the benefit
of their readers. Equally important is the implication of Meun's
method of reading the *Consolation*; we shall have to remain aware of
the possibility that late-medieval Boethian Apocalypses may be influenced not only by Boethius's book but also by its Christian commentators. Since commentators for centuries tended to allegorize it, in part
if not as a whole, there is the distinct possibility that works modeled
upon it may, because of this allegorical tendency in reading, be
consciously intended as allegorical works, in ways in which Boethius
himself did not intend his own work to be allegorical.

In spite of the possibility that a given Boethian Apocalypse may be
allegorical (in more than the very general sense of its being open to
commentary which generalizes the meaning of its specific statements
and actions, and which broadens the scope of applicability of its
doctrines), and in spite of the persistence and popularity of allegory as
a way of writing about ideas throughout the Middle Ages, we will
discover that Boethian Apocalypse retains for the most part its emphasis upon the literal level of its narrative. When authors make use of
allegory, it is usually personification allegory, which functions as a
vehicle for the rational instruction and consolation of narrators who,
whatever their exemplary qualities, are necessarily to be taken as
literal, "real," human beings. We shall deal with allegorical figures
and actions in the particular works as the occasions present themselves
and as the interpretation and analysis of the work's structure dictates,
while attempting to avoid the pitfalls of imposing upon them figurative meanings which their authors did not intend.

Part Two   Visions of Love and Nature

4

DE PLANCTU NATURAE

T he *De planctu naturae* of Alanus de Insulis occupies an important place in the development of the Boethian genre and provides a good deal of the impetus toward its broad dissemination as a vehicle for the poetic treatment of philosophical ideas. Far from being a mere imitator of Boethius, Alanus has completely taken over the Boethian form to express his ideas about his own philosophical concerns. His originality resides in the freedom with which he uses the genre to treat matters new to it, while remaining clearly within the structural framework provided by the *Consolation* and developing various tendencies inherent in it.[1]

The outer form of the work clearly reveals Alanus's debt to Boethius's *Consolation* and leads Paul Piehler to observe that the *De planctu* "seems to be not merely influenced by [the *Consolation*] but even a conscious attempt to produce something in the same genre."[2] Marc-René Jung treats only the most superficial aspect of the outer form of the *De planctu*, its Menippean verse and prose passages, but even this aspect of the work places it in a tradition which was well established and carried with it assumptions about literary content:

> The *Liber de planctu naturae* is a prosimetric work. It thus places itself, not directly in the line of descent of menippean satires, but in that of Martianus Capella and of the *Consolation* of Boethius. In the twelfth century this literary form, which consists of a prose text interrupted by pieces of verse in various meters, had already

49

been restored to respectability, for example, in the *Liber de querimonia et conflictu carnis et animae* of Hildebert de Lavardin, in the *De eodem et diverso* of Adelard of Bath, or in the *De mundi universitate* of Bernard Silvestris. The reader of that time, coming upon the *De planctu naturae*, would be able instinctively, through the tradition of prosimetric works which he would recognize, to place the text; he could expect a philosophical-moral work in which allegorical fabulation would occupy a prominent place. And the reader could himself confirm that Alain de Lille had respected the tradition.[3]

The Menippean form of the *De planctu* announces to the reader a work in which the subject matter is learned and philosophical — the goddess Nature, her relationship to humanity and to the cosmos. Thus its subject matter complements that of the *Consolation*, which concerns itself with the effect of vice upon a virtuous man, by taking up as its central theme questions of the origins of vice and its place in the cosmic scheme of things.

The earlier portions of the *De planctu* clearly indicate its formal debt to the *Consolation*. It begins with a metrical complaint by its narrator-visionary, who sees "the decrees of Nature in abeyance" ("...sua Naturae uideo decreta silere")[4] and unnatural sexuality — especially homosexuality — flourishing. The language of this complaint is highly figurative, and Alanus's use of the figure of Venus, though much more elaborate, parallels Boethius's use of Fortune in his opening metrum (1, m. 1). At once there appears a marvelous and awesome female authority figure, who later identifies herself as the goddess Natura. Alanus's description of this as yet unnamed figure parallels the shorter description of Philosophy in the *Consolation* and includes the important detail of the goddess's torn garment, which, as in the *Consolation*, signifies human abuse of or deviation from the abstract principle which the authority figure embodies. Nature's allegorical appearance is supplemented by a bit of symbolic action: she draws pictures which though given life by her cannot remain permanently and fade away, leaving no vestiges behind (4.3–8). Although the narrator is himself overwhelmed at the sight of her, the rest of the created world rejoices at the arrival of the goddess.

When Nature leaves her chariot and approaches the narrator, he falls into an ecstasy ("in extasis"; 6.5) similar to the mute astonishment of Boethius (1, pr. 1), from which she must revive him. Like Philosophy, Nature rebukes the visionary for failing to recognize her immediately and laments the mental condition responsible for this failure.

De planctu naturae

Alanus remarks upon the imaginative source of Nature's voice and the archetypal quality of her words: "When she realised that I had been brought back to myself, she fashioned for me, by the image of a real voice, mental concepts and brought forth audibly what one might call archetypal words that had been preconceived ideally" (6.11–13). This attempt to rationalize the means of communication between an allegorized abstraction and a "real" person has no counterpart in Boethius; Alanus perhaps interpreted the discourse of the authority figure in the *Consolation* in a similar way.

While at the corresponding point in the *Consolation* Boethius recognizes Philosophy (1, pr. 3), in the *De planctu*, Nature describes herself, emphasizing her creative powers, the nature of the men she creates, the relationship of human nature to that of the universe, and her personal inferiority to God and inability to comprehend spiritual matters. Finally she states her name. Her words bring the narrator out of his stupor, just as Philosophy's wiping of Boethius's eyes clears his mind (*De pl.* 6; *CP* 1, pr. 2–m. 3). Alanus's narrator then asks his instructress the reason for her visit (*De pl.* 7; *CP* 1, pr. 3). While Philosophy arrives specifically to aid Boethius, Nature has come for a more general reason: Man has by his sexual irregularities disobeyed her laws, and she has come to admonish, accuse, and punish him, for only he among all her creatures violates these laws. His violations, like the philosophical abuses against Philosophy, account for the rents in her garments (*De pl.* 8; *CP* 1, pr. 3).

In response to the narrator's questioning, Nature accounts for human vice and irrationality, which are identical in her view, by telling him the fable of Venus's defection from her service and subsequent adultery. This fable, which seems to be Alanus's invention, places Venus, Cupid, Hymen, and the newly coined Antigamus and Jocus in a cosmic perspective and explains, in secular terms, the origin of human vice. After completing her fable, Nature extends its implications beyond specifically sexual vice by complaining about the other human vices, which have emerged in the aftermath of Venus's defection. This allegory parallels Philosophy's anatomy of Fortune in the *Consolation*: the authority figure makes use of personification allegory to explain, in terms comprehensible to the human understanding of the narrator, a phenomenon pervasive in the world.

The final portion of the *De planctu* bears little resemblance to the *Consolation*. When Nature has finished castigating human vice (15), Hymenaeus, Castitas, Temperantia, Largitas, and Humilitas arrive to share Nature's grief over human defection from their service. Nature promises them that, since she has not the power to eliminate human

51

vice, she will take vengeance upon its practitioners. She sends Hymen with a letter to Genius, her priest and "other self" ("sibi alteri"; 16.188), summoning him to anathematize offenders against her and her cohorts. After Hymen departs (18), Nature and Largitas discuss, and finally condemn, Largitas's stepchild, Prodigalitas. Genius then arrives, and Alanus describes him in some detail; his function, like Nature's, is described allegorically as the drawing of images which soon fade away, but his images are restricted exclusively to human figures. He is assisted by his daughter Veritas, and opposed by Falsitas. Nature and Genius greet one another with an embrace signifying spiritual affection. Genius then puts on his sacerdotal robes and pronounces an anathema upon sinful humanity. The narrator, who has not participated in the action or dialogue since Hymen's arrival, then observes his vision fading away, as he passes from the state of ecstasy.

This final section of the *De planctu*, with its introduction of new allegorical figures and symbolic action and its departure from the pattern of dialogue between authority figure and narrator appears to owe more to the allegories of Martianus Capella and Bernardus Silvestris than to the *Consolation*. Nevertheless, the *Consolation* must have provided the primary generic model for Alanus. The *De planctu* presents an extended discussion of abstract, philosophical matters by means of a dialogue between a disturbed visionary-narrator and an allegorical authority figure. Allegorical elements are subordinated to this dialogue, and a resolution of sorts to the problems raised is finally achieved. Alanus's primary contribution to the Boethian genre is that he augments Boethius's generally discursive approach to philosophical subject matter, in which allegory functions in a fairly simple way, with a more pervasive and complex kind of allegory, derived from non-Boethian cosmic allegories and thoroughly integrated into the fabric of his work.

Alanus draws his theoretical justification for his more extended use of allegory from Macrobius's *Commentary on the Dream of Scipio*, a work which, along with the *Somnium* itself, likewise influences the *Consolation*.[5] Macrobius's defense of the use of *narratio fabulosa* for philosophical purposes, mentioned earlier, provides justification for the form of the *De planctu*, just as it could for the *Consolation*, and in fact Alanus borrows directly from this defense. Nature, while describing her works, remarks that she covers the face of her power in *figurae* to preserve its mystery:

> In all these things the effects of my power shine forth to an extent greater than words can express. However, for many I have de-

52

cided to cloak my face in figures in order to protect my secret from being cheapened, lest, if I should grant them an intimate knowledge of myself, what at first had been held in honour by them because they lacked knowledge of it, should when known be regarded as of less value. For, as the well-known proverb attests: "The divulgation of what is private gives rise to contempt for it." [6.121–27]

The abstract "Nature" which Alanus's figure embodies in all its attributes appears to men under the diverse veils of the phenomena of what men see as particular aspects of "nature." Alanus is here following Macrobius, whose similar comments upon the variegated garments of Nature provide part of his justification for philosophers' use of fabulous narratives (*Comm.* 1.2; ed. Stahl, pp. 86–87). In the *De planctu*, Alanus reverses this process; he presents Nature herself, the goddess behind the veils of natural phenomena, but in Macrobian terms he is still employing a fabulous narrative by representing a being which has no discrete physical form as if it had such form.[6]

In prose 4 the narrator inquires about the unnatural sexual behavior attributed to the gods, and Nature rebukes him for giving credence "to the poets' shadowy figments" (8.125). In the account of the relationship of poetry and truth which follows, Alanus again draws heavily upon Macrobius's discussion of *narratio fabulosa*. Nature first speaks of poetic fancies as a childish kind of learning which should be eradicated by the higher understanding of philosophy: "Do not a reappraisal from more profound discernment and a more advanced treatment by philosophy erase what has been learned in the childhood cradles of poetic teaching?" (8.126–28). Her remark suggests the class of fables which Macrobius says are intended only to gratify the ear, fables which "a philosophical treatise avoids and relegates to children's nurseries" (ed. Stahl, p. 84). She then mentions poets' cloaking of falsehood in credible garb to teach dishonorable ideas: "Or, how they cover falsehood with a kind of imitation of probability so that, by a presentation of precedents, they may seal the minds of men with a stamp from the anvil of false compliance" (8.131–33). This kind of poetry corresponds to the class of *narratio fabulosa* which treats "matters that are base and unworthy of divinities and are monstrosities of some sort," as is clear from the fact that Alanus's narrator has cited fables of this kind which deal with sexual irregularities, just as does Macrobius (ed. Stahl, p. 85). Finally, Nature speaks of poetry which, though false in its exterior, contains within it a kernel of truth: ". . . the poetic lyre gives a false note on the outer bark of the composition but within tells the listeners a secret of deeper significance so that when the outer shell of falsehood has been discarded the reader finds the sweeter kernel of truth hidden within" (8.133–36). This is the kind of fable approved by Macrobius, "a decent and dignified conception of holy truths, with respectable events and characters, . . . presented beneath a modest veil of allegory" (ed. Stahl, p. 85). This passage in Alanus in some measure serves to justify Nature's fable of Venus, which follows shortly after it (although Venus's conduct there is scarcely "respectable"), and in a larger context justifies Alanus's allegorical approach to philosophical truth as well.

In Nature's reticence toward theological matters and toward the Creator himself (pr. 3), Alanus follows Macrobius's dictum concerning matters inappropriate to fable: the Supreme God and Mind cannot be treated in fable but other, lesser, gods — Venus and Nature, for example, in the *De planctu* — can and should be so treated (ed. Stahl, pp. 85–86).[7] It seems then, that Alanus draws theoretical justification for his visionary work from a source with which Boethius himself was familiar and could have used for similar justification, while drawing upon Boethius's own masterpiece for his external form.

If Alanus modeled the outer form of the *De planctu* on Boethius's *Consolation*, and if the outer form of a work alerts the reader to what he should expect of its inner form — its content, audience, and subject matter — then we should expect the inner form of the *De planctu* to bear some relationship to that of the *Consolation*. On the simplest level both works deal philosophically with matters crucial to human life, and although their subjects differ, their ultimate purposes are similar. Each narrator begins from a view of the temporal world as being manifestly imperfect, and therefore personally disturbing. Boethius formulates the problem as one of justice and injustice, Alanus as one of natural and unnatural behavior. Boethius places worldly injustice and misfortune in a cosmic perspective in which they are perceived to be aspects of a higher good. From this perspective man rationally chooses good and virtue and avoids vice. Alanus likewise places his problem in a larger perspective, that of Nature and, ultimately, the divine order of the cosmos. He agrees with Boethius in identifying vicious behavior as irrational and associates rational behavior with what is natural.[8] Alanus's formulation of his initial problem, however, is finally less tractable than that of Boethius. Injustice may be a function of inadequate human knowledge, but unnatural vice, viewed within the epistemological limits Alanus imposes upon both his narrator and Nature herself, actually exists and cannot, within the confines of the *De planctu*, be assimilated into a perspective which

54

eliminates it as a problem. Both works attempt to expand the perspective from which one can view temporal phenomena and thereby point toward a fuller understanding of such phenomena, but Alanus's work seems less satisfactory in its resolution of its central problem.

Boethius's purpose in the *Consolation* is essentially practical; it is intended to provide a guide to the conduct of life in the temporal world. Whether Alanus has similar intentions in the *De planctu* is a question, the answer to which depends upon how one interprets its argument, and recent discussions have tended to emphasize its problematical philosophy and its theological implications, while playing down its practically instructive qualities. We shall consider this question at greater length a bit later on, but I shall anticipate my argument to assert here that, insofar as the doctrine presented in the *De planctu* suggests that men should practice certain virtues and avoid their corresponding vices, its purpose is at least partly to instruct one in the conduct of his temporal life.

Alanus's approach to his philosophical subject matter is essentially orderly and rational, not mystical. He relies much more heavily upon figurative language (especially metaphor) and allegorical fable than does Boethius, but his presentation seldom leaves any doubt about the meanings he wishes to convey by the use of such devices within their particular contexts. Alanus is careful to define the terms in which his figures of speech and thought are to be understood. For example, in describing the figures depicted on Nature's garments, he observes that the animals only seem to be alive — they live, so to speak, "allegorically," in pictures, and seem "literal," real ("These living things, although they had there a kind of figurative existence, nevertheless seemed to live there in the literal sense"; 2.193–95). The frequent laboring and grammatical metaphors for sexual activities are transparent enough to need no glossing. Finally, when introducing her fable of Venus's adultery, Nature speaks about the language she will be using, warning the narrator (and the reader) that she is moving to a different sort of discourse, presumably unlike the direct discourse she has used so far:

> As I am to begin from roots quite deep and wish to arrange the sequence of my narrative in a style above average, I first of all refuse to explain my theme on the plain of plain words or to vulgarise the vulgar with vulgar neologisms, but choose to gild things immodest with golden trappings of modest words and to clothe them with the varied colours of graceful diction. [8.182–86]

Here, as throughout the vision, Macrobius's justification of fable hovers in the background; cosmic truth is accommodated to merely human understanding. Alanus's ideas are not always simple, but they are neither esoteric nor clothed in obscure symbolism.

The doctrine Alanus presents is secular, like that of the *Consolation*; eschatology is never discussed, and theology is avoided. Given the limitations of the figures involved, the *De planctu* can deal with matters related to the created world only from a nonreligious, "natural" point of view.[9] To take the most controversial example, Nature's fable of Venus's defection from her laws almost inevitably calls to mind the parallel event in sacred history, the fall of man from divine grace. But Venus's fall is not an allegory of that other fall; rather, it is a fable that explains in secular terms a basic defect in humanity, a "natural" explanation of human sinfulness. Green rightly observes that "this is *narratio fabulosa* and it deals specifically with man's fall from virtue, not from grace."[10] Alanus neither glosses this fable in such a way as to connect it with sacred history, which for the medieval Christian subsumes mere "natural" history, nor allegorizes it as an account of the birth of theological *cupiditas* in the individual soul. He, like Boethius, excludes from his text specifically Christian doctrine. The medieval reader may have provided a Christian gloss to the *Consolation* and the *De planctu* as he read them, and Alanus may even want his reader to place the philosophical matter of his work in a Christian context, but he does not himself make this context explicit. In the Middle Ages any piece of secular literature could find a place in the larger Christian context which dominated the minds of educated readers, but obviously this does not mean that every piece of literature is, in a narrow sense, religious literature.

The actors in the *De planctu*, in their representation and in their functions in the drama, resemble those in the *Consolation*. Like Boethius, Alanus's narrator receives a vision, which he describes in the first person. Alanus is more specific concerning the nature of this vision; it comes in an "ecstasy," which fades away when the vision ends. The reader does not know this, however, until the very end of the work;[11] he cannot as he reads be certain of the precise physical state of the narrator. The narrator first alludes to his ecstatic state at the beginning of prose 3,[12] immediately before Nature begins speaking. One might read everything up to this point as a figurative account of the narrator's self-immersion in the natural world and thereby assume that the vision of Nature as authority figure begins with his falling into ecstasy and being revived by her,[13] but such a reading is difficult to reconcile with Alanus's treatment of Nature from the beginning as a personification. He simply does not differentiate "real" observation of nature from visionary confrontation with its essence, "Nature," or ecstasy from the waking state. This ambiguity surrounding the narrator's condition is thus similar to that which we observed in the *Consolation*.

Alanus's narrator is presented as a "real" person, a poet with a poet's interest in the fabulous materials of poetry, although his identity is less precisely established than that of his Boethian model. As the recipient and mediator of Nature's doctrine, he functions as a surrogate for the reader, as an enlightened Everyman whose perception of imperfection in his world parallels that of Boethius. The reader is expected to concur with his initial appraisal of the world, and this concurrence serves to unite reader and narrator. Alanus's narrator is deeply disturbed by his initial perceptions, although his unhappiness appears to grow exclusively out of his role as spectator, while Boethius is presented as one who suffers from injuries sustained as a participant in his world. Still, his state of mind indicates that he needs help to make sense of his chaotic environment. He does not specifically invoke the aid of a supernatural power, but clearly he cannot effect any sort of personal reconciliation without gaining a new, expanded perspective for his perceptions, and new knowledge about the meaning of temporal phenomena. Lady Nature appears in response to this need. Alanus's narrator receives symbolic aid from his authority figure—Nature kisses and raises him, just as Philosophy wipes Boethius's eyes. In the ensuing dialogue he takes an active part, questioning, urging Nature to debate or elaborate particular points, and enduring occasional rebukes when his ideas are faulty or stray from the subject. Whether or not he exhibits the sort of intellectual or psychic progress apparent in the *Consolation* and whether he is "cured" of his malady are questions which will be considered later on.

Nature, Alanus's principal authority figure, corresponding directly to Boethius's Philosophy, appears in response to the narrator's lament over the prevalence of unnatural sexual conduct in the world. She personifies the idea of the physical world in all its variety, as her name indicates. Like Philosophy, she subordinates everything in her presentation to her abstract identity and is consistent with it. She concerns herself primarily with the conformity of her creatures to her laws, especially the laws of propagation and, in human beings, of conduct, which is intimately related to the "natural" here. Her very specific limitations in knowledge of the cosmos and power over the created world are integral aspects of her identity. She is the vicar of God, his servant and functionary, vastly inferior to him in power. She cannot control human behavior, nor can she understand matters appropriate to the realms of faith and grace in which her laws and powers do not operate. She defines herself by her appearance, by what she says about herself, by her few actions, and by the customary actions and activities which she describes. By the end of the work the reader has learned virtually as much about her as she knows about herself.

The subordinate figures are, like Nature, personifications. These figures—Hymen, Genius, and the Virtues who attend Nature—represent concepts which in Alanus's scheme are closely related to the central concept of Nature. By introducing them into his narrative, Alanus follows Boethius's precedent, but he also opens up possibilities for the genre which Boethius had scarcely touched upon. Boethius's Muses exist primarily as a foil for Philosophy, but Alanus's Virtues contribute directly and positively to the reader's apprehension of Nature and to the development of the work. These figures are defined largely through Alanus's descriptions of them—with the exception of Genius, whose words and actions are central to our understanding of him. Alanus here emphasizes primary traits—the masculinity of Hymen, the moderate dress and bearing of Temperance, the abundance of Generosity—while the figures themselves do little more than reflect the moods of Nature. Only Genius and Hymen perform characteristic duties which point toward the essential aspects of their identities.

Finally, we have the figures whom Alanus presents only indirectly: Venus, Cupid, Antigamus, and Jocus in Nature's fable of the origin of vice. These figures are likewise personifications of forces in the phenomenal world, defined through the agency of Nature, who speaks of their ideal duties and functions, as well as their dereliction from them. Although she does not represent them as speaking in their own voices, Nature's portrayal of these figures closely parallels Philosophy's account of Fortune. In either case the primary authority figure presents in dramatic fashion, at one remove from the narrative present of the work itself, and presumably with complete accuracy, negative figures representing malignant influences upon humanity. Implicit in the perspective from which we see them is a value judgment concerning their place in the cosmic scheme of things, and the attitude appropriate for rational humanity to take toward them. Though not, strictly speaking, actors in the drama, they are forces whose influences dominate the motivation of the drama's principal participants.

Despite the similarities in form and technique between the *De planctu* and the *Consolation*, which suggest Alanus's dependence upon Boethius and thus confirm the generic relationship between the two works, Alanus uses the Boethian genre with considerable freedom and originality. The important differences between the two works reveal the particular direction in which Alanus has taken the genre and also certain weaknesses in his treatment of it. Presumably Alanus chose to imitate the form of the *Consolation* because he considered it appropriate to the philosophical subject matter with which he planned to deal and because he expected his audience to recognize by this form the particular sort of work it had at hand. The recognizable form would prepare the audience for the work's philosophical content. The question, then, is whether the Boethian genre proved in practice appropriate to this subject matter, or, put another way, whether Alanus successfully adapted his basic formal model to the demands of his theme, without either obscuring the highly useful conventions of the model or else making the conventions appear superfluous to the theme. Clearly he has avoided the former pitfall; the Boethian conventions of form are readily apparent and in themselves point to the nature of the work. But he has not, I think, entirely avoided the latter pitfall; there are legitimate questions to be asked about the organic, functional quality of some of the conventions he has chosen to incorporate in the work.

In the *Consolation* the visionary-narrator plays a central role. He provides a focus for the reader, who must receive the philosophy Boethius wishes to communicate through him. The narrator supplies the vital link between abstract argument and human experience, and in this respect Alanus's narrator does not altogether succeed. Alanus's narrator figures prominently in the opening of the *De planctu*, but he is not really central to the work. The focus of Alanus's dialogue is not so much upon the narrator's mental state as it is simply upon what Nature has to say. In spite of Alanus's sporadic efforts to make his narrator seem an appropriate recipient for Nature's discourse, he remains, as Nature herself says, her friend and confidant ("tecum quasi cum familiari et secretario meo"; 8.103–104), more reporter than consolee. The relationship between Nature's teaching and its recipient is not of the same order of intimacy as that which obtains between Boethius and the teachings of Philosophy.

This absence of a close, organic relationship between narrator and doctrine is remedied neither by the narrator's initial complaint nor by the occasionally animated interplay between the narrator and Nature. The content of the complaint might suggest, in the light of the corresponding complaint in the *Consolation*, that the narrator will be involved in some significant personal way in the doctrine of the dialogue, but in fact Alanus's complaint articulates a general mood of disquietude, brought about by the narrator's recognition of rampant vice around him. This perception affects him emotionally, and it raises important philosophical questions, but there is no personal problem inherent in the complaint, no psychological "illness," brought about by events in the narrator's own experience, to be "cured." Further, this complaint contains in compressed and sometimes enigmatic form many of the major points developed later in the *De planctu*. The body of the work thus might be described as a gloss upon, or expansion of, the narrator's initial poetic statement.[14] The narrator complains primarily of human deviation from Nature's laws concerning sexuality, as does Nature herself, in similarly figurative language, when her turn comes to complain. The narrator's grief is matched by Nature's own grief. His allusion to Venus fighting against Venus ("Venus in Venerem pugnans"; 1.5) is developed into Nature's fable of Venus's adultery. Finally, the suggestion that the vicious be anathematized by Genius ("Men like these, who refuse Genius his tithes and rites, deserve to be excommunicated from the temple of Genius"; 1.59–60) is literally carried out at the end of the work.

Given the summarizing quality of the narrator's initial statement, it is difficult to agree with Piehler[15] and Wetherbee[16] that the dialogue is "therapeutic," that the narrator really grows or changes psychically. His initial views are elaborated but do not develop in any real sense out of a process of inquiry and response. He and Nature agree from the outset that unnatural behavior is rampant in the world. If we take the narrator's opening statement at its face value, we must conclude that he already is intensely aware of the things which Nature tells him about human conduct. Further, there is no indication in his complaint that the narrator either practices or is somehow a victim of the sexual vices of which he speaks. His entire tone is that of censure, and his desire for untouched maiden lips, which contains a veiled reference to "natural" procreation, places him firmly in Nature's retinue:

> Why do so many kisses lie fallow on maidens' lips while no one wishes to harvest a crop from them? If these kisses were but once planted on me, they would grow honey-sweet with moisture, and grown honey-sweet, they would form a honeycomb in my mouth. My life breath, concentrating entirely on my mouth, would go out to meet the kisses and would disport itself entirely on my lips so that I might thus expire and that, when dead myself, my other self might enjoy in her a fruitful life. [1.43–50]

In view of the narrator's initial stance, Nature's occasional rebukes, and the occasional suggestions of her beneficial effects upon him, appear to depend upon their immediate contexts and not upon some basic aberration suffered by him. Alanus derives such passages from the *Consolation*, but where, for example, Philosophy's rebuke of Boethius is motivated by her analysis of his deplorable state of mind (1, pr. 1–pr. 2), Nature's parallel rebuke (6.13ff.) seems more appropriate to the "unnatural" portion of mankind than to one who has been her disciple from the beginning of the work and thus seems pointlessly severe. The immediate cause for her rebuke is his failure to recognize her, but this failure is not clearly the result of his having forgotten her. Alanus perhaps recognized the awkwardness here, for at the end of Nature's first long speech he gives the narrator an excuse for his behavior — his human frailty could not sustain the sudden vision of such divinity — which seems to satisfy Nature (6.170–98). Both narrators appear initially as sufferers, but while Boethius suffers because he has forgotten Philosophy and so has a distorted view of human life, Alanus's narrator suffers because he remembers Nature. The cause of his suffering is identical with that of Nature herself, it emerges from an accurate perception of human life, and it is completely justified.

The awkwardness involved in Alanus's treatment of his narrator seems to be in part the result of his attempt to parallel the general movement of thought found in the *Consolation*. Both works begin with a particular aspect of human experience and move outward from it toward a more general, all-encompassing view of the human condition. This movement is from a merely personal, self-centered view of the narrator's own experience toward a cosmic view in which that experience appears in its proper perspective. Thus the *Consolation* moves from Boethius's imprisonment to the related questions of Fortune and justice in the world and finally to its resolution in concepts of divine justice and providence. The *De planctu* moves from the narrator's perception of specifically sexual vice, through Nature's analysis of man's deviation from the natural laws governing his sexuality, then to the fable of Venus, which accounts for the cosmic origin of this unnatural behavior, and hence to a more general discussion of all the vices, which emerge in the aftermath of Venus's defection and, as species of inordinate, misdirected love, are related to that defection. The work ends with Nature, Genius, Hymen, and the Virtues joining to cast out all those who practice the vices from their elevated cosmic fellowship.[17]

Unquestionably the *De planctu* contains doctrine that should expand and deepen its narrator's understanding of his world. Whether, like Boethius, he becomes reconciled to this world and whether his philosophical questions are resolved, is, however, another matter.

Nature's knowledge and her powers are very precisely limited; as she herself admits, while she functions as God's vicar, the procreatrix and governess of the created world, her power depends from God, and her knowledge of the realm of grace, theology's realm, is virtually nonexistent (6.128–65). Because of her limitations she cannot correct defects of human Reason. Free Will, which is necessary to moral choice, cannot be controlled, even by Nature; she can only punish offenders against her law by denying them her favor:

> Accordingly, ignoring no pertinent fact and finding the proper motivation in myself, in so far as I can extend the arm of my power, I will smite men with a punishment commensurate with their crimes. However, since I cannot pass the limits of my strength and it is not in my power to eradicate completely the poison of this pestilence, I will attain what is allowed my power and will burn with the brand of anathema men who are ensnared in the tangle of the vices that I have mentioned. [16.169–74]

The anathema, which is pronounced by her priest, Genius, changes nothing; it merely punishes. The narrator's initial concerns have not been transcended in the way that those of Boethius have at the end of the *Consolation*.

Ironically, in spite of her considerable powers, Nature is ultimately inadequate as an authority figure. She can analyze the condition of sinful humanity, but only from a secular, "natural," point of view, and so she can do nothing to enforce her laws or to restore those who deviate from them. She and Genius are a kind of secular parody of God and his priests (or of God and his angels, as she describes them in prose 3): the priest administers divine law, but he cannot correct those who violate it. As Nature says, she controls birth and death, but the mystery of rebirth escapes her ("But my professional services are set aside in the mystery of this second birth. Such a birth needs no midwife of my kind. Rather I, Nature, am ignorant of the nature of this birth. When I try to understand these things, the keenness of my intellect grows dull, my enlightened reason is confounded" [6.144–48]). Clearly, divine grace is needed to effect this rebirth, but grace is not a subject with which Nature can deal. Just as in the *Consolation*, the authority figure's limitations require that her doctrine be supplemented by Christian revelation; this must be supplied by the reader, outside the limits imposed by the author upon his work.

Although the *De planctu* lacks the explicit, final resolution which only Christian doctrine could provide for it,[18] it points toward a partial, temporal resolution, which resembles the practical lesson of the *Consolation*, throughout. The formulation of this practical lesson is largely negative; the vicious are excluded from Nature's favor and, since Nature works God's will, they are implicitly excluded from his favor as well. Again and again Nature warns mankind to avoid vice and serve Reason and virtue. Man, as depicted on Nature's robe, has the capacity to avoid sensuality and through the agency of Reason to penetrate the secrets of the heavens (2.232–34). The victory of man's *ratio* over his *sensualitas* will be rewarded by his transfiguration into a god (6.55–61). The purpose of Nature's visit, and of her complaint is "so that men of restraint may revere the mark of modesty and that men without restraint may be kept away from trafficking in the brothels of immodesty. The knowledge of evil is advantageous as a preventive measure to punish the guilty, who are branded with the mark of shame, and to forearm the unaffected with the armour of precaution" [8.96–100]. She advises flight from Amor but modifies her position to allow for the sort of love that is governed by moderation (9–10.1–16). She ends her fable of Venus with the admonition to fight against the sort of vices she has described (10.165–83), and after more particular description of the vices she again counsels wisdom as protection against them (12.126–48). Finally, we witness the Virtues aligned with Nature, while the vicious are punished by anathema. The movement, then, is toward a practical, cautionary moral. The individual should exercise his free will and choose the life of virtue, Reason and Nature, avoiding the vices which will separate him from the cosmic harmony, "the kiss of celestial love" ("a superne dilectionis osculo"; 18.143–44), and the favor of Nature.

The status of the narrator in the cosmic scheme set forth by Nature is not altogether clear. There are indications in the text that he is a representative of the portion of humanity anathematized by Genius. Indeed, Nature and Genius at times speak as if all mankind were guilty of defecting from her laws, and certain symbolic details, such as the omission of man from Nature's welcoming committee (pr. 4, 5), and the rent in Nature's garment where man is depicted, may also point in this direction.[19] Likewise, one may read the fable of Venus as an allegory of the universal perversion of the human capacity for love, as a secular presentation of the doctrine of fallen man, in which case the estrangement of Nature and man, including the narrator, would appear total and irreversible without divine intervention. One can, however, take the general references to mankind as being less than universal in their application. The admonitions offered by Nature to men at the end of the fable would seem to favor this latter view. Even if, however, one takes such references and symbolic details in a limited rather than a universal sense, the possibility remains that the narrator belongs among those who have offended Nature, and again the details of his sometimes peculiar behavior, his shows of weakness and ignorance, and Nature's rebukes might suggest his personal culpability.

It would be possible to explain away each of the bits of evidence which could be brought forward against the narrator, but it is not, I think, necessary. If we take him either as a representative of universally unnatural humanity or as an individually unnatural soul, then Nature's visitation makes no sense. She cannot help him by anything she says or does; no psychic or philosophical solution is available to her, and her total inability to affect the course of his life becomes a prime source of irony throughout the work. Moreover, the narrator is Nature's ally, not her enemy, and her purpose is to strengthen her allies in the moral conduct of their lives. The narrator's complaint separates him from the vicious men whom he castigates. Nature's admonitions suggest that he is one of those who desire to follow Nature and eschew vice. Whether he is virtuous or vicious, however, the portrayal of the narrator as Boethian protagonist is incomplete and inconsistent. The indications early on of psychic progress and growing understanding of the world end with his request that Nature strengthen his mind against the assaults of vice (14.141–43). This desire to avoid vice is really no indication of spiritual progress, given the sentiments expressed in his opening complaint. The problem of vice in the world remains uncorrected and unresolved, and his attitude toward it, while more enlightened in terms of its origins and dangers, has not changed at all.

I have been treating the *De planctu* as a work which, like Boethius's *Consolation*, communicates its meaning primarily through literal rather than figurative means of expression. The bulk of the work consists of a dialogue through which a personified abstraction, Nature, instructs a human narrator about vice and virtue. Nature's words characterize her as a conceptual entity and explain her role in human life and conduct and her relationship to other conceptual entities, such as Reason and Venus, which affect human life. Her ostensible purpose in presenting this essentially philosophical information is practical and admonitory; she wishes to inform human beings how they should live so as to conform to her divinely established laws. She at times employs figurative language, including metaphor of various kinds, and allegorical fable. At the end of the work, together with several other personifications, she engages in allegorical action which complements the meaning of her literal, discursive statements. The *De planctu* thus fulfills the criteria for what Frank describes as personification allegory, in which characters who literally mean what their names say they mean engage in allegorical relationships and activities. The text provides the information the reader needs to understand what is being said and done, and it makes consistent sense on a primarily literal level.

Alanus departs from the practice of Boethius, however, by employing allegory of another sort, which complements and extends the meaning of his personification allegory. Throughout the *De planctu* runs a pattern of related images which, when taken in conjunction with the literal level of statement and activity, suggests a veiled or "other" level of meaning. This is not to say that the work means something basically different from what it literally says; Isidore's definition of allegory as *alieniloquium* would be misleading here. Nature remains what she says she is and means what she says she means. Rather, insofar as this other, veiled level can be spoken of as being separable from the literal level at all, it augments the implications of the figures, statements, and activities. Insofar as this pattern of images appears to direct the reader to interpret Alanus's figures at one level as symbols, when considering further their pattern of relationship and activity, the work must be taken, in part, as what Frank describes as symbol allegory. This interpretation is controlled—justified and limited—by Alanus's literal text.

The *De planctu* is rigorously secular in its point of view; it treats the natural world in rationalistic terms. Nature herself excludes theological doctrine from what she describes (6.89–91). She is a cosmological figure, not a religious one, and she imposes a secular, cosmological perspective upon all that transpires. The effect of this perspective is not to deny a relationship between her doctrine and Christian theology—as she says, she and Theology do not disagree—but rather to limit the boundaries of the discussion. The "natural" doctrine of the *De planctu* certainly can be subsumed by Christian theology and divine revelation, but the connections are not made within the work itself, and the reader must guard against assuming more meaning than is justified by the text. Alanus does not by his language and imagery point his reader toward meaning of a specifically Christian kind.[20] Thus the love which is misdirected in the story of Venus is not specifically the love of God (*caritas*), but rather the "natural" love between male and female which, when governed by Reason and so directed toward the perpetuation of the created world, mirrors divine love in this world. The story is a secular, psychological, and moral allegory of sin against the natural order of rational behavior; its implications for the spiritual order which lies beyond the natural order are not explored. The fall here is presented in terms not of divine grace but of Nature's grace. This lesser fall is indeed an aspect of the greater fall, but the latter is beyond the scope of the story and of Nature herself. By the same token, the grace of God, manifested in the Incarnation, makes possible the individual's salvation, without which Nature's admonitions would be pointless, but it, too, is beyond the scope of the work.

This is not to say that the *De planctu* contains no allegory, only that its allegory functions within its secular framework. The allegory, conveyed primarily by the work's imagery, is directly related to the element of moral suasion inherent in Nature's repeated admonitions, and is expressed in terms of the proper relationship of male and female.[21] Throughout the work imagery centered around the idea of lawful marriage attests to the function of marriage as a figure for the principle or order and harmony in the cosmos. Likewise, unbridled sensuality figures the violation of this cosmic principle. Thus the opposition set forth in the opening complaint is that of unchaste sensual love, especially sodomy, which in its sterility violates Nature's laws, and lawful human sexuality, which fulfills the dictates of Nature; this opposition gains significance through the course of the work. Evidence throughout the *De planctu* suggests that human marriage, the "natural" condition within which human sexuality has its lawful role, is, in Nature's Macrobian terms, the covering which masks the mystery of a cosmic kind of harmonious union requiring both a feminine and a masculine aspect.

The imagery which evokes the feminine aspect of this principle of order centers around Nature herself. She is a feminine figure, capable of producing procreative abundance but not of controlling her progeny. The need for a complementary masculine figure to complete the masculine-feminine paradigm of cosmic harmony is first suggested by the appearance of the charioteer in prose 2. He is "homo," who towers above Nature and her chariot and "a man, whose countenance had no flavour of earthliness but rather of the mysteries of the divine." Clearly, he must be some sort of representative of the supreme God from whom Nature derives her powers, perhaps an angel. The important point, however, is that as a divine surrogate this masculine figure is defined in terms of control; he is a force for order and guidance who, "supplying what is wanting to the female sex, by a series of moderate suggestions guided the car on its course" (4.11–14). In this conjunction of Nature and her charioteer, of feminine beauty and abundance and masculine discipline and control, we have the first reflection of the cosmic principle of which marriage is the mundane manifestation.

Again, in prose 3, when Nature describes her function in the creation of men, she speaks of the "marriage" ("nuptie"; 6.30, 41) of body and spirit in man, who is a "mirror of the world itself" (line 45). Implicit here as elsewhere is the idea of a union of masculine and feminine aspects, a marriage, in the microcosm as in the macrocosm. Similarly, the language used in Nature's complaint against man suggests that he has ignored or perverted the ideal of marriage in pursuing sexual vices: "However, from this universal law man alone exempts himself by a nonconformist withdrawal. He, stripping himself of the robe of chastity, exposes himself in unchastity for a professional male prostitute and dares to stir up the tumult of legal strife against the dignity of his queen, and, moreover, to fan the flame of civil war's rage against his mother" (8.12–15). Literal violation of the human law of marriage reflects the violation of Nature's laws in a general sense, and marriage itself stands for a cosmic principle.

Nature's story of Venus is the allegorical expression of this cosmic principle and its violation. God created the world as an ordered, harmonious whole, says Nature:

> Thus with an exchange of kisses, arising from a certain mutual affinity, He leagued together things hostile to one another by generic opposition, things whose position had placed them on opposite sides, and He changed the strife of contrariety into the peace of friendship. When all things, then, were harmonised by the fine chain of an invisible connection, in a peaceable union plurality made its way back to unity, diversity to identity, discord to concord. [8.210–16]

The creator "had wedded...in marriage" all things in their proper forms and proportions" (lines 218–19) and appointed Nature to perpetuate them under his (masculine) guidance: "However, under the mysterious power of God, I carried out the administration of this office in such a way that the right hand of the supreme authority should direct my hand in its work, for my writing-reed would instantly go off course if it were not guided by the finger of the superintendent on high" (lines 232–35). Nature in turn established Venus, along with her husband, Hymen, and her son, Cupid, to carry out her procreative duties among men, while at the same time instructing Venus at length in the laws governing propagation under "imperial precepts from my magisterial teaching" (10.35).

Venus's adultery, then, not only breaks the natural law of human marriage but also symbolizes the violation of the cosmic, divinely ordained principle of harmonious union. Love, willfully separating itself from its proper object and complementary principle, marriage-Hymen, gives birth to an illegitimate offspring, Jocus, and, as Nature further suggests, to all the various vices. We have here, then, an allegory of the original separation of the masculine and feminine aspects of cosmic union, original sin in cosmic terms. Further, since it is Venus, love as it manifests itself in human nature, who has defected from cosmic harmony and order, the allegory accounts for the exclusively human manifestation of disharmony and disorder.

The final section of the *De planctu* (pr. 8–9) emphasizes the allegory of cosmic harmony in the union of masculine and feminine agents. It begins with the sudden arrival of Hymen, Venus's lawful but estranged husband, whom Alanus presents in emphatically masculine terms:

> On his face there showed no signs of feminine softness; rather the authority of manly dignity alone held sway there. His face was neither drenched with the rain of tears nor calm with playful laughter but, resting modestly away from either extreme, was inclined more to tears.
>
> His hair had secured a truce to snarling and bespoke the energetic work of a mechanical comb. By the first offering of a modest dressing, his hair lay in orderly fashion to prevent it from appearing to degenerate into feminine softness by the vagaries of devious arrangements. To prevent a cloudlet of hair from burying his expanse of forehead, the ends of his hair had felt the scissors' bite.
>
> His face, as manly dignity demanded, was missing in no grace of beauty. [16.10–18]

The images of masculinity and discipline suggest that Hymen represents not simply Venus's mythological husband, nor the ceremonial concept of marriage, but, on a higher and more abstract level, the masculine, controlling principle from which human love has become separated. Hymen and Venus are complementary aspects of the overriding principle of cosmic harmony; the human concept of marriage figures, is an allegory for, this principle. The silence of the musicians who accompany Hymen here (16.34–37) is literally the result of the dissolution of Hymen's marriage to Venus, and allegorically it represents the breach of the principle of harmony figured forth in that dissolution.

The discussion between Nature and Largitas about Prodigalitas (18.1–56) is a final statement of the effect of the separation of masculine and feminine aspects of the principle of harmony. Prodigality is the foster-child of Generosity (Largitas), who is herself the "sister" of, and in the union of their desires virtually a twin to, Nature. Wetherbee remarks upon the "special bond" between these two figures, for

"Largitas is in the deepest sense a natural virtue, an emulation of the plenitude and the impulse to profusion of the goddess herself, and a quality essential to sexual and moral fulfillment."[22] Generosity should then be seen as a figure analogous to unfallen Venus, and Prodigality, her near relation, to fallen Venus. Like Venus, Generosity is an aspect of Nature; without a masculine controlling and disciplining principle, her qualities degenerate, and she "becomes" Prodigality, who abuses the gifts of Nature ("Naturae donis abutitur"; lines 32–33) by turning them to waste and excess, as do the vices, the daughters of Idolatria (12.5–125).

The conclusion of the *De planctu*, while it does not resolve the problem of human vice raised on the literal level, does offer a culmination of the allegory of unity and estrangement. Nature is joined by certain carefully selected virtues. Of these, Generosity reflects the abundant, feminine quality of Nature herself, and is thus subject to perversion (Prodigality), but Castitas, Temperantia, and Humilitas are not subject to excess. They are virtues which, though traditionally (and grammatically) female, embody a primary element of "masculine" discipline and self-control.[23] In this allegorical environment it becomes possible for Hymen, the representative of cosmic union, to bring Genius to Nature. Genius, whatever else he may represent — human nature, the human reproductive principle, the mediator between universal Nature and humanity, or between Nature and God[24] — is the masculine counterpart to feminine Nature. The opening of her letter to him makes clear both their close resemblance and the relationship between them:

> Nature, by the grace of God, vicar-governess of the city of earth: to Genius, her other self, greetings and wishes that in all things he may be befriended by the delights of fair fortune.
>
> Since like, with disdain for unlike, rejoices in a bond of relationship with like, finding myself your alter ego by the likeness of Nature that is reflected in you as in a mirror, I am bound to you in a knot of heartfelt love, both succeeding in your success and in like manner failing in your failure. Love, then, should be a circle so that you, responding with a return of love, should make our fortunes interchangeable. [16.187–94]

When Hymen departs to deliver this message, his attendant musicians at his bidding summon their instruments "to the strains of a harmonious melody" (line 220) announcing an impending "marriage."

Genius's arrival is marked by this music (18.57–59). The imagery used to describe him suggests order and discipline: "His height, kept within fitting limits by the rule of the mean, neither had a complaint to make about shortening by contraction nor was he saddened by superfluous elongation" (lines 59–61). He is in appearance a masculine complement to the glittering profusion of the beauty of Nature, and like her he draws images which quickly vanish, giving way to new ones. Nature greets him with a kiss, "indicative of the harmony of mystic love" (line 115), after which, as a preface to his assumption of his sacerdotal vestments, he remarks upon the bond of harmonious love between him and Nature:

> Nor is it surprising that I find a melody and harmony in the agreement and union of our wills since the conceptive exemplar of one idea brought us to birth and existence, since our status as administrators of one office brings us into accord, since it is no hypocritical love that joins us by a superficial bond of attachment but, rather, it is a pure and modest love that dwells in the deeper recesses of the soul. [Lines 130–34]

This mystical union of Nature and Genius in no way suggests that the literal problem of the *De planctu*, the prevalence of vice in the world, has been resolved. Genius, in his role as Nature's priest, can do no more than excommunicate the vicious from her favor. Their union, however, offers a figural representation of the cosmic principle of harmony, of which proper human sexual relationships, embodied in marriage, are the earthly manifestation. The union is the allegorical counterpart to the estrangement of Venus and Hymen; the earlier story presents an allegory of the violation of the cosmic principle of harmonious union through perverted love, while the later portion of the work presents the cosmic principle intact, preserved through properly directed love and mirrored in this world in marriage and, more generally, in the practice of virtue. The allegory of marriage — the natural, sanctioned union of male and female, of discipline and natural desire, and the principle of cosmic order which it figures, as opposed to adultery and licentiousness, disunity, uncontrolled desire and disorder — enforces the admonitory quality of the literal level of the *De planctu* by relating Nature's admonitions to a higher principle than mere socially conventional morality. Mankind receives cosmic justification for living virtuously and a cosmic example, in the union of Nature and Genius, toward which to aspire. This allegory is exemplary, on a higher plane than that of human phenomena, of the sort of love human beings should practice.

The *De planctu* contains allegory of a kind not apparent in its model, the *Consolation* of Boethius, and Alanus points the direction

De planctu naturae

which commentary upon the allegory should take. This direction is essentially secular, philosophical rather than theological. Human married love is brought into the perspective of cosmic harmony, of Nature, but not into that of the mystical union of the human soul with God, or of the Church with Christ. Alanus has limited his scope in such a way that divine grace, necessary in Christian doctrine for the continuing defeat of vice, is not discussed here. This is not to suggest that grace is unnecessary to the sort of virtuous life recommended by Nature; Nature simply cannot deal with a theological topic.[25] The relationship of Nature and grace is a major theme in Alanus's *Anticlaudianus*.[26] In this later work the irony of Nature's practical impotence is transcended: Nature and her cosmic allies create the earthly part of what is to be a perfect man, capable of defeating vice, but because of man's dual nature they cannot complete their work alone. God must contribute a soul, and so Phronesis and Reason are sent, on a chariot built of the seven liberal arts and powered by the five senses, on a journey to God-Nous. But Phronesis, Reason and the senses cannot journey unaided beyond the realm of the fixed stars (i.e., beyond Nature's boundaries); Reason and the senses (hearing excepted) must remain behind as Theology leads Phronesis into the realm of God. Here, aided by Theology and Faith, Phronesis petitions God and receives the gift of a perfect soul to complete Nature's creation. This perfect man subsequently accomplishes what Nature in the *De planctu* cannot do: he defeats the vices in combat. Thus the *Anticlaudianus* presents a resolution to the problem left unresolved in the *De planctu* by going beyond the realm of Nature to supply the spiritual grace of which Nature knows little or nothing. The *De planctu* is incomplete in the same way that the *Consolation* is incomplete; it provides adequate secular guidance for human life but leaves the mystery of divine revelation and theology for the reader to discover elsewhere. It offers its narrator-visionary a new perspective from which to view worldly phenomena and a practical guide for human conduct, but it does not present a total Christian perspective.

5

ROMAN DE LA ROSE

lanus's *De planctu naturae* was a central work in the development of the Boethian genre as it emerged in the twelfth
century and after. Alanus extended the scope of the genre by
dealing with subject matter wholly new to it and augmenting its
structure to accommodate this subject matter. The *De planctu*'s influence seems to have begun soon after its appearance and extended on
through the succeeding centuries; its theme, Nature, has left its mark
quite clearly upon the twelfth-century *Architrenius* of Johannis de
Altavilla, Jean de Meun's portion of the thirteenth-century *Roman de
la Rose*, Gower's *Confessio Amantis* and Chaucer's *Parliament of
Fowls*. The influence of the *Consolation of Philosophy* upon Latin and
vernacular literature was so pervasive that the works of Patch[1] and
Courcelle[2] can together only suggest it in very general terms, and
Alanus's successful adaptation of the *Consolation*'s generic characteristics must have intensified the formal aspect of that influence.

The development of the Boethian genre is influenced by two oppos-
ing tendencies, contraction and expansion; the former is of little
aesthetic interest, but the latter's aesthetic implications demand some
attention. By contraction I mean to suggest a closing up of the form's
basic structure and of the manner in which it presents its subject
matter. The elements which, taken together, characterize the genre (as
represented by its principal models) harden into rigid conventions.
Whatever flexibility the genre offers disappears as an author either
observes the obligatory conventions in a perfunctory manner or elabo-

73

rates them solely for the sake of demonstrating his own virtuosity. Works exhibiting this tendency are likely to appear as obvious imitations of their generic predecessors. The subject matter is poured into a preexisting, rigid mold, and while the genre of the work is readily apparent, the rationale for employing it is likely to be oversimplistic or even nonexistent insofar as the content is concerned.

This tendency toward contraction appears in the mid-fourteenth-century French *Liber Fortunae*.[3] In this poem an unjustly imprisoned narrator laments his situation; has a brief waking vision of a regal lady with a wheel, which he cannot comprehend; then in his sleep receives a vision of this lady, the goddess Fortuna, who rouses him from his lethargy and proceeds to lecture him for the remainder of the poem. The anonymous poet turns the Boethian form into a 115-line prologue, the purpose of which is to frame a 4,588-line didactic monologue over a wide range of philosophical and theological subjects. The poet has apparently chosen the Boethian form because he knows that it is traditionally appropriate to the kind of subject matter he wishes to treat, but he has little sense of the dynamics of how it works to convey meaning. Structure and content have for him only the most mechanical relationship; vision and personification allegory are merely devices to embellish a didactic treatise.

The tendency toward expansion, on the other hand, may result in the opening up of the form to new kinds of subject matter and new elements in its structure. This expansion may be achieved by elaborating elements already present, at least in embryonic form, in existing examples of the genre and by adding new elements drawn from other kinds of literature. Alanus's *De planctu* clearly moves the genre in the direction of expansion: his subject matter is wholly new to the genre, and he develops it by elaborating such elements of the *Consolation* as the opening complaint and the allegorical description of his authority figure, and by introducing largely unprecedented elements like the fable of Venus's adultery and the allegorical action at the end of the work. When it succeeds, this expansive tendency leads to the enrichment of the genre, in the potential kinds of material with which it may deal and in the manner in which the material may be presented. Expansions and innovations may, however, alter the appearance of the form so greatly that a particular work will be difficult if not impossible to recognize as belonging to a distinct generic tradition. The author must then forgo the advantages inherent in writing in a familiar tradition, and while he may produce a work which will become the foundation of a new genre (as did Boethius himself), there is every likelihood that his work will be sui generis and, as such, an oddity or puzzle for his readers.

The *Architrenius* of Johannis de Altavilla (Hauvilla in Latin, Jean de Hanville or Hautville in French), written in the later twelfth century, exhibits this tendency toward expansion and elaboration.[4] It is a transitional work, which draws upon the earlier Chartrian allegories of Alanus and Bernardus Silvestris and looks forward to the vernacular allegories of the next century in its structure and in the breadth of its subject matter. It seems to have been inspired by Alanus's two major poems, and may have influenced Jean de Meun's portion of the *Roman de la Rose*; its antecedents and its popularity,[5] together with its attempts to combine traditional poetic elements in new ways, make a brief examination of it worthwhile, before we turn to the *Roman*.

Johannis attempts to expand the Boethian form by augmenting it with new structural elements and thematic devices. The result of his ingenuity is a work in which elements of the *Consolation* and the *De planctu* are clearly discernible. Like the earlier examples of Boethian Apocalypse, this poem is essentially philosophical, and its purpose is essentially practical, addressing itself to the question of how one is to live morally in an immoral world.[6] The third-person hero, the "arch-weeper" Architrenius, is at the beginning of the work in despair over the corruption which he sees in himself and everywhere about him in the world. He accuses Nature of having failed to provide human beings with adequate inner defenses against the temptations of vice and resolves to seek her out for solace (1.1–349). His search departs radically in its form from the visions in earlier Boethian works, but it corresponds directly in its educational purpose to their dialogues. It takes him to a series of loci in which he observes, and rejects, various manifestations of "natural" behavior in his fellow men; he visits the dwellings of Venus (where he for the moment falls in love) and Gluttony, the university world of Paris, the mountain of Ambition and then the hill of Presumption, and finally Thule (Tylos), the island home of the ancient philosophers. Here he at last meets Nature herself, enthroned in a garden. She lectures him on the orderliness of the natural universe, promises to help him, and finally ends his weeping by giving him a bride, Moderancia.

Clearly the most prominent innovation here is Johannis's replacement of the Boethian dialogue, which occurs in a sort of spatial void, with a journey on which the consolee confronts a series of personifications, realistic human types, and actual historical persons. Architrenius must seek out his education in a world of human activity, rather than simply being visited by the supernatural figure evoked in his opening complaint. None of the earlier visionaries we have considered even contemplates a physical journey, allegorical or otherwise, as a means of seeking enlightenment. The journey theme has been grafted onto the Boethian genre from the allegorical epics of Martianus Capella and his twelfth-century heirs, Bernardus Silvestris and Alanus de Insulis, and, perhaps, in view of the fact that the journeys in the *De nuptiis Philologiae et Mercurii*, the *De mundi universitate* (or *Cosmographia*) and the *Anticlaudianus* are primarily celestial rather than terrestrial, from the chivalric quests of vernacular romance.

Architrenius's quest-journey is allegorical, even though it takes place in the physical world. Indeed, the journey framework is scarcely maintained once Architrenius begins moving from place to place with virtually no attention paid by the poet to the mechanics of physical travel. Architrenius is a young man who, having overcome the inertia of sloth (which is described in a sort of prologue as the parent of vice), wishes to discover a worthy mode of life but is hindered by human nature, his own as well as that of the world in general. Because he can see no aspect of Nature that has not been corrupted, he sets out to find the goddess herself, moving through her various human manifestations on the way, to learn how to live. The places and figures he encounters are at once aspects of Nature which humanity has corrupted and alternative courses of human experience, any one of which he might adopt as his own. In terms of the allegory, by visiting the locus of a particular aspect of human experience, Architrenius partakes of that experience, only to abandon it as being unworthy of his lasting devotion because of its corruption. His visit to each successive locus is directly equivalent to Boethius's exposure to, and transcending of, life under the auspices of Fortune. Because he appears more observer than participant in the experiences of these loci, his education through observation closely parallels the education of Boethius or Alanus's narrator through descriptive lectures. Architrenius's journey is an allegorical quest for a way of life which is both "natural" and virtuous, according to the hero's standards.[7]

The displacement of one kind of experience by another occurs in Boethius's *Consolation*, where first the Muses and then the figure of Fortune are transcended by the consolee, in the process of harmonizing his perceptions with true philosophy. Such displacement likewise appears in Alanus's *Anticlaudianus* when Phronesis must abandon Reason and be guided by Theology as she ascends from the created world to the realm of God. In the *Architrenius* this device is more closely associated with places than with successive authority figures, as

76

one locus of activity replaces another. The advantage inherent in the use of a series of figures or loci which displace one another is that experience can be treated in far greater variety than is possible when one personified power or allegorical locus controls the area to be explored. A clearer sense of progress through distinct stages of the educational process is possible. And if the various figures and loci are effectively integrated into the overall pattern of the work, complex relations between ideas or experiences can be presented in a way which does justice to their complexity, at the same time that they are being dissected for analysis. Dante, to take an obvious example, constructs the vision of his *Commedia* upon a pattern of loci within which his visionary is instructed by a series of clearly hierarchical figures.

Along with the possible advantages of using multiple authority figures or their equivalents to expand the scope of the Boethian educational process comes a tendency, which may or may not be beneficial, toward the encyclopedic. Encyclopedias, summas, and their literary relations, among which the episodic romance may be a distant cousin, reflect the late-medieval desire to assemble and systematically assimilate all knowledge concerning one or more realms of human inquiry. Such works attempt to anatomize all aspects of the particular conceptual or experiential realms which they take as their subjects; Martianus Capella's *De nuptiis Philologiae et Mercurii*, with its allegorical framework and copious analysis of each component of its larger theme, is perhaps the earliest example of this tendency, and it was highly influential in the later Middle Ages, especially upon the allegorical epics of the twelfth-century Chartrian poets. C. S. Lewis's amusing discussion of this work, which is too long to quote here, nicely captures the essence of this encyclopedic tendency in Martianus, who "established a disastrous precedent for endlessness and formlessness in literary work."[8] The desire to say everything that can be said on a given subject may not be inherently detrimental to literary art, but in practice it produced works which exhaust the reader with the digressiveness and copiousness deplored by Lewis. This is not the case when the encyclopedic tendency is firmly subordinated to a controlling structural plan and a sense of proportion; Boethius's *Consolation* itself attempts to epitomize philosophy in a comprehensive manner, without appearing prolix or loosely structured, and Alanus's *Anticlaudianus* holds together well despite its encyclopedic theme, the creation of a perfect man. The danger consists in completeness becoming an excuse for unnecessary erudition or ingenuity and in the writer's attempting to encompass too broad a subject and to analyze its components in too great detail.[9]

Boethian Apocalypse

In Boethian Apocalypse this encyclopedic tendency may obscure the central issues of the work, burying the visionary-narrator's problem under a mass of irrelevant detail and blunting the edge of the emotional anguish intended to involve the reader in this problem. In the *Architrenius* this is especially true since the problem to be solved is formulated in very generalized terms, so that its focus tends to blur. Architrenius seeks a suitable way of life in a world in which all human beings willfully corrupt whatever is natural in them. By allowing his hero unlimited opportunity for self-discovery and discovery of his world, Johannis leads him into what might have become an infinite series of examples of men perverting Nature. The only inherent limit to the kinds of human endeavor which Architrenius might encounter is, after all, the author's ingenuity in thinking of them. The copious detail with which each episode is presented tends to obscure the structure and the motivating purpose of the allegorical journey. It is easy to understand why the poem's nineteenth-century editor, Wright, classified it as a satire,[10] when local satire within its episodes looms so large as to veil its philosophical purpose. The problem is at times apparent in the *Roman de la Rose* as well, although the poem's authors never allow local effects to obscure entirely its controlling theme.

The *Roman de la Rose*, begun by Guillaume de Lorris in the third decade of the thirteenth century and completed by Jean de Meun over forty years later, is the earliest important vernacular poem exhibiting this encyclopedic tendency. Lorris's 4,000-line portion of the poem reveals little or none of the influence of either Boethius or Alanus. Meun's 18,000-line continuation, however, owes a considerable debt to both of these writers;[11] indeed, Meun transforms the *Roman* from Lorris's erotic allegory into, in part, a critical response to Alanus's *De planctu*, a response which begins with a Boethian dialogue. Thus, while I would stop short of identifying the whole work generically as a Boethian Apocalypse, I would place it in the mainstream of development of the Boethian tradition because of its literary and philosophical influences and because it exerted considerable influence upon all manner of later works, including Boethian visions. In this latter regard C. S. Lewis calls it a "germinal book" which "ranks second to none except the Bible and the *Consolation of Philosophy*" in the later Middle Ages.[12] The intricacies of the *Roman* have only recently begun to receive the attention they deserve from critics,[13] but our attention here must confine itself to those aspects of the poem which bear directly upon the Boethian generic tradition.

In the interests of setting the *Roman* into generic perspective, we should consider it in its relationship to the Boethian genre. Lorris very early refers to his poem as an "art": ". . . it is *The Romance of the Rose*, in which the whole art of love is contained" (lines 37–38).[14] Meun's Amor later offers an alternative title, "le *Miroer aus Amoreus*" (*The Mirror for Lovers*) (line 10621), but whatever the distinction in literary terms between "mirror" and "art,"[15] it seems clear enough that Meun has not altered the theme of the poem Lorris began. It attempts to analyze its subject, "amor," in its entirety;[16] its purpose is encyclopedic in scope. The kind of "amor" treated in this "art," however, is limited by the sphere of activity which circumscribes the narrative and is defined by the figures who act therein. This sphere is exclusively secular, and so the various manifestations of the subject and opinions about it must remain secular also. *Amor* in the Middle Ages is a complex subject, the implications of which go far beyond profane love to include divine love, *caritas*, in its earthly and heavenly forms. All lesser kinds of love are imperfect reflections of perfect divine love; still, divine love is never directly the subject of the *Roman*. Given this crucial limitation, however, the poem depicts through an allegorical account of the experience of the narrator the essence of secular *amor* in precise and comprehensive detail.

As Rosamond Tuve points out, whatever Lorris's skill in portraying psychological processes, the primary purpose of medieval allegory is not to dissect the actions and reactions of a unique hero pursuing a personal goal but rather to portray universal experience in a moral-philosophical context:

> The major strength of allegory is its brilliant resolution of the problem of the relation of particulars and the general or universal. . . . Moral allegory is the simplest form which that relation takes. A first disservice done by fastening our own conceptions of what is supremely interesting upon this earlier figurative artistry is that a divorce action is brought to separate moral from psychological allegory. The distinction is defined by a difference in the locus of the action: psychic or cosmic. But an extraordinary merit of allegory surely is that it does not part these. The extension of significance which gives great allegories their moving and permanent power to tell us something about man's relation to all else we call real depends directly on the power of allegory to get the psychic stage and the cosmic relevance of what happens there into one figure.[17]

The "art" of *amor* must therefore be large enough in its scope to embody general truths in the particulars of its narrative, and this requisite in itself points in the direction of encyclopedism.

Early in the *Roman*, Lorris asserts the originality of his work: "Its matter is good and new" (line 39). The "newness" of the *Roman* consists in its combining of elements already present in medieval literary tradition in a new way. Langlois long ago attempted to sort out the poem's major elements; his pioneering work treats the erotic tradition, *courtoisie*, arts of love, allegory and dream-vision.[18] Lewis clearly suggests that its importance lies in bringing together erotic subject matter and allegory in a thoroughgoing "allegorical love poem."[19] More recently, Jung, in his study of the backgrounds of French allegory, asserts that the *Roman* is in fact the first poem to combine all of its elements.[20] In combining the erotic tradition, as it had become colored by *courtoisie*, with radical allegory, Guillaume created a work so different in scope and texture from what had preceded it as to constitute a genre unto itself, regardless of its debts to earlier works.

The encyclopedic quality of the *Roman* is more apparent in Meun's continuation than in Lorris's lines. Langlois takes the view that Meun's portion is less an art of love than a compilation of discussions on various subjects, differing in character from Lorris's part and proving by its digressive quality that Meun had no clear plan in mind as he wrote.[21] Lorris, certainly, remains very close to the experience of the Lover throughout, while Meun at times appears to wander, to present figures whose views seem either incompatible with or irrelevant to those of the Lover. One must recognize, however, that Meun's excursions into philosophical lecturing and antifeminist or anticlerical invective, all of which are appropriate to the figures who offer them,[22] are a function of his desire to encompass all of the art of love, to achieve the stated purpose which he may well have taken more seriously and, as Gunn suggests, conceived in fuller terms, than did Lorris.[23] All of Meun's diverse material is justifiable as being important to the overall structure of the allegorical argument.[24]

Nonetheless, this abundance of learned disquisition, encyclopedic information, and satiric invective leads our attention away from Amant, the central consciousness of the work. In listening for thousands of lines to La Vielle's advice to Bel Acueil or to Nature's "confession" to Genius, one tends to forget the narrative circumstances which precipitated these passages. The problem is like that of the *Architrenius*: the poet's desire to get everything in gives the poem a kind of centrifugal force as the elements of its narrative argument spin in widening arcs away from its core. No matter how coherent the argument of the poem when seen as a whole, Meun's *Roman* cannot entirely escape the charges of digressiveness. One would not, however, wish to abridge the poem; to edit out parts of its carefully constructed arguments would perhaps restore Amant to a more central position in the "story," but it would destroy the intellectual depth and coherence which are its great virtue. This encyclopedic poem, which the *Roman* becomes in Meun's hands (whatever Lorris's original intentions), has its own structural logic. This logic, holding together and giving meaning to the work's various elements, differs significantly from that of Boethian Apocalypse.[25]

Langlois points out Meun's numerous borrowings from Boethius and Alanus.[26] He also attributes to their influence what he perceives as the change in the character of the *Roman* from Lorris's portion to Meun's—presumably the new philosophical, discursive quality—and notes a similarity to the *Consolation* and the *De planctu* in the *Roman*'s form as well.[27] Michael H. Means argues that the work as a whole, though "primarily not a true consolatio," derives its form in part from Boethius's *Consolation*.[28] Certainly there are some general similarities of the *Roman* to the Boethian genre, the most important being the narrator-visionary who is the focus of our attention. However, the potential emotional impact of the first-person narrator is partly dissipated by the use of allegory: when Amant in his own voice expresses his feelings and opinions, he resembles the Boethian narrator, but when these are personified in various figures, the affective potentialities of the human narrator are sacrificed for the sake of the analysis of his constituent parts.[29] Means further observes that, while Amant is not in need of consolation in the same sense that the Boethian narrator is, he does receive instruction through a series of dialogues, and the poem as a whole is instructional.[30] Still, it would be distorting the *Roman* to overemphasize the very general parallels between Amant and Boethius, or between the dialogues in which they take part. Much in the *Roman* is too radically different from anything in the *Consolation* and its successors for easy analogies in form to have more than superficial validity.

One entire section of the *Roman*, however, comes into very close contact with Boethius's *Consolation*, and that contact offers us insight into the limitations which Meun apparently saw in the Boethian genre. I am speaking of the second appearance of Reson, together with the material immediately preceding it. Lorris's allegorical account of the youthful experiences of Amant owes virtually nothing in form or substance to the Boethian genre. As this portion ends, Bel Acueil has been imprisoned and Amant is disconsolate over his apparent inability to achieve his erotic goal. Lorris breaks off in the midst of Amant's lament over his situation (lines 3975–4028). Meun completes Amant's lament (lines 4029–190) and immediately reintroduces the figure

Boethian Apocalypse

Reson. The sequence of events thus repeats that of Reson's first appearance, immediately following Amant's estrangement from Bel Acueil, in which she simply rebuked him for his folly in serving Amor (2982–3056), but here she engages him in what Langlois and D. W. Robertson accurately identify as a Boethian dialogue (4191–7200).[31] The dialogue begins with Reson's attempt to free Amant from the "prison" of Amor by exposing the god as he really is, a procedure identical with that used by Lady Philosophy in freeing Boethius from his slavery to Fortune (*Consolation* 2, pr. 1–pr. 2): "It is a good thing to know one's lord; if you knew this God of love well, you could escape easily from the prison where you are thus wasting away" (lines 4238–41). She goes on with her attempts to define the foolish, vicious love that Amant presently serves and the kind of virtuous, rational love that she wishes him to pursue instead. Reson is identical in all but name to Boethius's Philosophy, and much of her discourse is either taken directly from or inspired by books 2 and 3 of the *Consolation*.

This dialogue is a kind of parody of the *Consolation*. The verbal echo of Boethius's description of Philosophy's sudden arrival (*Consolation* 1, pr. 1) in Amant's reintroduction of Reson (lines 4191–98) is unmistakable. The reason for his evocation of Boethius in the midst of Lorris's anatomy of secular love can be found in part, at least, in Meun's preface to his translation of the *Consolation*, where he tells us how he read the Latin work.[32] He begins by pointing out that all things in Nature tend toward good, seeking what is good for them. Human beings, however, are not governed by necessity in seeking the good and are therefore likely to err in choosing *biens sensibles*, goods which appeal to the senses, rather than *biens entendibles*, the true goods perceived by the understanding. The *Consolation* teaches men to choose the true goods and avoid the false. Those who seek *biens entendibles* endure misfortune well and pass into the divine life. Man is thus divided into two parts, "that is, into a man tormented and controlled by sensual passions and into a man divinely elevated by intelligible goods." Because only Philosophy can lead us to *biens entendibles*, Boethius represents himself here as a man enslaved to his sensual desires, and Philosophy as a man pursuing *biens entendibles*. "So two persons are signified here, that is, the patient and the physician, because sorrow and infirmity of the heart on account of temporal goods are found in a man of weak and frail thought, but a man of noble and perfect understanding possesses the ability to console and strengthen himself against such sorrows." In Lorris's *Roman*, Amant has been pursuing his Rose, clearly a good which appeals to his senses, and is tormented by his loss of this temporal good. Meun, following

Lorris in separating the sensual and rational aspects of Amant, brings them together in a confrontation which, by recalling Boethius and Philosophy, underscores Amant's role as one of *li malades* who seek false goods. Thus it is not merely the doctrine espoused by Reson but the literary situation itself as well which has moral implications here.

What appears to have happened is that Amant's despairing complaint struck a familiar chord in Meun, reminding him of the opening complaint of the *Consolation*—which he seems to have already planned to translate[33]—and he began his continuation by taking this complaint as a point of departure for a philosophical dialogue which he intended his readers to recognize as being Boethian in its function. Lorris's entire narrative thus became in Meun's hands a sort of prologue to Amant's complaint, corresponding in content and function, though not in its placement before the complaint, to Boethius's account of the circumstances of his imprisonment (*Consolation* 1, pr. 4). We cannot, of course, know the precise sequence of ideas leading to Meun's final plan for Reson, but it seems entirely possible that his initial impulse was to complete the work by developing a dialogue, patterned on the *Consolation*, in which Reson would lead the confused, despairing narrator out of his temporal dilemma, bringing the poem to a satisfactorily philosophical, moral ending.

What Meun finally produced is, of course, quite different. The philosophical dialogue trails off into Amant's foolish quarrel with Reson over her use of unrefined language, and it has no beneficial effect upon the visionary-narrator, who rejects her. Lorris's careful analysis of Amant's mentality, in conjunction with Meun's intelligence and his ironic temperament, made any sort of rationalistic resolution to Amant's problem impossible.[34] Meun's inherited literary goal—to anatomize *amor*—could not be accomplished within the framework of the Boethian form, even as that form had been modified by Alanus. Lorris's complex allegory of the process of Amant's falling in love and pursuing his goal in the face of both internal and external impediments could be reduced to the mere setting out of a problem for rational solution only by ignoring the complexity and subtlety which is its unique virtue. It might have been possible for Meun's Amant to have abandoned Amor for Reson and thus joined the Boethian narrator as one who had been educated to see through his initial errors, but it is clear throughout the dialogue that, however interested Amant may at times be in Reson's discourse, he will not be won over by her.[35]

To make Amant follow Reson's way out of his dilemma, Meun would have had to ignore the realities of the experience of secular, sensual love as Lorris had presented them.[36] Boethius recognizes

Boethian Apocalypse

human emotion as an impediment to the attainment of a rational view of his narrator's predicament; Philosophy must drive away the Muses, and the Boethian persona at first balks at accepting her "easy medicine" (*Consolation* 2, pr. 3–pr. 4). Lorris, too, had earlier brought Reson down from her tower to remonstrate with Amant, and his rejection of her warnings then underscored the irrationality of one who is firmly committed to the kind of love represented by Amor (lines 2955–3082). Amant remains enslaved by his passions and therefore incapable of responding to his rational impulses. Meun, like Lorris, is "realistic" (in a modern sense) in that he presents the experience of "love" as it commonly manifests itself in ordinary human beings; he does not transform it into what it ought to be in an ideally rational lover.

Moreover, as Tuve points out, although Reson offers a rational alternative to Amor's kind of love, even she is inadequate as an instructress, for she does not understand irrational passion.[37] Her attempt to expose Amant's god, Amor, as he really is turns out to be nothing more than a conventional list of the paradoxes to which those who follow him are subject (lines 4263–328), drawn directly from Alanus's Nature's *descriptio Cupidinis* (*De planctu*, m. 5). Paradoxes are not, of course, reasonable, and Amant is right to object (with an implicit criticism of Alanus's earlier attempt to explain the rationally inexplicable)[38] that he has described but not defined Amor: "But since you have described love to me, and have praised and blamed it so much, I beg you to define it in such a way that I may better remember it, for I have never heard it defined" (lines 4341–45).

Her further attempts to define legitimate love (natural affection, friendship, love of all mankind) and distinguish it from illegitimate love (sensuality, love of Fortune's gifts) satisfy Amant no better. Although he cannot himself see the implications of what he says, Amant's later objection that Reson's Boethian view of the relationship of love, Fortune, and true happiness sets goals too lofty for him, that such rational love is beyond the capability of most human beings, is also just: that sort of love left the world when the gods, "Right and Charity and Faith" and "Justice," fled to the heavens (lines 5358–74). This suggests that the sort of untainted rationality that underlies all of Reson's conceptions about legitimate love has not since the Golden Age been available to ordinary humanity. The Golden Age is a common medieval figure for man's prelapsarian state, and the Reason of a postlapsarian Amant simply does not hold the uncontested sway over his passions that, from Reson's point of view, it should.[39] Amant is no Boethius, and Reson is wasting her time. Amant's final rejection of

84

Reson is entirely appropriate to the experience being analyzed and opens the way for Meun to continue the exploration and definition of love as it manifests itself in the secular sphere of a fallen world. Meun finally refuses to turn Lorris's "art of love" in the direction of a perfunctory statement of a single, purportedly valid philosophical position. His parody of the Boethian dialogue emphasizes the moral and intellectual distance between the philosophical Boethius and the sensual Amant.[40]

Lorris and Meun both employ several kinds of figures in their attempt to encompass the entire experience of profane love. The proliferation of figures is apparent to even a casual reader. At the center of the narrative is a "real" human being, Amant, who as Lorris's persona narrates the generalized experience of a youthful lover. The voices of the poets can occasionally be distinguished from that of Amant, creating at times a certain ambivalence in the point of view of the narrative. Lorris purports to be relating a dream he had about himself; since he was twenty when he had the dream (line 21), and is recounting it five years later (line 46), after it had come true (lines 28–30), there is at times some distance between Lorris-Amant's perceptions of what is happening to him and the retrospective perceptions of Lorris the poet. On the simplest level, the poet can for example see Amor stalking Amant, while of course Amant is unaware of his danger (lines 1299ff.). More complex is Lorris's account of the pool of Narcissus (lines 1423ff.), in which Amant easily dismisses his momentary fears of the place as "folie" (line 1520), while at the same time the poet alerts the reader to Amant's error:

> I wanted to remain there forever, gazing at the fountain and the crystals, which showed me the hundred thousand things that appeared there; but it was a painful hour when I admired myself there. Alas! How I have sighed since then because of that deceiving mirror. If I had known its powers and qualities, I would never have approached it, for now I have fallen into the snare that has captured and betrayed many a man. [Lines 1601–12]

At times it is difficult to tell precisely whose observations are being expressed; when Reson first arrives, comments upon her angelic appearance may reflect Amant's immediate impression of her beauty (lines 2962–72), but it is difficult to reconcile the next statement with the consciousness of Amant, who wants nothing to do with her: "Know, if the letter does not lie, that God made her personally in his likeness and in his image and gave her such advantage that she has the power and the lordship to keep man from folly, provided that he be such that he believe her" (lines 2973-79). Either this is Lorris the poet interrupting Amant, or else Amant himself has recognized the divinity of Reson, but chooses nevertheless to ignore her advice. The important point is that Lorris is quite willing to sacrifice consistency in narrative point of view to manipulate the reader's attitude toward his youthful hero.

Such complications are compounded by Meun, since he is performing the unlikely task of completing the retrospective account of a dream dreamed almost half a century before by someone else. Meun too relates events, like the confession of Nature to Genius (lines 15861-19408), of which Amant could not logically have been aware, but he seems more careful than Lorris to avoid the ambiguities inherent in mingling Amant's narrative with authorial observations. Still, when he addresses the reader directly, as he does in defending the *Roman* against criticism (lines 15105-272) or in moralizing the story of Venus and Adonis (lines 15721-34), as the poet who has dreamed and then experienced whatever is at the moment happening to Amant, it is impossible to tell whether he is speaking (ironically or otherwise) as Jean de Meun or as Guillaume de Lorris. Thus within the *Roman* we have several human voices (as opposed to the voices of allegorical figures) among which we may choose: Lorris-Amant, who experiences and comments upon events as they transpire; Lorris the poet, who relates and comments upon his dream; Meun-Amant, who is virtually identical with Lorris-Amant; Meun speaking in the role of Lorris the poet, commenting sometimes ironically and sometimes directly upon the dream action; and, possibly, Meun the poet in a role like that of Lorris the poet. Finally, in Meun's portion, we have a new voice, that of Amant speaking in retrospect and without the critical edge characteristic of the voices of the two poets. This Amant, older and more experienced, but completely sympathetic with the attitudes of his younger self, emerges most clearly toward the end of the *Roman*, in his paean to his scrip and staff (lines 21347-97) and in his comments on the relative merits of old and young women (lines 21405-552); he is the logical development of the young Amant at the end of his long and educational quest for the Rose. In reading the *Roman*, one must constantly be aware of the possibility of shifts between these narratorial voices to recognize the ironies inherent in the distances between the poets and their first-person narrators.[41]

The Rose creates problems of a different sort by being neither a realistic human being nor a simple personification but rather a symbol. Langlois identified the Rose as Amant's lady, while Lewis identified it as the lady's love.[42] But at the very end of the poem the Rose is viewed quite cynically by Amant (and Venus a bit earlier), if not as the female genitalia themselves, at least, in a more general sense, as the object of his sexual desire, so that it would be justifiable to equate the Rose and the lady's sexual favors. Gunn emphasizes the multiplicity of associations which the Rose accumulates in the course of the poem.[43] Finally, Tuve is certainly right in her observation that "proper allegorical ambiguity is superbly illustrated in Jean de Meun's own Rose, which is played upon by the shifting lights of first one character's conception of her, then another."[44] In neither Lorris nor Meun has the Rose one uniquely "correct" meaning, beyond its narrative function as the object of Amant's desire. For every figure in the poem it is an object to be either sought or avoided, but for each figure the idea of what it is, and therefore what attitude to assume toward it, is different. Amant's view of it changes through the course of his education, as he is affected by the various other views expressed to him or otherwise enforced upon him. The Rose "is" whatever its particular observer thinks it is, and so, in its ambiguity and multiplicity of meaning, it functions as a true literary symbol.

The other figures in the *Roman* are less difficult to identify. First, we have personified aspects of the psychology of Amant and his Rose lady. Lewis divides these figures into three groups: qualities belonging to the hero, qualities belonging to the heroine, and "neutral qualities" belonging to both.[45] Some of these figures, like Dangier, Bel Acueil, and Amor's barons, have only limited roles as emotional or intellectual responses of the human figure of Amant or the human aspect of the Rose, but some are genuinely cosmic forces. Reson, Amor, Venus, Nature, and Genius represent important philosophical concepts. As principles operative throughout the visible world, they exert influences that may extend beyond the garden of Deduit, but these influences cannot be recognized apart from their manifestations in a realm available to human perception and activity, and therefore they are not really separable from the human narrative, where they appear in intimate association with Amant and his Rose lady. In addition, we have figures representing external social and psychological conditions which affect the love affair, as, for example, Oiseuse and Deduit, conditions of the milieu in which love flourishes, and Jalousie, an aspect of the lady's guardians which inhibits the affair. Also we have realistic type figures, Ami and La Vielle, who influence the course of the affair and extend the range of views of love presented in the poem. Finally, although they are not part of the action of the narrative, we have figures in the various mythological fables and exemplary descriptions, like Narcissus, Pygmalion, and the Jealous Husband described by Ami, who likewise extend the range of views in, and function as commentary upon the action of, the poem. The complexity of the relationships between all these figures far exceeds anything we have encountered in the Boethian Apocalypse, and defines the totality of the experience being examined in the allegory.

The locus of the allegorical action in the *Roman* is likewise more complex than we have seen in earlier works.[46] In one sense the entire action takes place in the mind of Guillaume de Lorris, who claims to have dreamed it. This enveloping locus has little bearing upon the meaning of the vision; some medieval visionary literature appears within a dream framework, and some does not, and it does not seem to me that the intended audience for such works would concern themselves with this distinction. Within the vision the locus is problematical. In the *Consolation* the literal locus is Boethius's prison, and in the *De planctu* the action is not localized at all; one might interpret either vision as an internal one. In neither case does it seem necessary to reinterpret the setting of the vision to arrive at its meaning, and in both the important point is that everything transpires in the immediate vicinity of the visionary narrator. Even in the *Architrenius*, where the shifting locus of action includes in its compass much of the known world, this world appears to the hero (and to the reader) only as he enters it, one place at a time, and each place remains significant only so long as he remains in it. In the cosmic allegories of Bernardus and Alanus the case is different, for the narrator is an omniscient third person, and the locus includes the entire, orderly cosmos appropriate to the action. The poet's eye moves freely after his figures as they pass through this cosmic locus.

In the *Roman*, however, the locus of action at any given point may be vague or nonexistent. The general area in which the action takes place is, literally, the walled garden of Deduit, which Lewis takes to represent "the world of courtly society,"[47] and which Robertson tends to identify with the traditional evil gardens of fleshly delight.[48] Given the sorts of things excluded from this garden,[49] as well as what goes on within it, it must represent a socially limited world in which the particular kind of love under examination can exist. Beyond the social requisites for entry, however, defining the garden in specific terms is difficult. It is the specific locus of *amor*, and since this *amor* is defined by the entire poem, a definition of the garden cannot be more limited and precise than the totality of the experience contained within it. It is simply the metaphorical space which contains and confines the subject matter of the vision. Everything that happens, and every figure that appears, within its walls has some role in the experience of *amor*.

Within this metaphorical space the reader tends to lose physical orientation, not because he does not know precisely the geographical relationships between the gate, Deduit's dancing area, the pool of Narcissus, the hedged rose plot, and the Rose's castle prison — these, after all, need no physically precise placement in an allegory — but because, in Meun's portion especially, one cannot keep track of where the narrator stands with respect to the action. At times the action may be taking place, figuratively, within his mind, as in the case of his two debates with Reson. Certainly Reson cannot be a native resident of the garden like Deduit and Amor, for she consistently opposes all that these figures represent. She has entered here as an aspect of Amant's consciousness which he can suppress but never really escape; the symbolic *tour* in which she dwells suggests perhaps Amant's head, certainly her elevated status and view of the world, and also her isolation from the life of the garden. Virtually all of the action in Lorris, and much of it in Meun, takes place in the immediate vicinity of Amant, with him as a (sometimes unwitting) participant. Thus he converses with Amor and Ami, joins Deduit's dance, is pursued by Amor, and tries repeatedly to get his hands on the Rose.

Increasingly in Meun's portion actions directly related to Amant's goals take place at some unspecified distance from him; he is not, for exampie, present at La Vielle's interviews with Ami and Bel Acueil. Venus must be summoned from her home to aid Amor's forces, but it is not clear that her dwelling on Mount Cythera is within the garden (lines 15629–44); since she is clearly the force of sexual desire, divorced from social mores and classes, one assumes that it is not. A cosmic power, she is everywhere but manifests herself only in human beings who come under her influence. Likewise, Nature's workshop is not localized; her realm encompasses not only the garden but all of the created world. The complexity, in relationship to Amant, of the figures who either appear or are discussed in the narrative, and of the loci of action, reflects the complexity and sweep of the allegory as a whole. With so many aspects of the amatory experience being examined, it is no surprise that we may lose track of Amant himself for long stretches at a time, thus moving far away from what would be the emotional and intellectual center of a Boethian poem. Nonetheless, such complexity and variety later enters the Boethian tradition in English.

Aside from its erotic subject matter, probably the most important influence exerted by the *Roman* upon Boethian Apocalypse, and especially upon Chaucer's excursions into this genre, is a sustained irony which keeps the reader at an objective distance from the narrative. Through irony every figure in the poem is exposed as being inadequate, foolish, or genuinely sinful in his or her view of love. As Tuve observes, everyone in Meun's part of the poem attempts in some fashion to define love for Amant:

> The Lover is shown as falling for one after another insufficient or damaging definition of the Rose, and we are never unaware of the large element of truth or attractiveness each contains, nor of the interesting fact that people have always so fallen; one's own memory of how true the definitions sometime seemed is an ironic note struck. Jean shows some gaping hole in every definer's equipment, and his methods for uncovering holes have the widest comic variety.[50]

We need add here only the reminder that Meun builds on a foundation laid by Lorris. Behind the use of irony in the *Roman* lies at least a partial source in the *Consolation* and the *De planctu*.

We observed that Lorris, as the poet looking backward in time upon himself as a younger Amant, occasionally injects comments upon the actions and opinions of Amant which underscore his folly. Amant begins innocently enough as a youth attracted to a life of self-indulgent pleasure. In this environment he falls in love, as any adolescent might, for scarcely adequate reasons and devotes himself obsessively to the pursuit of the object of his narcissistic desires. Lorris portrays a willful, arbitrary, adolescent psyche, newly arrived at an age when love (of a sort) commands its attention; after all, for the allegory to be convincing as an anatomy of love, it must appear valid in its presentation of the particular example. Amant's enslavement to his passions is comparable to that of Boethius early in the *Consolation*; it is serious but not irrevocable. The narrator-visionaries of Lorris, Boethius, and Alanus are recognizably human in their emotional outbursts and intellectual errors, and are all to some extent objects of irony, insofar as they make mistakes in judgment which the reader either perceives for himself or is alerted to by the various authority figures.

While the irony inherent in a comically obtuse or willful narrator occurs only occasionally in the *Consolation* and the *De planctu*, this same kind of irony is emphasized and sustained in the *Roman*. In both Lorris and Meun, Amant follows the dictates of his passions rather than being guided by Reson. In his choice and in his inability to perceive its folly, Amant as a fictional character is doubtless truer to human nature than the Boethian figure, who is finally idealized as a more or less perfect recipient of true philosophy. Amant's obstinate refusal to consider Reson's advice has no parallel in earlier works, and it places him in the position of having to follow an irrational course toward a misdirected goal. Because his goal is unworthy of a rational, virtuous man, he must accept aid and direction from unworthy guides, continually compromising himself by following whatever course is expedient, as when, in his dialogue with Ami, he recognizes and momentarily rebels at the duplicitous nature of Ami's advice (lines 7765–88 et seq.), but after his encounter with Richece he resigned himself to following the course of "Traïson" (lines 10267–76).

At the end of the poem Amant attains his goal. By this time, however, as the imagery of the assault on the tower and of Amant's erotic "pilgrimage" makes clear (lines 20755–21232, 21316–750), the Rose symbol has declined from its earlier, elevated position as the object of a more innocent Amant's apparently genuine devotion to its final role as the mere receptacle for his pent-up sexual juices. The stories of Pygmalion and of Cynyras and Myrrha, together with the complex, extended image of the Rose lady as a female idol whose genitalia form "un saintuaire" for Amant's devotion (lines 20755–21232), point up the idolatrous quality of Amant's *amor*, suggest that what he experiences is a kind of incestuous desire for an object created in his own fantasies, and remind the reader (lines 20843–49) of Lorris's earlier evocation of Narcissus.[51] Finally, through his remarks upon his staff, scrip and hammers ("...thank God, I know how to forge. I tell you truly that I count my two hammers and my sack dearer than my citole or my harp. Nature did me a great honor when she equipped me with this armor and so taught me its use that she made me a good and wise workman.... Since then it has often comforted me in many places where I have carried it" [21343–50, 367–68]), as well those on the relative value and conquest of older women and those on the benefits of variety if one prefers younger women (lines 21398–552), Amant reveals that he has gained considerable sexual experience in the interval between this first conquest and the present time at which he is narrating his dream (cf. lines 21ff.). His allusions to his more recent amorous successes imply that his Rose has not satisfied him for long. He has become as cynically worldly as Ami and La Vielle. His ultimate success is merely sexual, his love has emerged as lust and idolatry, and he has become morally and spiritually degraded by all of the false enlightenment he has absorbed along the way. The movement of the Boethian narrator is upward toward light, that of Amant downward into darkness.[52]

The figures who undertake to assist Amant all for one reason or another prove inadequate in their views of love, and again we may see the possible influence of Boethian works behind this phenomenon. Lady Philosophy's limitations are appropriate to what she represents and do not impair her efficacy as purveyor of the highest kind of secular wisdom. The similar limitations of Alanus's Nature do somewhat impair her ability to resolve the problems posed by the narrator of the *De planctu* and result in the final irony of her ability to exhort and condemn human beings, but not to change them. The irony of at least Meun's portion of the *Roman* consists in his presentation of a series of self-styled authorities on love, whose views of the subject mingle valid and invalid ideas, conflict with one another, and cannot successfully explain the problems, paradoxes, and contradictions inherent in the attempt to define love in an exclusively secular context. Thus Nature affirms a totally amoral kind of love. As Tuve observes, she understands no higher law than her own, and her only concern is that this law, the law of procreation of the species, be fulfilled.[53] So far as she knows, death, not damnation, is the supreme danger to humanity. Meun has stripped this figure of the close association with Reason which she had in his source for her, Alanus's *De planctu*.[54] Meun's Nature does not provide man's understanding, she cannot comprehend the supranatural incarnation (lines 19025–160), and, deprived of the moral position which her alliance with Reason entailed, she supports Venus, Amor, and Amant. But procreation is never the goal, though it may be an accidental result, of the activities of these figures, and so Nature and Genius, her priest, become the servants of an indiscriminate sexual desire whose real goal is simply physical pleasure. Nature's religion of procreation is a temporal, materialistic belief which knows no moral or spiritual dimension for man, and her alliance with Amant and his supporters, whatever its success from her point of view, is one of mutual convenience and self-interest.[55]

John Fleming treats Reson as the authoritative figure in the *Roman*, as the dispenser to Amant of "the store of traditional Christian wisdom,"[56] but it is clear from a careful reading of the colloquy between Reson and Amant that she, too, is an inadequate instructor on the subject of *amor*. Her wisdom is not exclusively or uniquely Christian; rather, it is the sort of rational wisdom available to the great pagan writers who, either directly or indirectly through the works of writers like Boethius and Alanus, supply Meun with the substance of her discourse. She is limited precisely because she cannot discuss love from a Christian perspective. She may well be Amant's best adviser, but, as Tuve points out,[57] she cannot persuade Amant to pursue a more virtuous kind of love because she does not understand irrational passion. In a postlapsarian world — which Deduit's garden certainly is — Reson does not hold uncontested sway over human emotions.

Ultimately no figure emerges to provide an authoritative definition of *amor*, because none can be drawn from this context, from the realm of postlapsarian Nature. Likewise, there can be no final resolution of the relationships among the various figures into a higher, all-embracing unity. Reson is excluded from the experience of passionate *amor*, while the other figures, including the worldly cynics Amis and La Vielle and the alien but useful Faus Semblant, are drawn into the retinue of Amor and Venus to pursue a common goal which each understands according to his own allegorical "character" and which in its attainment fails to reveal any common element to harmonize their views.[58]

In this way all the local ironies of the *Roman* are drawn by Meun into the larger irony of the whole:

> It might be claimed, and I do not know the answer, that Jean fully intended as one of his points the one great and shocking omission from his book: any character who loves anyone. It would be very like this writer, and whether or not it was meant to satirize men's excesses and misapprehensions, it surely does so. The world of the *Roman* is quite loveless, lacking markedly its multi-tudinous common forms of disinterested affection, kindness, generosity, kept faith, good will. Self-love and self-interest are anatomized time and again. There is no attempt whatsoever to portray caritas. This was certainly glaringly apparent to any medi-eval reader.[59]

Tuve's analysis of Meun's *Roman* bears out this perception. Various figures profess to know all about *amor*, but no one view is wholly adequate, and all must finally be unacceptable. Within the restricted locus, which encloses only secular views of love, without reference to the forms of *caritas* constituting a truly Christian kind of love, Reson offers the most elevated view of the subject. But Reson's view is necessarily "philosophical" and secular, in that its rationalism pre-cludes the emotional dimension of human desires as well as the theological understanding offered by revelation, and it therefore can-not resolve the paradoxes inherent in the experience of fallen human-ity. Boethian stoicism and rationalism, Ciceronian friendship, disin-terested benevolence, and naturalism are the best substitutes Reson can offer for Amor's eroticism. Nature, by the same token, can offer only a limited, narrowly single-minded conception of love. The principal forces operative in the *Roman*—Reson, Amor, Venus, Nature, and Genius—remain to the very end suspended in solution, never combining to yield a new unity.

Spiritual love, the love of man for God and God for man, together with its earthly manifestations in genuine human affection, is excluded from the garden and so from the immediate, ironic context of the *Roman*'s analysis of temporal love. Nevertheless, Meun draws attention to this higher, more rewarding kind of love in a way which avoids violating the consistency of his carefully circumscribed allegory. One might justifiably question Fleming's assertion that Nature's "account of 'things created' is clearly intended to move the reader to the contemplation of the 'invisible things of God,' His majesty and His infinitely wise ordering of the universe,"[60] but there can be little question that Genius's "sermon" is designed to do precisely that. Very near the final action of the poem Genius describes the Park of the Good Shepherd, which on the basis of its traditional imagery must be identified as the Christian Heaven, and which Genius contrasts to the garden of Deduit (lines 19877–20637).

Genius's precise significance and function are multiple and interrelated. As Nature's confessor he is in one sense superior to her spiritually, but as her priest he is in another sense her servant. He is not merely the morally neutral natural desire of fallen man, as Fleming claims,[61] but is, as Wetherbee observes, "a symbol of all that is best in human nature, with the capabilities and limitations which the fact implies."[62] He links the natural order in which he exerts his influence and the divine order toward which he aspires, but he is not naturally aware of divine grace, and he functions in a fallen world. Meun appears to be suggesting that he has some memory of what the prelapsarian world was like, and a sense of what Heaven may be like; but since he is only a "natural" power, Genius in the sense of human nature, his view, like Nature's, is limited. He knows nothing of Christian revelation or theology (lines 19589–98); the highest law he knows is that of Nature, and the greatest enemy, Atropos (lines 19733–47). His evocation of the Golden Age (lines 20002–190) reveals that he knows the pagan mythological story of Jupiter and Saturn, not the scriptural one of Adam and Eve. He lacks the revealed truth necessary to a full understanding of humanity's history and destiny. He mistakenly believes that in preaching Nature's laws to man he is offering him the true way to the heavenly park (lines 20597–629). And it is certainly an ironic comment upon the "natural" *genius humanum* that, while extolling Nature's laws as man's supreme guide, he conceives of Heaven (correctly) as a place where these laws do not function, where all is perfect, uncorruptible, and timeless (lines 19901–20006). Without revelation man's genius can only posit a general idea of Heaven and cannot know how to attain it.

Despite his limitations, however, a secular Genius, like Reson, is capable of recognizing that the garden of Deduit cannot fulfill the aspirations of human love. Deduit's garden is the locus of sensual pleasure, but sensual pleasure, as Reson observes much earlier (lines 4373–91), should serve the higher goal of procreation. Procreation is Nature's law, and Genius is the force which impels human beings to fulfill that law. At the same time this natural force links the phenomenal world and the spiritual world which lies behind it. The human genius recognizes that the temporal *locus amoenus* can be no more than the imperfect imitation of the truly paradisal garden. In comparing the two gardens, Genius clearly suggests that everything that happens in Deduit's garden and every figure native to it is finally bogus and inadequate. No figure in the poem seems at all aware of the implications of this judgment—Genius himself fails to recognize the paradox of his and Nature's demands being achieved in this false paradise—but surely the reader must recognize them. If all that happens here is a sham, subject to time and decay, then one ought to seek a better place, a more permanent and worthy kind of experience. Genius recognizes the need for something better and has a good idea of what it must be like, but he is incapable of leading anyone to it. Still Genius can point humanity in the right general direction. The clear identity of the park of the Lamb as Heaven should suggest to a Christian reader, aware of the revealed truth as Genius is not, not only the proper goal but also the true way to attain it.

The final, pervasive irony of the *Roman* is that the reader learns about love by learning what it is not. Throughout the poem he observes the wrong sort of lover seeking the wrong object in the wrong place. As Tuve says: "We find ourselves building a definition for love by negatives, as we progress through the ironic presentation of unrelieved inadequacies and deceptions and rationalizations and errors. Genius and Nature for example are not being condemned (intentionally at any rate) for evil ideas but shown as laughably dominated by inadequate ones."[63] Accurate evaluation of irony, in a work as remote in time and cultural milieu from our own as the *Roman*, is often problematical, and it is evident that even some of Meun's near contemporaries had difficulties understanding his ironic technique.[64] Nonetheless, I would argue that Meun's rhetorical technique throughout his *Roman* points toward an ironic reading of the work, even though the relationship between technique and interpretation may not become wholly apparent until the very end of the poem.

Meun was readily conversant with the learning available to literate men of his time,[65] and recent scholarship has pointed out his debt to formal rhetorical practice. Gunn demonstrates the central position of formal rhetoric in the construction of the argument of both parts of the *Roman*.[66] I would add that the device of argument and definition by contraries pervades the entire poem and leads to a final, theoretical statement which offers a valuable insight at once into Meun's rhetorical technique and his irony. Lionel Friedman some years ago noted that this device, "an expository method characteristic of medieval argumentation and of this particular romance: reasoning or demonstration by contraries, the τοὐναντίον of the ancient rhetoricians,"[67] explains the appearance of the Jealous Husband, whom Ami presents as the antithesis to his thesis that male sovereignty destroys love (lines 8425–9462). Paré had shown earlier that the idea of definition by means of opposites, as it appears in Meun's portion of the *Roman*, has its origins in Aristotelian and Scholastic logic,[68] and it would seem that the always implicit theme of defining love accounts for the frequent use of contraries and contrasts in the larger units of the poem's structure.

The oppositions between many of the figures in the poem at least partly define their essential qualities. This is true for figures like Amor and Reson, who never directly confront one another in allegorical combat, as well as figures like Pitié and Dangier or Honte and Delit, who do. In Lorris's portion of the *Roman*, the figures portrayed upon the outer side of the garden wall point toward a definition of this locus by indicating which "vices" are excluded from it (lines 129–460), and the paired sets of arrows of Amor help define the god's particular kind of love (lines 907–84). In both parts of the poem exemplary stories and figures like Narcissus and Adonis are employed to teach lovers what they should not do (lines 1505–1508, 15721–34). All the authorities in Meun's part use the device of contrast. Reson contrasts the folly of youth with the wisdom of age (lines 4400–598) and true friendship with its opposite (lines 4655–806). Ami offers the way of Trop Doner as the alternative to his own way of deceit and trickery in the quest for Bel Acueil (lines 7855–930 et seq.). La Vielle offers her advice to Bel Acueil as a corrective to the sort of life she herself led in her youth (lines 12706–14516). Meun introduces Nature by contrasting her works with those inferior products of Art (lines 15983–16118). Nature's "confession" is structured upon the opposition between the decorous natural behavior of all realms of the created world and the unnatural conduct of man (lines 16771–18991 et seq.).

All such examples of argument and definition by contraries might conceivably be dismissed as fortuitous, the result simply of ingrained, unconscious rhetorical habit, were it not that they lead up to Genius's final, all-important evaluation of Deduit's garden by contrast to its heavenly contrary, and to a final, theoretical statement of the method of definition and evaluation itself. We have already discussed Genius's contrasting of the two gardens and its implications — the perfect park of the Lamb defines the inadequate quality of the garden of Deduit. This passage is preceded by and closely related to the contrast Genius draws between the postlapsarian Iron Age and the lost Golden Age, and to the contrast he draws between the beauty of the landscape of the Golden Age and that of the heavenly park (lines 19997–20248). Immediately following Genius's "sermon," the story of Pygmalion is prefaced by a statement of the superiority of the beauty of Amant's idol to that of Pygmalion's statue (lines 21188–97), and this story brings us to the final assault upon the tower-prison and the curious concluding description by Amant of his victory.

The final four hundred lines of the *Roman* are not entirely straightforward in their purpose. Amant begins by presenting himself "like a good pilgrim" (line 21317) on the way to his journey's end, pausing almost immediately to sing the praises of the pilgrim's staff and scrip (lines 21323–97) and thereby characterizing himself as the cynical lecher he has become. He maintains this extended pilgrim-staff metaphor to describe the beginning of the deflowering of his shrine (lines 21553–639) and then reverts to the rose metaphor to describe its completion (lines 21640–750), but before getting on with his work, Amant digresses for a few moments to discuss mistresses old and young (lines 21405–552). Besides revealing his cynicism and profligacy, this digression serves several purposes, the most obvious of which is to delay the climactic action and heighten the reader's sense of anticipation. Since his first Rose, Amant has become an expert on "old roads" (line 21407), as well as a connoisseur of "new paths" (line 21515). Fleming is therefore quite right to observe that Amant has become "the last of the *doctores amoris*";[69] he no longer needs the various teachers he has encountered, for he has learned their lessons thoroughly and now has the credentials for teaching his own theory of *amor*.

When Amant moves from the subject of old women to that of younger ones, he appears to go even farther afield of his pilgrimage, but in so doing he brings the reader back to the theme of contraries. If one prefers younger girls, he says, one ought to try them all, like a gourmet testing various dishes, for in women as in food, or anything else, "he who has not tried evil will hardly ever know anything of the good" (lines 21533–34). The theory follows: "Thus things go by contraries; one is the gloss of the other. If one wants to define one of the pair, he must remember the other, or he will never, by any intention, assign a definition to it; for he who has no understanding of the two will never understand the difference between them, and without this difference no definition that one may make can come to anything" [21.543–52]. This is the last theoretical statement in a long poem filled with theories; coming as it does at a point in the narrative where it seems digressive and wholly unrelated to the action which follows, it demands the reader's attention. Amant, without intending to do so, unaware of the implications of his statement, has made explicit what has been implicitly suggested by the rhetoric of the *Roman* about the poem's theme. Surely this is a key passage for the entire poem: the *Roman* defines love by describing in detail its opposite.

Through Genius's evocation of the park of the Lamb, which exists beyond Deduit's garden and is infinitely superior to it, and through the finally negative, ironic view of temporal, erotic love which emerges from his narrative, Meun succeeds in pointing the reader toward a source of resolution and harmony standing counterpoised against the problems, paradoxes, inadequacies, and chaotic activity of the *Roman*. He manages to do this without violating the limits imposed by the *locus* of action of his allegory, and without violating the decorum of his ironic approach to his subject matter. Genius remains an ironic figure; he is limited by his sphere of activity, he is wrong about the purpose of love and its proper practice, and he does not really know enough about Paradise to know how to achieve it, but he does know that it exists and that it is superior to the natural world. The reader knows what Genius knows, and should be reminded by his truth as well as his errors that revelation teaches him much more than his natural impulses can. It teaches him in a positive way what the *Roman* teaches him only negatively and by implication: the kind of love that will lead him to the park of the Lamb. Meun's ironic method appears to have been too subtle and liable to misinterpretation to have become popular with most later poets, but at least one, Chaucer, appears to have mastered it and put it to good use.

6

CONFESSIO AMANTIS

In his continuation of Guillaume de Lorris's *Roman de la Rose*, Jean de Meun undertakes to reexamine ideas about secular love, nature, and reason which he apparently found in Alanus's *De planctu naturae*. His conclusions concerning these cosmic forces, their relationships to one another, and their moral implications for humanity differ in significant ways from those of Alanus but certainly do not lay to rest the questions which he had raised. In the 1380s both Geoffrey Chaucer in *The Parliament of Fowls* and John Gower in the *Confessio Amantis* enter into the discussion of love and nature, and each employs the Boethian form of vision poem as his vehicle in seeking to clarify his own views. It is to these two English poems that we now turn. Although Gower's poem was almost certainly written a few years after that of his friend Chaucer, and therefore might well have been undertaken as, in part at least, a response to it, the *Confessio* in fact reveals little influence from the *Parliament's* treatment of love. Like Chaucer, Gower appears to be responding to the *De planctu* and the *Roman*, and since his vision poem is less difficult, structurally and conceptually, than the *Parliament*, we shall deal with it first here.

The *Confessio Amantis*, Gower's only long poem in English, has the dubious distinction of being over 11,000 lines longer than the *Roman de la Rose*. That the *Confessio* runs to over 33,000 lines has long interfered with attempts to view it as a unified work; its principal editor, G. C. Macaulay, describes it as a collection of stories within a narrative frame: "[Gower] found his true vocation . . . as a teller of stories. The rest is all machinery, sometimes poetical and interesting, sometimes tiresome and clumsy, but the stories are the main thing."[1] For over half a century C. S. Lewis stood virtually alone in defending the *Confessio* as a unified whole, but since the appearance of John H. Fisher's important study of Gower in 1964, scholars have begun to reassess the nature of the poem's "machinery," its prologue, narrative framework, and characters.[2] One important result of the reassessment has been the recognition by Russell A. Peck and Michael H. Means of its place in a generic tradition which derives from Boethius.[3] Written and revised between about 1385 and 1393,[4] the *Confessio* appears in the wake of Chaucer's experiments with the vision form and may well owe its generic inspiration to them. It is structurally innovative, an attempt to expand the essentially Boethian form, although one may agree with Lewis that, while "showing a concern for form and unity," Gower "almost succeeds" in producing a unified whole.[5]

The principal Boethian elements of the *Confessio* need be reviewed only briefly here. To ignore for the moment Gower's Prologue and introductory remarks in book 1, the narrative "plot" appears quite straightforward. The narrator, Amans, wanders in May in a forest where he can his "wo compleigne" (1.114). He suffers from unrequited love, and, so miserable that he wishes to die, he prays to Venus and Cupid (lines 93–137), who immediately appear before him. Cupid casts "A firy Dart" through his heart and passes on. Venus casts "no goodly chiere" upon him but pauses to interrogate him about his plight, after which she turns him over to her priest, Genius, so that he can confess and be shriven of his sins against her (lines 138–202). For the next 31,000 lines Genius instructs Amans in the seven deadly sins as they apply to love, and in various other points of wisdom, while Amans either admits or denies his guilt, asks questions, or comments upon Genius's lore. After the confession Genius, at Amans's request, delivers another complaint, written in tears, to Venus, who returns to effect the resolution of Amans's problem and so conclude the vision. A brief epilogue follows.

Venus and Genius share the role of Boethian authority figure. Although Gower does not describe her physical appearance, Venus recalls Lady Philosophy: she arrives in immediate response to the narrator's complaint, asks "What art thou, Sone?" rousing him as if from sleep (1.154–55; cf. *Consolation* 1, pr. 2 et seq.), and urges him to tell his "maladie" so that she can apply her "medicine" (1.164–67, 184–85; cf. *Consolation* 1, pr. 4). Her general tone of suspicion toward Amans parallels Philosophy's impatience with Boethius. At the end of the vision her revelation that he is old finally resolves Amans's suffer-

ing. Genius provides the bulk of the doctrine which prepares Amans
for his final release; taking over from Venus, he instructs the visionary
in moral philosophy and related matters. The interplay between
Genius and his pupil keeps the visionary experience moving toward its
climax. The purpose of the vision is essentially practical; Amans learns
what he needs to know to master himself and come to terms with his
life in the world. Gower is explicit about the practical, exemplary
purpose of his writing:

> For in good feith this wolde I rede,
> That every man ensample take
> Of wisdom which him is betake,
> And that he wot of good aprise
> To teche it forth, for such emprise
> Is forto preise; and therfore I
> Woll wryte and schewe al openly
> How love and I togedre mette,
> Wherof the world ensample fette
> Mai after this. . . .
>
> [1.78–87]

As in all other Boethian narratives, the focus here is upon the
consciousness of the narrator. Amans's suffering precipitates his vision.
Since unrequited love causes his anguish, his vision is presided over by
the goddess of love, and its doctrine is formulated in terms of sins
against love, although, as Pearsall observes, Gower "is not providing
instruction in the art of love, but using love as bait for instruction in
the art of living."[6] Amans cannot help himself. He needs external aid,
for his mind is confused and divided against itself:

> . . .I am destourbed
> In al myn herte, and so contourbed,
> That I ne may my wittes gete,
> So schal I moche thing foryete:
>
> . . . .
>
> Bot now my wittes ben so blinde,
> That I ne can miselven teche.
>
> [1.221–29]

He believes that he needs Venus to grant him success in his love affair
(1.124–37, 168–71); after his confession he becomes aware of the
alternative, that he might be released from bondage to Venus's cause.
Thus the ostensible purpose of the confession is to purge his guilt for
sins against love, while it becomes clear that Genius wishes to purge

101

him of love itself. By the end of the vision Amans has in fact been purged of his love for his uncooperative lady. He gains a new perspective upon himself: his circumstances are unchanged, but his concerns have shifted from earthly to moral wisdom.

The *Confessio* is encyclopedic in its scope. The seven deadly sins provide the organizing principle for the vision; Genius breaks each sin (except the last) into several subcategories, analyzing and illustrating each of these with at least one exemplary tale. Genius also treats the corresponding virtues. Not all of Genius's tales deal directly with love, but all deal with sin in its larger moral context;[7] the *Confessio* is thus a compendium of the vices and virtues. Further, material which pertains to wisdom but does not quite fit the basic structural scheme appears in expository sections often characterized as digressions:[8] discussions of war and homicide (3.2201–2621), the arts and labors of men (4.2363–2700), and the religions of the world (5.729–1959) and a description of the education of Alexander, summarizing "the whole field of human knowledge,"[9] which occupies all of book 7.

In his Prologue, Gower attempts to link the microcosm of the individual, Amans, with the macrocosm, the larger world of English society. His book, "Somwhat of lust, somwhat of lore" (line 19), is to treat new matter, though it is modeled upon the examples of old books. It is written "for Engelondes sake" (line 24) in times of turbulence, so that "The wyse man mai ben avised" (line 65). The Prologue is devoted entirely to "wisdom," the body of the work to love; the book is dedicated to Henry of Lancaster (lines 66–92). The present world is in a state of decline; chaos rules and the old values have decayed:

> Now stant the crop under the rote,
> The world is changed overal,
> And therof most in special
> That love is falle into discord.
> [lines 118–21]

Blind Fortune rules every realm; the rulers who should uphold "thassise / Of love, which is al the chief / To kepe a regne out of meschief" (lines 148–50), fail to do so. Gower prays that God will remedy the universal war and suffering brought by this failure (lines 93–192). He then turns from the estate of the nobility to that of the clergy; here, too, disorder rules, with dire effect upon the laity (lines 193–498). The commons are also in disorder, not because of the influence of Fortune or the stars but because "man is overal / His oghne cause of wel and wo" (lines 499–584, 546–47). The biblical story of

Nebuchadnezzar's dream predicts the decline of the world through the ages, down to the present day, in which all is crumbling into dust (lines 585–880). The reason for the present situation is clear:

> And why the worschipe is aweie,
> If that a man the sothe seie,
> The cause hath ben divisioun,
> Which moder of confusioun
> Is wher sche cometh overal,
> Noght only of the temporal
> Bot of the spirital also.
> [lines 849–55]

The Church is contaminated by worldliness, and the end of the world approaches (lines 856–904). Man himself causes the decline and disorder in the world; he is the microcosm which influences the macrocosm:

> Thus of his propre qualitie
> The man, as telleth the clergie,
> Is as a world in his partie,
> And whan this litel world mistorneth,
> The grete world al overtorneth.
>
> . . . .
>
> The man is cause of alle wo,
> Why this world is divided so.
> [lines 954–66]

Division causes the decline of the larger world, just as strife between body and soul caused man's fall from Paradise, which in turn brought sin and division into the world. We now await rewards and punishments at the final Judgment (lines 967–1052). The Prologue closes with Gower's wish for another singer like Arion to restore peace and order in the world (lines 1053–88).

As Peck observes, this Prologue presents "a complex social analogue" to the plight of the lover in the visionary portion of the *Confessio*.[10] Gower explicitly states the relationship between macrocosm and microcosm in his Prologue; early in book 1 we are exposed to the "divisioun" within Amans which mirrors that of the larger world. Gower obviously sees himself as a new Arion, bringing men by means of his poetry out of "divisioun," back to the rule of love.[11] Important elements from the Prologue reappear in the expository sections of the poem: the discussion of war (3.2251–2360) recalls the state of the contemporary world, and the next three expository sections pertain to the three estates, Commons (the arts and labors of men,

4.2363–2700), Clergy (religions, 5.729–1959), and Nobility (the education of a prince, bk 7).[12] After the vision Gower returns to the macrocosm in his prayer for the estates of England, recapitulating the themes of "divisioun" and "singuler profit" (8.2971–3105).[13]

Through his Prologue and epilogue Gower calls attention to the relationship between the plight of Amans and the plight of society at large, but in so doing he creates problems of aesthetic consistency which cannot quite be resolved. Although the poet of the Prologue and epilogue must certainly be the same person as Amans, the visionary-narrator,[14] their two voices are not at all the same. The voice of the Prologue is that of John Gower, the moralist of the *Mirour de l'omme* and *Vox Clamantis*, who criticizes with righteous indignation the world in which he lives. This voice persists through the first ninety-two lines of book 1, but is dropped when Amans, the confused, suffering lover, takes over. Thus Gower's initial voice is not that of the unenlightened prospective visionary but that of the enlightened poet who emerges at the end of the vision to offer the final prayer for England.

One might argue that the voice of "John Gower" is that of the poet's persona at present while that of "Amans" is the same persona in the past, before his visionary experience; this is logical, but it does not quite solve the problem created for the reader. The decorum of the Boethian Apocalypse demands that the reader experience the visionary process of enlightenment along with the narrator, that he see, hear and learn through him. The reader should not know the route and goal of the mental journey before it is begun, if the work is to be entirely effective. Gower's reader, however, must make a chronological adjustment, from present to past, at the very beginning, before he is really supposed to know the final disposition of Amans's problem. If he identifies the voice of the Prologue as that of an enlightened Amans, then he knows from the outset not only Amans's problem—"divisioun" in his mind—but also its solution—the restoration of "love" which serves the "comun profit" (Prol. 377). Unless one ignores the Prologue altogether, in which case he must disregard the social analogue as well, his perspective upon the vision will prevent him from participating in the Boethian experience.

Gower may have been aware of this problem; he attempts at the beginning of book 1 to convince his reader that, as he promised earlier (Prol. 66–80), he is changing his subject:

> I may noght strecche up to the hevene
> Min hand, ne setten al in evene

Confessio Amantis

This world, which evere is in balance:
It stant noght in my sufficance
So grete thinges to compasse,
Bot I mot lete it overpasse
And treten upon othre thinges.
Forthi the Stile of my writinges
Fro this day forth I thenke change
And speke of thing is noght so strange,
Which every kinde hath upon honde,
And wherupon the world mot stonde,
And hath don sithen it began,
And schal whil ther is any man;
And that is love, of which I mene
To trete, as after schal be sene.

[1.1–16]

This only compounds the inconsistency. If the new, less difficult ("strange," line 10) subject is unrelated to the Prologue, then the Prologue is irrelevant. If the subject of the vision is in reality related to that of the Prologue, and there is ample evidence that it is, then these lines are deliberately misleading; they are Gower's attempt to make a new beginning which will not compromise the aesthetic integrity of the vision which is to follow. Further, the fact that the new subject and the earlier subject are both called "love," without an adequate distinction being drawn between the love which is lacking in the world and the love whose "lawe is out of reule" (1.18), adds to the initial confusion. Gower's transition from Prologue to vision, from macrocosm to microcosm, is at best clumsy.

To assess the coherence of Gower's argument, one must first sort out the principal ideas. First, there is the problem of the word "love" itself. In the Prologue and epilogue "love" connotes Christian *caritas*, the divine love which, among men, overcomes "divisioun," bringing peace, order and "comun profit." Gower uses the word "charite" as a synonym for this "love" in the Prologue (lines 257, 902, 903), and he returns to "thilke love which . . . stant of charite confermed" at the very end of the poem, contrasting it with the love which turns one "Fro reson in to lawe of kynde" (8.3138–72). The latter sort of love is that which Gower describes in book 1 as a source of suffering which men can neither avoid nor control, a blind force, unpredictable as Fortune itself (1.17–60). This love, which even in the Prologue "doth many a wonder / And many a wys man hath put under" (Prol. 75–76), cannot be the theological opposite of *caritas*, *cupiditas*. Rather, it is *Naturatus*

105

amor, "natural (or created) love," which Gower describes in the Latin epigram preceding book 1:

> Natural love by natural laws subjects the world, and incites all to be beasts: Love seems to be the Prince of this world, from whom the rich, the poor and all others need aid. Love and fortune are equals in their agony, luring blind people to the snare or the wheel. Love is a diseased health, a troubled peace, a holy error, a warlike peace, a sweet wound, a pleasant evil.

In the succeeding English verses it is likewise associated with Nature — as "thing which god in lawe of kinde / Hath set" (1.31–32) — and with Fortune (lines 47–57). It "wol no reson understonde" (line 46; see also lines 769–75). It has its own laws and acts according to its own will (5.4546–60). Because it is a natural phenomenon, it is neither inherently virtuous nor vicious. At its worst it can blind one's wits so that he loses his "reson" (3.1312–28), but at its best it is to be pursued through manliness and "gentilesse," and it promotes virtue (4.2014–2700). The highest sort of this kind of love, "love honeste" (line 2297), is in accord with both Nature and Reason, and according to Genius is the only genuinely worthy love for Amans (8.2009–28).[15]

Throughout the *Confessio*, Venus embodies *amor naturatus*. In commenting upon the tale of Rosiphelee, Genius observes that Venus and Cupid demand that a woman in "hir lusti age" should desire either marriage or paramours (4.1260–71), while a bit later he adds that, while love must be served, married love, "Wherof the love is al honeste," is by far the preferable sort (lines 1447–84). Venus herself appears to have no special preference between love "paramours" and love "honeste"; her personally indiscriminate sexuality includes incestuous union with her own offspring, Cupid, and her law approves even prostitution (5.1382–1443). She is, however, not evil but morally neutral, amenable to all sorts of sexual love. As she tells Amans, she seeks only her own "lustes"; where she finds no "lustes," no physical facility for service in her court, she has no interest at all (8.2398–2439).

Gower offers no clear indication in the *Confessio* that Cupid is to be distinguished from Venus in concept or function. He is "kyng of love," and she is "qweene" (1.139); the two either act in concert or are spoken of as if they were interchangeable. Cupid appears twice in the visionary narrative, first, to thrust his dart through Amans's heart (1.138–47), and much later, in Amans's swoon, to confer with Venus and then withdraw the dart (8.2783–2807). As the god "Which may hurte and hele / In loves cause" (lines 2745–46), he may perhaps represent the active agent of the love represented more comprehensively by his mother, but there is little clear evidence for even this distinction. Peck seems to associate him with cupidity,[16] but there is no reason to think him any less a morally neutral force than Venus.

Nature never appears in the *Confessio*, but Gower has a good deal to say about her. The portrayals of the goddess in Alanus and Jean de Meun may both have contributed to Gower's conception of her, but his Nature is closer to Meun's amoral figure than to Alanus's moral, rational one. Gower's Nature is still superior to Venus in the celestial hierarchy; her sphere of influence is broader than, and inclusive of, that of Venus. Venus herself says that she has no influence over Nature, who is "under the Mone / Maistresse of every lives kinde" (lines 2330–31), except for holy men who withdraw their "kindly lust ayein hir lawe" (line 2334).[17] Nonetheless, Venus and Nature are here in accord; those who offend against Nature are unwelcome in Venus's court (8.2337–49). Nature, like Venus, is a morally neutral power, as she is in Meun. She inspire incestuous love in Canace and Machaire:

> In chambre thei togedre wone,
> And as thei scholden pleide hem ofte,
> Til thei be growen up alofte
> Into the youthe of lusti age,
> Whan kinde assaileth the corage
> With love and doth him forto bowe,
> That he no reson can allowe,
> Bot halt the lawes of nature....
> [3.150–57]

Cupid bids them kiss, and then Nature takes her course:

> And after sche which is Maistresse
> In kinde and techeth every lif
> Withoute lawe positif,
> Of which sche takth nomaner charge,
> Bot kepth hire lawes al at large,
> Nature, tok hem into lore
> And tawht hem so, that overmore
> Sche hath hem in such wise daunted,
> That thei were, as who seith, enchaunted.
> [Lines 170–78]

Without "lawe positif," the *lex positiva* of the Church,[18] Nature does not oppose incest. Again, at the beginning of book 8, Genius observes that originally incest, brought about by the natural impulse to procreation, was not forbidden, though it is now proscribed under Christian law (8.48–147).

In the *Confessio*, as in Meun's *Roman*, Reason is entirely separate from, and morally superior to, Venus and Nature. Reason separates men from beasts and makes them resemble the angels (Prol. 945–50). Throughout the poem Genius argues that Reason ought to control the Will and that Nature and Venus ought to be subservient to Reason:

> Thou dost, my Sone, ayein the riht;
> Bot love is of so gret a miht,
> His lawe mai noman refuse,
> So miht thou thee the betre excuse.
> And natheles thou schalt be lerned
> That will scholde evere be governed
> Of reson more than of kinde....
>   [3.1193–99]

> For wit that is with will oppressed,
> Whan coveitise him hath adressed,
> And alle resoun put aweie,
> He can wel finde such a weie
> To werre....
>   [lines 2335–39]

> ...Delicacie in loves cas
> Withoute reson is and was;
> For wher that love his herte set
> Him thenkth it myhte be no bet;
> And thogh it be noght fulli mete,
> The lust of love is evere swete.
>   Lo, thus togedre of felaschipe
> Delacacie and drunkeschipe,
> Wherof reson stant out of herre,
> Have mad full many a wisman erre
> In loves cause most of alle:
> For thanne hou so that evere it falle,
> Wit can no reson understonde,
> Bot let the governance stonde
> To Will, which thanne wext so wylde,
> That he can noght himselve schylde
> Fro no peril....
>   [6.1229–45]

At times Reason and Nature agree, as on homicide, which both oppose (3.2251–61, 2580–98), but when they differ, Reason, the moral faculty, should curb Nature:

> For god the lawes hath assissed
> Als wel to reson as to kinde,
> Bot he the bestes wolde binde
> Only to lawes of nature,
> Bot to the mannes creature
> God yaf him reson forth withal,
> Wherof that he nature schal
> Upon the causes modefie,
> That he schal do no lecherie,
> And yit he schal hise lustes have.
> [7.5372–81]

In the *Confessio*, Amans's Reason is at odds with his Will, specifically his inclination to serve Venus. After telling the story of Apollonius, Genius warns him against loving "ayein kinde" and urges that love and Reason should be in accord (8.2009–28); Amans should "withdrawe, / And set [his] herte under that lawe, / The which of reson is governed / And noght of will" (lines 2133–36). Genius and Amans argue because Amans's Will opposes his Reason (lines 2189–99). After his final "cure," Amans's Reason returns to him, and he no longer knows love (lines 2858–77). Finally, Reason, Nature, and Venus are brought into harmony in Amans: Venus, who always agrees with Nature, observes that an old man like Amans should seek her medicine only if it accords with Reason (lines 2367–71). Amans's love is both irrational and unnatural, since he is "noght sufficant / To holde love his covenant" (lines 2419–20), so Venus rejects him, sending him off to be guided by Reason (lines 2908–40). Contrary to the view taken by several recent scholars,[19] neither Venus nor Nature is permanently allied with Reason in the *Confessio*. They are allied only when Reason dominates Will and leads to married, "honeste" love in youth, or the abandonment of love in old age.

Genius, Venus's priest and Amans's confessor, is the most problematical figure in the poem. Gower defines his functions more clearly than his conceptual identity, perhaps because the device of the lover's confession took precedence in his mind over philosophical clarity. George D. Economou has shown just how far Genius's literary background can help us to understand Gower's characterization of the figure: Alanus's Genius, Natura's "other self," shares the features of the goddess pertaining to procreation and acts as her priest on Earth.

Meun expands Genius's role to include that of Nature's confessor, but he separates Reason from Nature, who therefore represents "the pro-creative instinct without reference to the institution of marriage or a thorough awareness of Christian morality."[20] Nature and her priest "stand for sexual but not rational power," and Nature is no longer *pronuba*.[21] Genius finally becomes in Meun the priest of a Venus who is "the descendant of Alan's fallen Venus...a figure of *luxuria*."[22] Gower restores the old relationship between Venus and Natura, which Meun had followed Alanus in abandoning; he sees their relationship "in a way similar to Alan's original Natura-Venus relationship."[23] Thus far one must agree with Economou, as he must with the conclusion that Gower makes Genius Venus's priest because "that is where he found him in Jean's *Roman*," and that Gower's Venus is different from Meun's, "a Venus who is in basic agreement with a Nature strongly resembling [Genius's] original Chartrian mistress" in the *De planctu naturae*.[24] But this resemblance is not identity, for, as we have seen, in the *Confessio*, Nature and Venus are not entirely reconciled with Reason, though they are reconciled with one another, and Genius does not entirely agree with them.

Genius functions in the *Confessio* as Amans's moral instructor, and his views are essentially Christian. He opposes Venus and Nature when they promote immoral behavior ungoverned by Reason or Christian law. He recommends married love over love "paramours" (4.1467–84), and, while acknowledging that incest is natural "Withoute lawe positif" (3.172), he qualifies this by observing that it is not "honeste" to be angry with creatures who "doth the lore / Of kinde, in which is no malice," unless what they do is vicious ("Bot only that it is a vice"), because even a "resonable" man is "menable / To love, wher he wole or non" (lines 384–91). He expresses shame over Venus's licentiousness (5.1374–1451), remarks that Reason should modify Nature's dictates to prevent lechery (7.5366–81), praises virginity (5.6359–6486) and discourses at length on the virtue of chastity (7.4215–5397). Throughout the poem, Genius is more fully the champion of Reason and Christianity than of Nature and Venus.

Macaulay observes that Gower does not entirely harmonize Genius's dual role as priest of Venus and Christian confessor: "The Confessor is continually forgetting one or the other of his two characters, and the moralist is found justifying unlawful love or the servant of Venus singing the praises of virginity,"[25] although lapses of the latter sort are more common, and in general Genius emphasizes the power of Venus (and Nature) over men, not her rectitude. This duality leads him, for example, to castigate avarice for gold while apparently condoning avarice for love (5.60–124). He equivocates about whether his role as Venus's servant should take precedence over that of Christian priest (1.233–80); he later disavows his knowledge of "wisdom" as alien to those who serve Venus's law (6.2420–40); and in his final advice to Amans he again alludes to his dual role (8.2072–83). Though he usually tries to adhere to the pattern of sins against Venus, he generally defines sins from a Christian perspective, explicitly disapproves of Venus's sexual morals, and emphasizes repeatedly the superiority of "honeste" love. Secular sin and theological sin, despite analogies between them, are not quite the same thing in the *Confessio*. Venus introduces Genius to purify Amans of sins against her law, and Genius maintains this function, not altogether successfully, until the end of the confession, when his final words make it clear that he wants to free Amans from Venus herself (lines 2009–2148).

Genius appears as an authority figure throughout the poem, without ever quite reconciling his dual nature or defining himself through his words and actions. His traditional roles are many and varied,[26] and Gower draws upon most of them. His role as god of procreation is minimally stressed but emerges in his remarks upon the importance of childbearing (4.1485–1595). His role as moral instructor derives from his position in Alanus as the "other self" of a rational Natura. As in Alanus and Meun, he mediates between man and divinity; he hears confessions for Venus, teaches her laws, and carries Amans's "Complaint" from Earth to the heavens (8.2300–2309). Finally, he may be by implication the god of human nature, in that he leads Amans from the folly of an inappropriately youthful love to the pursuit of moral virtue appropriate to old age, a movement which at least one of Gower's contemporaries, the poet of *The Parliament of the Three Ages*, presents as being natural to human beings. Moreover, viewing Genius here as "human nature" might justify his duality; like most human beings, he pays allegiance to two principal masters, a natural Venus and a Christian God.

Gower's personified figures never quite define themselves through the visionary process depicted in the *Confessio*. Personifications are static, fully developed concepts which Gower presumably understands from the outset but illuminates for the reader only intermittently and incidentally. While the authority figures of works like the *Consolation*, *De planctu*, and the *Roman* are self-revealing, Gower's, on the whole, are not. The abstract identities of Genius and Venus do not emerge clearly through their interaction with Amans. Gower seems to assume that his reader will know what Venus and Genius represent, but given the variety of sometimes complex ideas and attitudes associated with them in earlier writings, it is difficult to believe that even a contemporary would recognize early on in the poem precisely which Venus or Genius he is confronting.

The modes of instruction employed in the *Confessio*, expository dialogue and exemplary tales, are basic to the Boethian genre. Gower does not rely upon multileveled allegory; the meaning of the *Confessio* is expressed on the literal level of the narrative, although what goes on there may require some explanation. This is personification allegory of the most basic kind; the few personifications possess stable identities which are circumscribed by their names and intellectual traditions. If one is uncertain about the precise meanings of Venus or Genius or Cupid, it is not because they are concealed beneath a veil of allegory but rather because Gower does not offer enough information about them. Amans requires no allegorical exegesis; he is a prototypical Boethian narrator, a whole human being, obsessed by the love which gives him his name. Because he is an exemplary figure ("A-man"?) rather than an abstraction, he can emerge at the end of the vision as the poet himself, John Gower (8.2321).[27]

The ideas in Gower's Boethian dialogue are expressed literally and explicitly. Genius and Venus mean precisely what they say to Amans. Gower is fond of using analogy, most obviously the analogy between microcosm and macrocosm, but this, I think, is not allegory or even metaphor. Gower seems to believe quite literally in the relationship he describes between the individual and the larger world; what is true for the one in the Prologue is true for the other in the vision. Amans's problem is not merely analogous to the problem besetting England but the same problem, internal disorder caused by an absence of the proper kind of love, charity. By the same token, the stories Genius tells are not allegories of the vices but literal examples in which "real" characters either commit or avoid committing them.[28] This literal approach to meaning is the rule rather than the exception in Boethian visions; Gower breaks no new ground here. Even the device of the confession is somewhat derivative, insofar as Genius had appeared as Nature's confessor in the *Roman*. Gower's innovation, a "masterstroke," as Lewis observes, of considerable originality,[29] is to adopt the confession for his principal structural device by transferring it from the goddess to the Boethian visionary.

Of particular interest to a study of the structure of Boethian Apocalypse is Amans's swoon-vision near the end of the poem (8.2440–2861). Amans faints and experiences a vision within his larger vision. This inner vision is essentially symbolic; it provides a final revelation, different in kind from what has preceded it, which succeeds in bringing the earlier instruction to fruition in the visionary. As Peck says, it "designates Amans' recognition of the moral implications of what he has learned,"[30] and it does so by externalizing the changes taking place at this point in Amans's mind. The parliament of lovers recapitulates symbolically Genius's teachings, by bringing the actors back into the forefront of Amans's consciousness. Amans takes momentary comfort in the knowledge that even the great authorities of the past have been servants of love (lines 2705–25), but at the same time he himself can now refer to his condition as "sotie" (line 2759). Moreover, even these old lovers express diverse opinions about his case, echoing the mental conflict he had recognized a bit earlier (lines 2189–99); some think that an old man ought not "assote" himself for love, while others excuse him because of love's great power (lines 2760–79). Finally, Cupid and Venus, the powers which have bound him, themselves agree to release him: Cupid withdraws his lance, and then Venus applies an ointment to his wounds and gives him a mirror in which he sees himself as the old man he really is (lines 2783–2857). In symbolic terms, as the powers of love abate in the aged lover, he recognizes what before he has been unable or unwilling to see, and his "cure" is then complete. When Amans wakens from this inner revelation, Reason returns to his mind, and love is forgotten.

The *Confessio's* encyclopedic scope brings with it attendant aesthetic and thematic problems. So long as one reads the work as a collection of stories, the framework seems an unnecessary distraction, but if one reads it as a Boethian Apocalypse in which the exempla play a subordinate part, then a different problem comes to light. The enormous bulk of the exemplary material obscures the primary narrative of Amans's vision. The task of illustrating all the varieties of all the sins by at least one tale requires far too much subordinate narrative. It becomes difficult to follow Amans's consciousness from beginning to end, unless one skips parts of the poem. The problem here is not that the reader loses sight of the visionary, as he does in the *Architrenius*; Amans is constantly present, occasionally describing his life as a lover or asking Genius questions, but most often simply admitting or denying his guilt of the sin under discussion. The whole process, however, seems uncomfortably protracted and repetitious, dissipating one's sense of continuity and progress in the Boethian argument. The overall impression of watching the visionary's mind at work is thus considerably weakened.

Also contributing to the diffuse quality of the *Confessio* are the expository sections, the discussions of war, the arts, religions, and the education of a prince. These excursions into matters not directly related to the lover's confession form a large part of the summa of knowledge which Amans needs to resolve his difficulties and are therefore thematically justifiable. Nonetheless, they break the orderly exposition of the sins, the poem's basic organizing principle. Gower himself appears to be aware of the intrusive quality of the education of Alexander section (bk. 7); he has Genius excuse himself for treating a subject that "is noght to the matiere / Of love, why we sitten hiere / To schryve, so as Venus bad" (7.7–9). The relevance of this section becomes clear later, in book 8, when Genius tells Amans that every man has a kingdom to rule, namely, himself (lines 2109–25). The analogy between Amans, the microcosm, and the macrocosm is appropriate enough, but Gower has waited rather a long time to point it out. However one accounts for the presence of the longer expository sections, their intrusion into the narrative must seem somewhat contrived.

Gower's structural pattern itself seems to break down in book 8. This last book should treat the sin of Lechery, the only sin as yet unaccounted for, but it appears to deal only with incest. As Lewis observes, lechery "naturally cannot be a sin against Venus,"[31] or at any rate not against Gower's Venus, who indifferently approves love "paramours" and love "honeste" (4.1260–71), and whose licentious career embarrasses own priest (5.1374–1443). Many of Genius's exempla have presented lechery, but never in the context of a discussion of that particular sin. It should be recognized, however, that the first part of book 8 is really a continuation of book 7. The last point of a ruler's policy with which Genius deals is Chastity, and the last bit of wisdom he bestows upon Amans in book 7 is that Reason must "modefie" Nature so that a man will avoid "lecherie" (7.4215–5397). If one ignores the brief conclusion to book 7 (lines 5398–438), the continuity between Genius's discourse on Chastity (and its opposite, Lechery) and his remarks on the once-accepted "natural" practice of incest should be obvious. In book 8, Genius returns to the pattern of the confession, but his subject remains the relationship of Reason and Nature in matters of love; incest is acceptable to Nature but not to Christian law, which presumably is rational law. But though the section on incest is in effect part of the larger discussion of Chastity, this does not explain the absence of the seventh sin from the confession format of the poem.

The situation is that Genius, as he himself says, has abandoned his role as Venus's priest to discuss "wisdom," at the beginning of book 7 (lines 1–22); this frees him so that he can deal with Chastity as a virtue. He resumes his role as confessor in book 8, but does not resume his service to Venus. Incest is not a sin against Nature; Venus agrees with

Confessio Amantis

Nature, and has herself committed incest with Cupid. As Venus's servant, Genius could not logically discuss lechery as a sin, and he treats incest in a peculiar way, as the most blatant and heinous of lecherous sins against a Nature (and Venus) which is subordinated to Reason and Christian law. Genius has in effect broken with Venus in book 7, where he approves only lawful marriage, and he remains an opponent of all love that is not reasonable in his remarks to Amans at the end of the story of Apollonius (8.2009–28). The story of Apollonius itself begins as a warning against incest but goes far beyond this particular sin to present a model for Amans to follow.[32] The length of the Apollonius tale (lines 271–2008) and its position as the last exemplum set it apart from all the earlier exempla. Its hero, who weathers an incredible series of catastrophes without ever straying from the path of virtue, offers a model not for servants of Venus but for followers of Genius, the spokesman for rational, Christian, and regal morality.

Although Genius has separated himself philosophically from Venus, Gower remains unable or unwilling to acknowledge this ideological separation by breaking with the formal device of the confession of sins against Venus over which Genius presides. After the tale of Apollonius, Genius once more remarks that he has gone beyond the confines of his role as Venus's priest "To vertu more than to vice / Encline, and teche thee mi lore" (lines 2082–83), explicitly calls Amans's love "sinne" (line 2088), and urges him to "withdrawe, / And set thin herte under that lawe, / The which of reson is governed / And noght of will" (lines 2133–36). Nevertheless, he resumes his role as Venus's priest and intermediary to deliver Amans's verse complaint to her, and though he says almost nothing more, he remains in her company when she returns to Amans (lines 2808–10), indicating that he remains her servant. Gower has sacrificed thematic consistency, and consistency of character in his authority figures, to his structural device of the lover's confession. Rather than removing Genius finally from the shadow of his goddess, he manipulates Venus's attitudes—in the particular case of Amans—to bring them into line with those of the Christian confessor.

The device of the confession makes the *Confessio* a much more static work than most other Boethian Apocalypses. In such works we expect a steady, usually marked, development in the ideological argument and, consequently, in the narrator's consciousness. Such development supplies a norm against which, when the narrator falters in his progress, his poem continues to work. Peck argues that "the progress of Amans' confession may be measured by the expository sections of the poem," the digressions which grow progressively longer and more complex "as if to imply that Amans, in coming out of his lethargy, is capable of benefiting from larger areas of experience."[33] Further, Amans initiates these sections by his questions and requests for information. Still, however, given the nature of the confession, there is little reason to expect significant progress from the "sinner" until he has been completely purged of all sins. And even after this process has been completed, Amans remains almost as confused as he was at the beginning of the vision (8.2029–59, 2149–2300). He now recognizes the nature of his inner conflict — Reason and Will are in opposition (lines 2189–99) — but he can do nothing about it, and he turns away from Genius's teaching to appeal again to Venus and Cupid for aid. His progress up to this point consists in the analysis of his personal sins, but he has not himself transcended the idea of sins against, and purification for, Venus to reach the idea of the purgation of Venus's power from his psyche. Through the course of the confession his emotional and intellectual condition has been revealed in detail, but no real transformation has been effected. Gower recognizes and makes use of the emotional aspect of the Boethian genre in presenting his visionary's emotional condition as a continuing barrier to understanding and acceptance of his lot in the temporal world. It takes him an extraordinarily long time to make this point, however, since the entire confession must first run its course.

The manner in which Gower finally resolves Amans's problem seems to me arbitrary and unsatisfactory — either a trick played upon the reader or else a retreat from Gower's own articulated belief in man's moral responsibilities. After his confession, Amans recognizes the nature of his problem (inner "divisioun") and knows himself better than before but still persists in his irrational desires. The barrier to his full recognition of what he is and what he should do remains, despite Genius's advice to "tak love where it mai noght faile" (8.2086). Amans turns to Venus and Cupid, asking now not simply for success in love as he had in book 1 but for either success or release from their power (lines 2287–90). Venus returns and "halvinge a game" asks his name, which he can now give as "John Gower" (lines 2318–21; cf. 1.160–62). She remarks upon her alliance with Nature, excuses him of conduct unbecoming members of her court, and promises, somewhat ambiguously, "medicine" appropriate to "suche olde sieke," in accord with "reson" (8.2322–76).[34] Gower's remarks at this point on Venus's blindness and capriciousness perhaps are intended to suggest that he expects the worst from her (lines 2377–95), as indeed he should. Venus rejects him from her service, and her reasons are purely biological; it is unnatural for an old man to seek her sort of love, since he is incapable "to holde love his covenant" (lines 2398–2439, 2420). The inner vision, discussed above, follows: Amans symbolically recognizes and accepts Genius's teaching about love and sin as valid, is cured of his amorous desires, and recognizes that he is old. When he awakens, his Reason returns, he no longer knows what love is, and so he withdraws from Venus's service. He receives Genius's absolution (presumably for all sins, Christian and secular), and is given by Venus beads and the advice to follow Reason and "go ther vertu moral duelleth" (line 2925), leaving love behind. The two authority figures leave him, and his initial amazement quickly gives way to a smile which indicates his final recognition of his proper course in life (lines 2870–2970).

As Schueler has shown, there are indications throughout the *Confessio* that Amans is an old man,[35] and so the reader should recognize from the outset that his suffering over unrequited love is ridiculously inappropriate. Still, the resolution to his problem seems arbitrary and evasive. It depends entirely upon the fact that Amans is old and so begs the question of what one is to do in Amans's situation if he is not old. Since Venus and Nature demand service — the sexual desires that lead to procreation — from the young, they cannot release all victims of unrequited love as easily as they release Amans. Venus, Nature, Genius, and Reason are in harmony in "honeste," married love, and in the rejection of earthly love in the elderly, but this is no final reconciliation of the forces and concepts these figures represent. Their relationship is hierarchical, and although Reason should control the Will, the province of "natural" impulses, it sometimes cannot, as Genius observes frequently in the poem. Indeed, Venus, who by her own admission seeks only her own "lustes" (8.2399), steps out of character when Gower makes her agree with Genius in sending Amans to Reason and moral virtue, since these are really not within her sphere of influence.[36] Her advice is appropriate for the aged Amans, but she would not, could not, give the same advice to a young man, even if the love he sought were not "honeste."

The alternative, I think, to viewing Amans's salvation as a sort of trick, a merely local remedy for a more far-reaching condition, is to argue that Gower has abandoned his moral demands upon the individual in favor of a more "naturalistic" solution to the problem of earthly desires. Especially if we take Genius to represent "human nature," we could argue that human beings like Amans are presented by Gower as being naturally inclined to turn from venereal passion to rational virtue as they grow old. The movement from essentially natural, secular values to spiritual values, represented by Amans's confession and its aftermath, is itself natural once one recognizes that he can no longer participate in the pursuits of youth.[37] Certainly, this view gives us a very humane John Gower, tolerant of the follies of youth, in expectation that they will give way to the wisdom and consequent virtue of old age. However, it does not seem consistent with the assertions of the Prologue and epilogue, and of Genius throughout the *Confessio*, that Reason and Charity must reign, in each estate and in all men, if the world is to be set right. In this "naturalistic" view individual morality becomes a function of natural impulses rather than their governor. An optimistic trust in Providence (which created the natural order) to bring men to Reason and virtue replaces to some extent individual responsibility. Gower himself seems to reject this position in his Prologue:

> . . .the man is overal
> His oghne cause of wel and wo.
> That we fortune clepe so
> Out of the man himself it groweth. . . .
> [Prol. 546–49]

> And fro the ferste regne of alle
> Into this day, hou so befalle,
> Of that the regnes be muable
> The man himself hath be coupable,
> Which of his propre governance
> Fortuneth al the worldes chance.
> [Prol. 579–84][38]

If the rational instruction of Genius requires the acquiescence of Nature and Venus to be effectual, then no man can be held responsible if his impulses, his "Will," reject Reason.

118

7

THE PARLIAMENT OF FOWLS

Chaucer's *Parliament of Fowls* was probably written in the early 1380s,[1] when he also translated Boethius's *Consolation* in its entirety. The *Parliament*'s structural sequence of opening remarks, summary of a text which the narrator-visionary has read, vision, and concluding comments closely parallels that of his first vision poem, *The Book of the Duchess*. Its ostensible subject, as announced in its opening lines, is "Love."

The first thirty-five lines of the *Parliament* introduce a bemused, Chaucerian narrator and the themes which will be central to his visionary experience. The two opening stanzas function as a Boethian "complaint":

> The lyf so short, the craft so long to lerne,
> Th'assay so hard, so sharp the conquerynge,
> The dredful joye, alwey that slit so yerne:
> Al this mene I by Love, that my felynge
> Astonyeth with his wonderful werkynge
> So sore, iwis, that whan I on hym thynke
> Nat wot I wel wher that I flete or synke.
>
> For al be that I knowe nat Love in dede,
> Ne wot how that he quiteth folk here hyre,
> Yit happeth me ful ofte in bokes reede
> Of his myrakles and his crewel yre.

Boethian Apocalypse

> There rede I wel he wol be lord and syre;
> I dar nat seyn, his strokes been so sore,
> But "God save swich a lord!" — I can na moore.
>
> [lines 1–14]

These lines are in the present tense, which the narrator abandons at line 17 to describe the circumstances, "Nat yoore / Agon" (lines 17–18), leading up to his vision. Except for one stanza (lines 113–19), he speaks in the past tense until the end of the poem, when he describes his return to his customary pursuits (lines 695–99).

While the astonishment and confusion of the narrator emerge clearly enough in the first stanza, their source remains vague because of the ambiguity of the word "Love." Like "Fortune" in the *Consolation* or "Natura" and "Venus" in the *De planctu*, "Love" will become the subject for visionary analysis; one cannot at this early stage know precisely what the word means, or should mean, to the confused narrator. He appears to be thinking of secular love, the sort of literary *amor* treated in the *Roman de la Rose*, a personified figure who works "myrakles and . . . crewel yre," "wol be lord and syre," and delivers "strokes . . . sore." His awe of this figure reduces him to a sort of mental paralysis; his most profound comment on Love is a trite, almost nonsensical, "God save such a lord!"

A Boethian narrator usually does not understand the subject of his opening complaint; that is why he needs visionary enlightenment. Chaucer's narrator needs help to understand the mysterious workings of love, and so one might expect a personified god of love to appear in a vision, but this expectation, like many others throughout the poem, goes unfulfilled. As Robert Frank observes: "Surprise, the failure of expectation, the occurrence of the unanticipated, is the pattern of the poem's movement. (This pattern imitates the failure of expectation in love which, among other things, the poem examines.)"[2] One aspect of the narrator's difficulty is his conception of "Love" as a single, apprehensible phenomenon. Unlike Amor in the *Roman*, or Fortune, the "Love" which baffles this visionary will not manifest itself as a single allegorical figure, capable of coherent characterization or analysis.

The narrator's confusion about love arises from his reading about it, for he does not know love "in dede" (line 8). He observes that he reads frequently, both for "lust" and for "lore" (lines 15–16); presumably reading about love should satisfy these motives, but it has not. Recently he picked up an old book, "a certeyn thing to lerne" (line 20). Some take the phrase "a certeyn thing" to mean "some particular (though unstated) bit of information," but in light of his disturbed state of mind it must mean rather "something reliable." He had been seeking an authoritative statement on the subject which confuses him, love.[3] The book he had selected held the promise of "newe science" (line 25) for him, and he read it throughout the day (lines 22–28). One expects it to have been a work dealing with secular love, and so it comes as a shock when we learn what book it was:

> . . . "Tullyus of the Drem of Scipioun."
> Chapitres sevene it hadde, of hevene and helle
> And erthe, and soules that therinne dwelle. . . .
> [Lines 31–33]

More surprisingly, he next summarizes this work.

The lines leading up to the summary of the *Somnium Scipionis*, besides revealing the narrator's preoccupation with love, introduce his concern with time. The first line of the poem relates the "craft" of love to the limitations inherent in the finite span of human life. The narrator reads "ofte" (lines 10, 16), "Of usage" (line 15); he read this book, written with "lettres olde" (line 19), "Nat yoore / Agon" (lines 17–18), spending "The longe day" (line 21) on it. His pleasure in it made "al that day me thoughte but a lyte" (line 28). He pursues this pastime because, just as from "olde feldes" comes "newe corn from yer to yere," so from "olde bokes" comes "newe science" (lines 22–25). One can distinguish from these references two sorts of time: fixed periods with beginnings and ends (a day, a lifetime), and cyclical, repeated periods (frequent reading, the emergence of new from old). To these the *Somnium* will add a third sort, cosmic time, which merges into a timeless eternity, adding to what will prove one of the poem's principle motifs.

The *Somnium* provides the narrator with the "lust" he seeks in books, but its "lore" is difficult to reconcile with his waking preoccupations and his vision. Brewer observes that "there is nothing about Nature or love in the Dream of Scipio."[4] The narrator himself introduces it as a book about Heaven, Hell, Earth, and the souls dwelling in these realms (lines 32–33) and later observes that it did not provide the "thing" he wanted to find (lines 88–91). Yet Chaucer devotes seven stanzas to the summary, which would seem excessive if the *Somnium* were not pertinent to the larger theme of the *Parliament*. Chaucer's treatment of Cicero's work here should suggest its relevance to a poem about "Love."

Chaucer compresses Cicero's "Chapitres sevene" (line 32) into forty-nine lines (lines 36–84), rearranging materials slightly, but does not distort Cicero's meaning in any very obvious way. The setting for

Boethian Apocalypse

Scipio's vision comes from chapter 1 of the *Somnium*. Chaucer reduces Africanus's prophecy of Scipio's future, which occupies all of chapter 2, to the statement that Scipio, "from a sterry place," learned "of al his grace" (lines 43–45), thereby retaining the basic idea of the vision's relevance to the visionary's life. The lines describing the heavenly rewards promised to those who "lovede commune profyt" (lines 46–49) parallel the opening of chapter 3. Chaucer derives his phrase "commune profyt" from Cicero's "all who have maintained, aided, or enlarged the commonwealth";[5] there is no Latin equivalent for "loved." Chaucer omits Cicero's statement that nothing is more gratifying (*acceptius*) "to the supreme god" than the establishment of commonwealths (*civitates*) and, as Clemen points out, extends the promise of rewards not only to the leaders of society, as in the original, but to all those who love the common good; this alteration "expands Cicero's purely individual promise to the dimensions of established Christian belief."[6] The stanza which affirms the existence of an afterlife and describes earthly life as "but a maner deth" (lines 50–56) greatly compresses the material of chapter 3.

Scipio's view from the "Galaxye" (line 56) of the nine spheres, and his hearing their divine harmony (lines 57–63), comes from chapters 3 to 5. Chaucer eliminates Cicero's detailed description of the spheres, together with much of the discussion of their harmony, but retains the point that celestial harmony is related to earthly harmony and music. Cicero says that humans imitate this harmony through music, but mortal ears cannot hear the music of the spheres: ". . . learned men, imitating it on stringed instruments or in songs, have prepared a return to this place, as have others who with their superior talents have pursued divine studies in human life. Though filled with this sound, the ears of men have become deaf to it" (p. 12). Chaucer ignores the suggestion that musicians, as well as students of divine truths, have by their pursuits gained their return to the celestial regions, and he adds the point that the spheres' "melodye" is "welle" of earthly music and harmony.[7]

Africanus's exhortation that Scipio should not "in the world delyte" (lines 64–66) is implicit in chapters 6 and 7. Chaucer omits much of chapters 6 and 7, while introducing the detail of the world's "torment and . . . harde grace" (line 65). Boethian and Christian influence seems likely here,[8] and the line links the Ciceronian view of earthly life with the torments and severe "grace" of love in the larger poem. The idea that at the end of a celestial year all memory of mankind's deeds will have vanished (lines 67–70) comes from chapter 7. Chaucer makes this phenomenon sound a bit more like the end of the created world than does Cicero, who more clearly suggests the cyclical nature of the celestial year.[9] Africanus's promise of heavenly immortality as the reward for working for the "commune profit" (lines 71–77) is paraphrased from chapters 8 and 9. Chaucer eliminates Cicero's Platonic doctrine of immortality and derives his reference to the common profit form Cicero's "however the noblest concerns are for the welfare of the commonwealth" (p. 19). His description of Cicero's Heaven as "that place deere / That ful of blysse is and of soules cleere" (lines 76–77) appears to be based upon suggestions throughout the *Somnium*, colored by commonplace Christian notions of Heaven.

In his closing stanza (lines 78–84), Chaucer elaborates upon Cicero's brief reference in chapter 9 to the fate of those who pursue bodily pleasure and break the laws of gods and men:

> But the souls of those who have surrendered themselves to bodily pleasures and those who yielded themselves like servants and by impulse obedient to the pleasures of desire have violated the laws of gods and men, having left their bodies, will roll about this earth, nor will they arrive in this place until after many ages of torment. [Pp. 19–20]

The idea that these souls "Shul whirle aboute th'erthe alwey in peyne" (line 80) could come directly from Cicero's *volutantur* and *exagitati*, but it is perhaps also colored by Chaucer's memory of the lecherous souls in Dante (*Inferno* 5.31–36).[10] Chaucer preserves the Platonic view of this punishment as temporary, a sort of Purgatory, and by adding the specific reference to forgiveness (line 82), and the final prayer to God for these souls (line 84), he further Christianizes this idea.

Chaucer has adjusted the language and the emphases of the *Somnium* just enough to turn Ciceronian virtue and vice into varieties of "love," when that term is allowed its broadest latitude. Public service has become love of the "commune profyt," the surest means of attaining the Ciceronian Heaven (lines 46–49). The pursuit of bodily pleasure, on the other hand, hinders the soul's ascent to that "blysful place." Chaucer has taken a single sentence, very near the end of the *Somnium*, on vice and made it central to one-seventh of his summary, thereby giving "likerous folk" (line 79) prominence all out of proportion to their place in the original. Still, he does not suggest that sexual vice leads to theological damnation, but rather, following Cicero, he treats it as an aberration which must be purged before one can enter Heaven. The *Somnium* speaks of a heaven and a sort of purgatory, but not of "helle" (line 32) in any Christian sense of the term.[11]

Boethian Apocalypse

Love of the commonweal and love of bodily pleasure appear as alternatives which will lead to reward or punishment in the essentially Platonic afterlife. Despite the bits of Christian coloring, the formulations of the *Somnium* remain Ciceronian in the summary. The *Somnium* offers a rigorously polarized view of human activity; Scipio can devote himself either to the public welfare or to worldly pleasures. There is no extension of the idea of public service to embrace any sort of legitimate private activity, nor is there any indication that physical or psychological gratification can be a part of legitimate earthly behavior. The sort of "Love" which manifests itself in "myrakles" and "crewel yre" seems to have no place in Scipio's world.

The immediate relevance of Scipio's cosmic vision to the *Parliament*'s narrator is far from clear. The narrator, after all, is not a Roman statesman. He might learn from the *Somnium* to work for the common good in his own sphere of activity and to avoid lechery, but he could learn such general precepts anywhere, and they tell him virtually nothing about the sort of love he is concerned with. Scipio's vision offers the Roman personal guidance; the narrator needs a vision of his own, answering to his own circumstances and concerns. The reader must assume at this point that whatever thematic importance the *Somnium* might hold for the narrator will emerge from, and be clarified by, his own visionary experience.

Time, or, more precisely, the relationship of time to the individual, furnishes one link between the *Somnium* and Chaucer's narrator. The narrator is acutely aware of time's passage as it relates to his own activity. He reads the *Somnium* all day long and reports its "sentence" "shortly" (lines 34–35). His technique in summarizing the work, with its peculiarly frequent time references, calls attention to his reading as a process taking place over a period of time. He begins, "Fyrst telleth it, whan" (line 36), goes on to "Thanne telleth it" (line 39), and continues through eight more similar references (lines 43, 50, 57, 59, 60, 64, 67, 71). Though the day seems to him "but a lyte" (line 28), he appears nonetheless very conscious of its passage. Within the *Somnium*, Scipio's experience is likewise firmly bound to the temporal; diurnal time frames his vision and ties it to his waking life. He and Masinissa talk "til the day gan misse" (line 40), after which he receives his vision "that nyght" (line 42), and, though Chaucer does not bother to state what is obvious, he must awaken to another day to act upon Africanus's advice and fulfill his prophecies.

Within his vision Scipio learns about his temporal and eternal future (lines 45–49). Africanus tells him that "oure present worldes lyves space / Nis but a maner deth" (lines 53–54) but nonetheless urges him

124

to spend his time serving the common profit. Man's finite life is linked to, and subsumed by, what A. C. Cawley calls "cosmic time";[12] virtuous earthly life earns eternal happiness, "a blysful place. . . / Ther as joye is that last withouten ende" (lines 48–49; cf. lines 55–56), while the vicious are punished "Tyl many a world be passed" (line 81) and, forgiven, they "come into this blysful place" (line 83). Eventually, "in certeyn yeres space" (line 67), the great cycle of the Mundane Year will end, and with it all memory of human deeds and, perhaps, the temporal world itself (lines 67–70). For Scipio earthly time provides the opportunity to prepare for cosmic time, the happy eternity Africanus inhabits in "hevene." In this context, Scipio is both time-bound and eternal, limited by the finite span of his life but capable of using his allotted years to earn eternal happiness. The difference between Scipio and the narrator is that, after his vision, Scipio knows how he must spend his time, while the narrator is confused about his temporal pursuits and therefore feels restricted by his "lyf so short" (line 1).

The narrator read the *Somnium* until "The day gan faylen" (line 85) and the night interrupted his "business," reading, just as it had ended Scipio's conversation with Masinissa (line 40). More generally, the coming of night always "reveth bestes from here besynesse" (line 86); men's and beast's (and bird's) lives are controlled by the diurnal round. He leaves his reading, dissatisfied with what he has found there:

> . . . And to my bed I gan me for to dresse,
> Fulfyld of thought and busy hevynesse;
> For bothe I hadde thyng which that I nolde,
> And ek I nadde that thyng that I wolde.
> [Lines 88–91]

He remains, then, in the same state of mind in which he began reading. His studies have failed to provide the enlightenment he needs. He may have found authoritative doctrine in Cicero's work, but not the "certeyn thing" he sought. Clearly, the sort of love he wishes to know about is not the sort of love treated in the *Somnium*, not love of the "commune profyt" and not mere lechery, either.

The narrator falls asleep, and Africanus appears to him in a dream, standing at his "beddes syde" (line 98) in an attitude clearly reminiscent of Lady Philosophy. In the usual Boethian situation, the visionary fails to recognize his authority figure, but Chaucer's narrator immediately identifies Africanus by the "aray" he claims Scipio had described (lines 96–97). This recognition, bound as it is to the narrator's memory of the *Somnium*, reminds the reader that the visionary already knows the doctrine associated with Africanus and has found it irrelevant to his search for knowledge about love. Why, we must wonder, is Africanus here at all? He says that he has come to "quyte" the narrator's "labour" (lines 109–12), while the narrator speculates that he dreamed of Africanus because of his reading about him during the day (lines 99–108).

The unexpected invocation of Cytherea (lines 113–19) offers yet another explanation for the narrator's vision. Speaking in the present tense as a poet recording his former experience, he attributes the vision to the agency of this goddess (line 115), whose conceptual identity is never entirely clear. Her "fyrbrond" (line 114) suggests that she is the sexual Venus of Jean de Meun and of Chaucer's *Merchant's Tale* (*CT* E1723–29), but the narrator's reference to having seen her "north-north-west" (line 117) suggests the wholly benevolent planetary goddess of love.[13] Her name appears intended to distinguish her from the Venus figure who appears later in the vision. Whoever or whatever the narrator means by Cytherea, she does not appear in the vision. The attribution of the dream to Cytherea reflects the narrator's obsession with "Love" and indicates that he, at least, believes that his vision deals with that subject.

The invocation over, the "forseyde Affrican" brings the narrator to the gate of a walled garden (lines 120–22). This enclosed place is the symbolic locus of action for the vision, and, appearing as it does immediately after the invocation to Cytherea, one expects it to be some sort of garden of love. The inscriptions in gold and black (line 141), over "eyther half" (line 125) of the garden's single gate, confirm this expectation:

"Thorgh me men gon into that blysful place
Of hertes hele and dedly woundes cure;
Thorgh me men gon unto the welle of grace,
There grene and lusty May shal evere endure.
This is the wey to al good aventure.
Be glad, thow redere, and thy sorwe of-caste;
Al open am I—passe in, and sped thee faste!"

"Thorgh me men gon," than spak that other side,
"Unto the mortal strokes of the spere
Of which Disdayn and Daunger is the gyde,
Ther nevere tre shal fruyt ne leves bere.
This strem yow ledeth to the soreweful were

126

The Parliament of Fowls

There as the fish in prysoun is al drye;
Th'eschewing is only the remedye!"
[Lines 127–40]

These inscriptions define the nature of the place. In the *Roman* the garden wall keeps out the things painted on its exterior; here the inscriptions describe what is contained within. This garden encloses the experience of worldly love. The sets of opposed images in the two inscriptions define two aspects of the experience, one healing, fertile, and happy, the other painful, sterile, and sorrowful. One invites the neophyte in; the other warns him away. The gold side promises a "blysful place" (line 127) reminiscent of Cicero's Heaven, while the black side warns of "mortal strokes" (line 135) reminiscent of the "peyne" of Cicero's place of punishment (line 80).

These inscriptions amplify the twin aspects of "Love," "his myrakles and his crewel yre" (line 11). The entrant to this symbolic garden may expect either or both of these fates. The visionary has arrived at the right place in which to learn about the subject which confuses him. However, the ambivalence of the experience of love persists even within his vision. The two inscriptions over a single gate suggest that he will find within no absolute separation of the positive and negative aspects of the sort of love about which he has read. Taken together, they mark the boundaries of an entire range of potential experience to which a lover subjects himself.

The narrator's reading of the inscriptions repeats within his vision the pattern of his waking life. He reads about love and becomes confused ("astoned," line 142; "Astonyeth," line 5) over the contradictory fates offered Love's "folk" (line 9); unable "to chese, / To entre or flen, or me to save or lese" (lines 146–47), not knowing whether he floats or sinks (lines 6–7), he finds himself reduced to a sort of mental paralysis (lines 148–53; cf. lines 13–14). In the vision, however, he further confuses his pursuit of knowledge about love in books with the pursuit of love "in dede" (line 8). He takes the attitude of a prospective initiate into love's mysteries, assuming that the inscriptions confront him with a conscious decision. In his waking state he had turned to a book about Africanus for knowledge which might resolve his perplexity; in the vision Africanus himself intervenes to end his paralysis and provide him with information.

Chaucer once again defeats our expectations by revealing that the narrator has misperceived his own relationship to the locus of his visionary experience and, by implication, to his waking researches as well. Africanus reminds him that he is a reader about love, not a lover (lines 155–61). Of the inscriptions he observes that "this writyng nys nothyng ment bi the, / Ne by non, but he Loves servaunt be" (lines 158–59); this comment clarifies his relationship not only to "writyng" about "Love" but also to "writyng" about Scipio. He is not "Loves servaunt," nor is he a political leader like Scipio, and therefore the doctrine of the *Somnium* has no direct relevance to his own waking life. He can read and learn about political and amatory experiences without being directly involved in them. He will not have to experience love "in dede" in order to "se" it in vision and, if he has "connyng," to write of what he sees (lines 162–68). Seeing, in allegory, sometimes implies actually experiencing whatever it is the protagonist sees, but here seeing, like reading, holds only the possibility of understanding the experience. The decision about whether he should enter the garden is thus made for the narrator at the same time that his role in his own vision is defined as observer rather than participant.

The expectation that Africanus is to play the role of Boethian authority figure, by explaining what transpires in the allegory, proves false. He is not in any real sense the visionary's guide in this poem, and no other figure takes over the conventional function of the authority figure. Africanus disappears as soon as he has led his visionary to the entrance to the garden, calmed his fears, and pushed him inside. The most obvious explanation for Africanus's withdrawal is that he has already performed as visionary guide in the *Somnium*, and no purpose would be served by having him reiterate or elaborate upon his wisdom. I suspect that Chaucer conceived of Africanus in much the same way that he did of Lady Philosophy and the other personifications and allegorical deities which populate vision poetry. That is, he associated Africanus with a well-defined area of abstract knowledge, beyond which poetic decorum prevents taking him. He is no more an appropriate guide to the garden of love than Fortune would be to a garden of Theology.

The quesion remains, then, why Chaucer chooses to introduce him into the vision at all. The reasons given — because he was on the narrator's mind, or to reward the narrator — evade the question. The answer, I think, is that, despite the irrelevance of Scipio's life to that of the narrator, Chaucer wishes to make a connection between the realm of cosmic wisdom of the *Somnium* and the garden of the *Parliament*, and Africanus provides a link between the two visions. The narrator implies that he is dissatisfied with the *Somnium* because there is something missing from it. That something must be "love," as the narrator himself conceives of the subjet — neither mere lechery nor love of the common good, but an as yet undefined area between the two and not totally unrelated to either. Africanus can, in a figurative sense, lead him to the right gate but cannot guide him through the park in which this hiatus in his knowledge can be filled.

Significantly, no figure appears within the park to take over the role of authority figure which Africanus has so abruptly abandoned. The narrator meets no "Love" and no Cytherea; in fact, he speaks with no one here. The absence of a single authority figure implies that there is no one authority to whom he can turn for that certain knowledge he seeks. The vision offers no simple way to make sense of the complex experience which he is to witness. The experience of worldly love is a "poetic" one and cannot be reduced to rational discourse.[14] Complexity is its salient quality; it cannot be explained; it can only be presented through related and contrasting images. This vision will take the narrator deeper into the heart of the experience of love, revealing its facets more fully to him than his reading has, at the same time that it confirms (as only authoritative vision can) that his initial state of bewilderment is not an aberration, that one should not be astonished at being astonished by love.

The park appears initially, through the first six stanzas describing it (lines 169–210), to be an earthly paradise, reminiscent of the many Edenic loci of medieval literature.[15] In its eternal fertility it corresponds to the "blysful place" (line 127) promised in the gold inscription over the gate. The inscription's ever-enduring "grene and lusty May" (line 130) manifests itself here in the green "leves that ay shal laste" of the trees (line 173), the springtime abundance of all vegetable and animal life, and the eternal temperance of the climate in a place where night never falls (lines 204–10). The "colde welle-stremes" (line 187) recall the promised "welle of grace" (line 129), while the absence of sickness and old age (line 207) suggests the "hertes hele and dedly woundes cure" (line 128) of the inscription. Further, this place, where there is "joye more than a thousandfold / Than man can telle" (lines 208–209), with its images of fertility, harmony, and fulfillment, glances back beyond the "blysful place" (line 127) of the inscription to the "blysful place" (lines 48, 83), Heaven, of the *Somnium*. The harmony of the spheres in the *Somnium* finds its earthly manifestation in the ravishing music of the garden:

> Of instruments of strenges in acord
> Herde I so pleye a ravyshyng swetnesse,
> That God, that makere is of al and lord,
> Ne herde nevere beter, as I gesse.

Therwith a wynd, unnethe it myghte be lesse,
Made in the leves grene a noyse softe
Acordaunt to the foules song alofte.
[Lines 197–203]

The permanent joy and fruition here (lines 204–10) likewise evoke Cicero's place "There as joye is that last withouten ende" (line 49).

Chaucer keeps his reader constantly aware of the presence of the narrator within this landscape. The frequency of first-person pronouns in this descriptive portion of the poem emphasizes the personal aspect of the vision; scarcely a stanza does not contain a personal reference to what he saw, heard, or found. His response to the paradisal aspect of the park is wholly positive. He takes "confort" from Africanus's grasp (lines 169–70) and once inside repeatedly expresses his delight at the sights and sounds (lines 171, 175, 198–200, 208–209). Only the catalog of trees, with its emphasis upon their varied uses in the everyday world of men (lines 176–82), reveals that he remains conscious of the less pleasant aspects of human life, of pain and death. The images of "the cofre unto carayne" the "whippes lashe," "the cipresse, deth to playne," and "the asp for shaftes pleyne" prepare the way for the more disturbing features of the landscape which are to come.

The paradisal landscape soon gives way to scenes and images which, while still located within this same park, evoke darkness, disharmony, and suffering. We are here dealing with symbolic space. The inscriptions define in terms of place the most extreme states to be found within the garden: eternally perfect happiness and fertility in love, and eternal sterility and suffering in love. These are the figurative boundaries of this locus; earthly love manifests itself between them.[16] The paradisal landscape itself is symbolic, in the same way that the gold inscription is symbolic, as the setting for, and correlative of, perfect earthly love. It is an ideal, one extreme boundary for a range of experience bounded at the other extreme by its antithesis, the landscape which corresponds to the black inscription. Moreover, as one might expect, the golden, Edenic landscape contains no inhabitants, no human figures (except the narrator, who is no lover), just as there are no perfectly, eternally happy lovers in the world of everyday reality. This portion of the garden seems most like Heaven in its images of eternal fertility and harmony because the dream of perfect earthly love traditionally expresses itself as a mirror, in earthly terms, of the joys of Heaven. It is here that the ideal of earthly love most closely approaches the blissful state described in the cosmic Heaven of the *Somnium*.

On his tour of the park the narrator moves from the Edenic garden through a sort of middle ground and on into the temple of Venus, where the imagery recalls the black inscription. These symbolic loci are not sharply separated from one another; they are in fact linked by shared images, indicating that they are parts of a conceptual continuum which spans the entire park. The narrator sees Cupid, Wille, and various lesser figures in some unspecified part of the originally paradisal landscape, but once they appear, the landscape no longer seems perfect. He has moved imperceptibly into a conceptual area somewhere between love's earthly paradise and Venus's temple. Thus the general effect of the lines describing his approach to Venus's temple is ambivalent (lines 211–45). The "tre" and "welle" (line 211) beside which Cupid and Wille appear recall the "welle of grace" and "grene and lusty May" of the gold inscription (lines 129–30), and the trees and "welle-stremes" (lines 172–89) of the idyllic garden, but Wille uses the well to temper Cupid's arrows. These arrows, weapons like the "sphere" of the black inscription (line 135) introduce a negative note. They "sle, . . . wounde and kerve" (line 217), suggesting the obverse of the golden "hertes hele and dedly woundes cure" (line 128), the "mortal strokes" (line 135) of the black inscription. Death, which must here be taken in a figurative sense, had only indirectly been hinted at in the catalog of trees; now it becomes more prominent in the imagery of the park.

Cupid is perhaps somewhat less foreboding here than in, for example, Gower, but Chaucer says too little about him to define him very clearly. His traditional association with his mother, Venus, tells us little of his conceptual identity. Separated from Venus and designated "oure lord" (line 212), he perhaps represents "love" in the broadest secular sense, the "lord" whose "strokes been so sore" of the opening stanzas, with whom Economou identifies him.[17] His arrows suggest, as in Gower and the *Roman*, that he personifies the active force or cause of love; he inflicts the "wounds" that trouble his unsuspecting victims. Wille, his daughter, is carnal desire,[18] a fairly straightforward personification. She is Cupid's daughter, presumably because love begets desire, and it seems likely that she tempers his arrows because desire "sharpens" the effect of love.

The various other figures represent aspects of the experience of worldly love. Chaucer, while following Boccaccio, makes no attempt at comprehensiveness in gathering them together. These figures are essentially emblematic, serving to fill out the abstract idea of love embodied in Cupid. Chaucer refrains from naming three of them (lines 228–29), perhaps so that the reader can fill in this gallery to satisfy himself. As traditional personifications associated with amatory allegory, they have mixed natures.[19] Craft, who is "Disfigurat," Foolhardynesse, Flaterye, and Meede appear largely negative, distasteful figures, while Curteysie and Gentilesse are desirable qualities in most medieval contexts, and the others are more or less neutral or ambivalent. Disdayn and Daunger, the personifications of the black inscription (line 136), while unmentioned, would not seem out of place in this company.

Venus's "temple of bras" (lines 230–94) appears to isolate her domain and therefore her influence upon the realm of love, but this isolation is more apparent than real. The women who dance about the temple (lines 232–36) are the first human beings we see. That they do "here offyce alwey, yer by yeere" (line 236) suggests the perpetuity of Venus's power over humanity, while providing the first reference to the passage of time here. The doves, Venus's birds,[20] sit on her temple (lines 237–38) and recall the many birds throughout the park (lines 190–91). Dame Pees represents a condition necessary for the flourishing of Venus's influence (lines 239–40); she looks back to the "olyve of pes" (line 181) in the garden and foreshadows one of Nature's primary concerns. Likewise, Dame Pacience is a quality desirable in those who seek Venus's favor (lines 241–43), and she too will play a role later in the poem. Her hill of sand suggests the insecurity from which the prospective lover suffers, and perhaps, in contrast to Nature's "hil of floures" (line 302), the possible barrenness of his success.[21] She is, moreover, a particularly time-related virtue, existing only where waiting for the passage of time may have some significance. Byheste and Art, and the "route" of their folk, round out, without limiting, the population of figures outside the temple (lines 244–45).

The interior of Venus's temple seems largely oppressive, filled with images of sexuality and suffering, in marked contrast to the idyllic garden. The sounds here first claim the narrator's attention:

> Withinne the temple, of sykes hoote as fyr
> I herde a swogh that gan aboute renne,
> Whiche sikes were engendered with desyr,
> That maden every auter for to brenne
> Of newe flaume, and wel espyed I thenne
> That al the cause of sorwes that they drye
> Cam of the bittere goddesse Jelosye.
>
> [Lines 246–52]

Such sounds contrast with the music in the garden, as do the "sorwes" that "drye" them with the garden's thousandfold joys, and the images of heat with the "attempre" air outside. Priapus, enshrined here with his "sceptre" in his hand (line 256), is obviously a phallic god. His attitude, "as whan the asse hym shente" (line 255), suggests both sexual shame and the sexual frustration promised in the black inscription. Yet living men, the male equivalents of the female dancers outside, attempt to honor him, and their garlands of fresh flowers recall the flowers outside (lines 257–59).[22]

The narrator discovers Venus herself "in disport" with "hire porter Richesse" (lines 260–62), a figure reminiscent of Meede (line 228), whose haughtiness (line 262) recalls the figures Disdayn and Daunger (line 136). The sense of confinement of Venus here, "in a prive corner" (line 260), contrasts with the openness of the exterior landscape, as does the darkness (lines 263–64) with the daylight outside, which she avoids. That she waits "Til that the hote sonne gan to weste" (line 266) again introduces the note of temporality, reminding us that Venus prefers a particular portion of the diurnal round for her works. Her appearance is voluptuous and sexually suggestive (lines 267–73). "Bachus" and Ceres traditionally attend her[23] but are not in themselves negative figures (line 274–76). Like Priapus, she has her representative human worshipers, who appear in an attitude of servitude which implies desperation and the fear of frustration (lines 278–79). The broken bows hanging on the walls celebrate Venus's victories over Diana, sexuality overcoming chastity (lines 281–84). The sentiment — surely that of Venus herself — that Diana's maidens "gonne here tymes waste / In hyre servyse" (lines 283–84) again reveals the consciousness of time associated with the venereal aspect of the park.

Finally, the narrator observes the painted stories of martyrs who died because of love (lines 284–94). Chaucer has moved this list from its earlier position in Boccaccio, augmented it with names not found there, and added the explicit reference to their deaths.[24] Placed as it is at the very end of his description of the park, this list brings the narrator to the low point in his tour of the realm of earthly love, to the sterility, frustration, and sorrow promised in the black inscription. This description forms a self-contained unit, just as the park itself is a self-contained locus in which he can observe worldly love. He moves from one extreme boundary to the other, from a landscape symbolic of miracles to paintings of cruel ire, from the Heaven of the gold inscription to the Hell of the black, from ravishing sweet music to sighs of sorrow, from eternal May where lovers never age nor grow ill to a realm where time leads to sorrowful death. Within this locus there are no clear boundaries; images of death appear in the garden, flowers in the temple. There are no living human beings in the Edenic part of the garden, and no actual corpses in the temple either, although the ideal of the garden is obviously less attainable than its antithesis, depicted on the temple walls. Human erotic activity takes place within these extremes, between the ideal of eternal happiness and erotic death.

In this context Venus, given the figures and images which surround her, must represent the sexual aspect of love. As such, she appears remote from the idyllic perfection of the earlier description of the garden, bound to time, suffering, and death. However, while Chaucer presents Venus's temple and its goddess in a rather unpleasant, ominous light, he offers no clear moral condemnation of what she represents. Thus Loomis denies that Venus as sexual desire is here "necessarily evil or corrupt."[25] Venus, taken in isolation from her symbolic setting in the poem, resembles the fallen, morally reprehensible Venus of Alanus and Meun, but Chaucer's context complicates matters. Venus cannot be wholly evil; she is a permanent, inseparable part of the symbolic garden which encompasses love's complex experience. Moral distinctions have nothing to do with the allegorical "subject" of the garden, which symbolizes the "real" world of love, presided over by a beneficent Nature. As Kearney observes, Venus is "a very necessary aspect of the garden...under the dominion of Nature."[26] "Th'eschewing is only the remedye" (line 140) by which one can be certain of avoiding the fate of love's unhappy martyrs, but if one does not enter the garden, he also eschews the promise of the gold inscription.

This locus of worldly experience abuts—to preserve Chaucer's own spatial metaphor—at its extreme boundaries the two spiritual realms into which the *Somnium* polarizes the afterlife. The golden landscape is an earthly paradise, analogous to the spiritual Heaven. This landscape represents an unattainable ideal for the living and so appears without human inhabitants, but it offers a spatial correlative for the highest human aspirations in love. From here the narrator moves through the everyday, "real" world of love, past the well of Cupid, and into the temple of Venus, where, finally, he arrives at the scenes of sorrowful death. At this point he has arrived at the other extreme boundary of human experience in love, the figurative Purgatory which lovers wish to avoid but may be consigned to. Whether unfortunate lovers actually die of love or only figuratively suffer the pains of death seems beside the point. Either way, the Purgatory of sorrow and sterility which they inhabit abuts, and is analogous to, the realm of the *Somnium* in which the lawless and lecherous are punished after death. The landscape of the park thus fills the metaphorical space between Africanus's Heaven and Purgatory; it is that portion of "the lytel erthe" in which legitimate erotic activity takes place.

The narrator has, in spatial terms, traversed the whole realm of love, and in so doing has for a second time reenacted his waking experience of reading about Love's miracles and cruel ire. His reactions to this tour correspond to what one would expect of an avid, sensitive reader. He rejoices in the Edenic realm of Love's miracles and describes it fully. Moving into the less ideal realm of Cupid, he at first seems willing to describe even the unattractive aspects of the landscape, and so "nyl nat lye" about Craft's disfigurement (line 222). However, as the landscape grows more disturbing, he seems (within the limits imposed by the necessity that he survey the whole place) to grow more reticent. He flatly refuses to give the names of the three figures who follow Messagerye and Meede (lines 228–29) and slips past the "route" of folk with Byheste and Art (line 245). Having seen Venus in her temple, he seems in a hurry to dismiss her with something approaching contempt or even fear: "thus I let hire lye" (line 279). When he is outside once more, his desire "myselven to solace" (line 297) suggests relief at having left a depressing place where he "read" depressing stories about "Love's cruel ire." Still he offers no moral judgment about what he has seen.[27] He remains an observer, and there is more to see. He has seen love in broad, emblematic panorama; now he will see it in depth, as it manifests itself dynamically, within everyday society.

The *Parliament*'s geography and its relationship to the poem's meaning at the point when the narrator emerges from the temple require some clarification. If, as many readers seem to think, the "place . . . that was so sote and grene" where he finds himself is the paradisal portion of the park, he remains there only momentarily; his walk (line 297) takes him into the more ambivalent middle ground. The parliament portion of the poem certainly takes place within the realm of Nature, the presiding deity here, and not in the temple, which Bennett seems to think is the realm of "Love."[28] The entire garden is the realm of love, however, and the temple is only one aspect of that realm. The realm of Nature includes, but is not limited to, earthly love; it encompasses all earthly phenomena, and all of the created world as well, as Alanus and Meun make abundantly clear. It does not matter precisely where the glade and hill of Nature (line 302) are located; they are simply in the park, with the hill elevated above it to suggest Nature's rule here.

Nature appears as "a queene" who "fayrer was than any creature" (line 298–301). In Chaucer, as in Alanus, Meun, and Gower, Nature is clearly distinguished from Venus and superior to her in her beauty and the scope of her power. Their precise relationship, as in Alanus and Meun, is a philosophical problem, which Chaucer approaches less directly than they. The two figures do not appear together; rather, we see the manifestations of Venus's influence within the parameters of the mating ritual over which Nature presides. Venus, as well as the various other figures occupying places in the symbolic landscape, is thus subsumed beneath the beneficent figure of Nature, the last abstract figure, and highest deity, to emerge in the allegory.

Chaucer identifies his Nature specifically with the Nature of Alanus's "Pleynt of Kynde" (lines 316–18), a significant indication not only of his literary source but of his conceptual position as well. Like Alanus's figure, she is "the vicaire of the almyghty Lord" (line 379). As *procreatrix* she presides over orderly, lawful mating, thus associating herself more closely with Alanus's figure than with the amoral Nature of Meun and, later, Gower.[29] As God's vicar, she is the goddess whose sphere of influence extends to the very limits of the created world, which is itself an expression of the providential order. She "hot, cold, hevy, lyght, moyst, and dreye / Hath knyt by evene noumbres of acord" (line 380–81). That she customarily assembles the birds on Saint Valentine's Day, each in "his owne place" (line 320), to choose mates expresses this divinely ordained natural order.

Nature's orderliness manifests itself dynamically, in time, embracing the phenomena of the everyday world within a larger whole. As the *Somnium* reveals, the music of the spheres—themselves part of the "natural" world—is the source of harmony on earth, though it is inaudible here. This harmony, itself a reflection of divine concord, manifests itself only dimly on earth, through the workings of Nature's laws. The birds represent not only a microcosm of human society but more generally the entire realm of Nature. From the outset they are a noisy, disorderly crowd (lines 309–15), placed and kept in hierarchical order by the goddess (lines 319–29). Within the overriding order the various species exhibit every sort of character trait, good and bad (lines 330–64), according to their individual natures.

From the time that she begins the assembly (lines 319–20), one expects a visionary expression of the harmony of Nature in the world of secular love. The gathering of birds is a ritual, social expression of lawful earthly love, which contrasts with the private, dangerous love earlier associated with Venus. Still, this choosing of mates cannot be entirely dissociated from sexuality, since its goal is procreation. Chaucer appears to be following Alanus in presenting marriage, sanctioned by Nature, as a figure for the principle of cosmic order. However, unlike Alanus, he does not present an absolute opposition between his moral, orderly Nature and his sexual Venus. Rather, he follows Meun insofar as he recognizes sexuality as an essential element in the sort of love which leads to procreation. Venus inhabits Chaucer's garden of love, but the sexuality she represents is controlled and made legitimate by Nature *pronuba*. In the *Parliament*, God's benevolent vicar presides over earthly love; her views on earthly lust are never stated, though one might infer from her presence at the mating ritual that she opposes illicit coupling.

The formality of Nature's speeches and her insistence upon her rules reflect her divine orderliness. The cyclical nature of this assembly, "fro yer to yeere" (lines 321, 411), suggests a permanent, orderly pattern behind the particulars of individual, time-bound experience, even though on the individual level all is less than orderly and serene. Just as the individual traits of the birds introduce elements of tension into the orderly assembly (lines 330–64), so tension of another sort emerges as Nature rehearses the rules, her "ryghtful ordenaunce" (line 390), for the proceedings. It is obvious from the outset that the formel (lines 372–78) and the royal tercel (lines 393–99) are superior in "degre," appearance, and character to the other birds and that Nature intends them for one another.[30] Nature, however, intimates that things are far from certain even in this ceremonial expression of legitimate love:

> And after hym by ordre shul ye chese,
> After youre kynde, everich as yow lyketh,
> And, as youre hap is, shul ye wynne or lese.
> But which of yow that love most entriketh,
> God sende hym hire that sorest for hym syketh!
> [Lines 400–404]

There is at least the possibility of disappointment for the suitors. The elements of free choice and mutual agreement promise amatory complications:

> But natheles, in this condicioun
> Mot be the choys of everich that is heere,
> That she agre to his eleccioun,
> Who so he be that shulde be hire feere.
> This is oure usage alwey, fro yer to yeere,
> And whoso may at this tyme have his grace,
> In blisful tyme he cam into this place!
> [Lines 407–13]

Nature's governance and guidance do not guarantee love's miracles; love's cruel ire may well be the lot of individual participants in this mating process.

The entire parliament is an allegory of legitimate earthly love,

137

presented in all its complexity and ambiguity through the avian microcosm. It begins with the royal tercel, highest in "degre" and worthiest of all the noble birds (lines 393–99), declaring his love for the formel eagle. In his speech (lines 416–41) he employs the idiom of courteous, aristocratic literary lovemaking appropriate to his position in the social hierarchy. He humbly declares his eternal, faithful service to his "soverayn lady" (line 416), who has the power to "do me lyve or sterve" (line 420), beseeches her "merci" and "grace," alludes to the "payne" (line 424) and "wo" (line 427) he presently suffers, and claims his love for her to be greater than that of any other suitor. His language and sentiments are those of Venus and Cupid, of the conventions of amatory literature embodied in those figures, and they link his individual case to the more general aspects of worldly love seen earlier in the narrator's tour of the park. He prays for the miracles of love and fears the cruel ire which, so he believes, could lead to his death (lines 420, 423, 424). His "korven" heart (line 425) directly recalls Cupid's arrows, which "kerve" (line 217), and nothing he says is inappropriate to the realm of Cupid and Venus, since that, figuratively, is where he stands.

The formel does not respond at once to the tercel's declaration, and so the second and third tercels introduce the note of competition into the mating process by declaring that they, too, desire her as a mate (lines 449–83). The perceptible differences in speaking style which distinguish these birds from the royal tercel are appropriate to suitors "Of lower kynde" (line 450) and underscore Nature's assertion of his superiority, but still these somewhat comical suitors are of the nobility, their sentiments are essentially identical to those of the royal tercel, however clumsily they may express them, and they have the right to present their suits. The three tercels debate from morning until sundown (lines 484–90); the question is, basically, which of them loves the formel best, and it cannot be resolved by rational means. They can only assert the intensity of their amorous feelings. The element of rivalry has created a dilemma whose apparent irresolubility becomes the central point in the proceedings. What began as an apparently simple, orderly process has reached an impasse.

The "noyse of foules for to ben delyvered" (line 491) signals the entry of the other, lower, classes of birds into the debate, further confusing matters and contributing to the near breakdown of the temporal order. The social purpose for which the birds have assembled is not being accomplished. The disorderly "noyse" (lines 491, 500) is so great that the landscape of love itself seems about to come apart: "wel wende I the wode hadde al toshyvered" (line 493). What to the disinterested narrator had seemed "gentil ple" (line 485) to the birds seems "cursede pletynge" (line 495), and they collectively reognize that, "withouten any preve," no judge can render a verdict in the dispute. The goose and cuckoo offer to render verdicts nonetheless (lines 501–509), but are forestalled by the turtledove, who rebukes them for meddling in matters they do not understand (lines 510–18), cutting across class lines to express the respect of one of the commons for an apparently aristocratic point of contention.[31]

Nature, aware of the discontent among the commons, intervenes to stem the "noyse" and, once again, to propose an orderly procedure which will avert chaotic argumentation. A representative of each order will be chosen to speak for his fellows (lines 519–25). The "tercelet of the faucoun," speaking first for the noble birds of ravine, agrees that it is too difficult "to preve by resoun" who loves the formel best, and he quickly dismisses "batayle" as an alternative, apparently because "pes" (line 547) is the rule in Nature's orderly realm (lines 533–46). The only criterion amenable to rational judgment is the relative worthiness of the rivals:

> ...I seye, as to my wit,
> Me wolde thynke how that the worthieste
> Of knyghthod, and lengest had used it,
> Most of estat, of blod the gentilleste,
> Were sittyngest for hire, if that her leste;
> And of these thre she wot hireself, I trowe,
> Which that he be, for it is light to knowe.
> [Lines 547–53]

Rationally, the formel should choose her worthiest suitor, who is clearly the royal tercel, but whether she "leste" choose him is another matter.

From this point the parliament strikes out upon a tangential question from which it never returns. The next speaker, the goose, does not address the question of whom the formel should choose; apparently assuming that she will choose one of the three suitors, she directs her words to the losers, advising them, "Bot she wol love hym, lat hym love another!" (line 567). The subject has shifted to that of the fate of the rejected suitors. The noble birds, along with the turtledove, insist that a lover should remain faithful to his lady until death, while the commons oppose them. Insults are exchanged, the birds begin interrupting one another, and the gulf between the idealistic, "gentil," nobles and the churlish but practical commons becomes a chasm. The two camps express irreconcilable views of love, and neither can understand or sympathize with the other. The tercelet, responding to the duck's churlishness, makes the point, by implication, that his ignoble view of love is of no value to the nobility: "Thy kynde is of so low a wrechednesse / That what love is, thow canst nat seen ne gesse" (lines 601–602). Finally, the cuckoo, speaking for worm fowl, gives up in complete exasperation and declares that, so long as he can have his mate "in pes," those birds who cannot "acorde" can be "soleyn" all their lives, for all he cares (lines 603–609). The merlioun, unable to contain his anger at the cuckoo's insensitivity and self-centeredness, responds with a brief, vitriolic, personal attack upon the cuckoo's character (lines 610–16), and once again the proceedings come to a standstill.

For the final time, Nature commands "pes" (line 617). Again the orderly process has degenerated into near chaos, and, as Nature herself admits, the birds are "nevere the neer" a solution (lines 618–19). Her decision, therefore, is that the formel shall have "eleccioun / Of whom hire lest," regardless of the consequences (lines 620–30). The formel is back where she began, and the question of the fate of her rejected suitors is simply brushed aside. Nature agrees with the tercelet that there is no purpose to be served in debating over who loves the formel best (lines 624–25) and reiterates his rational advice:

> But as for conseyl for to chese a make,
> If I were Resoun, certes, thanne wolde I
> Conseyle yow the royal tercel take,
> As seyde the tercelet ful skylfully,
> As for the gentilleste and most worthi,
> Which I have wrought so wel to my plesaunce,
> That to yow hit oughte to been a suffisaunce.
> [Lines 631–37]

The whole parliament seems to be going around in circles.

The formel's behavior is consistently enigmatic. Her reaction to the tercel's speech is to blush "for shame" and remain silent, "So sore abasht was she," while Nature reassures her that she has nothing to fear (lines 442–48). Her embarrassment probably reflects a maiden's modesty before a public declaration of love, and Nature's remark "drede yow noght" (line 448) suggests that, since there is nothing specific in the tercel's speech to inspire fear, she wishes to calm the vague general apprehension of a prospective bride. Still, her blush and silence remain a bit mysterious. Her refusal to choose one of the suitors is even more mystifying; it seems the vision's crowning manifestation of the ambiguous nature of earthly love, of its resistance to easy comprehensibility. Like "everich other creature" she must be under Nature's "yerde" so long as "lyf may dure" (lines 639–42). Yet she simply refuses to go along with the rational choice of the royal tercel, insisting instead upon a year's "respit for to avise me" before choosing, even if Nature should "do me deye" (lines 646–51).

The formel offers no real explanation for her unexpected decision. Her refusal to serve Venus and Cupid "as yit, by no manere weye" (lines 652–53), cannot, I think, imply a negative judgment upon the character of her suitors or upon the influence of the god and goddess of love. Venus and Cupid are very much a part of the experience presented within the park of love, and by rejecting service to them, the formel at the same time rejects Nature's advice; were she to accept "hym on whom hire herte is set" (line 627), she would be serving Venus, Cupid, and Nature. Moreover, she says that she will make her "choys" (line 649) in a year; she does not renounce love permanently. All one can infer from her words is that she is not yet ready to enter into the procreative, sexual process of lawful mating. Like Alanus's Nature, Chaucer's figure, despite her great power and responsibility, apparently cannot compel her subjects to adhere to her laws contrary to their wishes. She must agree, "syn it may non otherwise betyde" (line 654), to allow the formel her respite, thereby excluding her and her suitors temporarily from the procreative process. The formel has not rejected Nature's laws, but in her own individual case she has forestalled them.

The unresolved problem of the eagles' mating stands as a paradigm for the confusing nature of worldly love. Their affairs will remain in abeyance for a year. The formel's decision not to decide remains unexplained and probably inexplicable. Neither Nature, Reason, Cupid, nor Venus can at this juncture successfully resolve the complications which have arisen. Robert Frank is no doubt right that Chaucer's point in not having the formel make a choice is to show that Nature is not Reason, that love is irrational.[32] Indeed, the only appropriate resolution to this central, individual problem in the *Parliament* is no resolution at all. Any resolution that Chaucer might offer would cut arbitrarily through the ambiguity and complexity of the subject of worldly love itself. Chaucer does not wish to satisfy his narrator's quest for "a certeyn thing" by reducing love in all its variety to conformity to the dictates of any or all of a series of abstract figures and concepts.

At the end of the vision Nature simply sets aside the dilemma of the tercels, whose futures continue to hold the possibilities of love's miracles and cruel ire. She turns to the other birds, whom she wishes to see mated and to depart without "taryinge lengere heere" (lines 654–57). She dismisses the tercels, admonishing them that "A yer is nat so longe to endure" (line 661); they must practice patience. Her "werk" ends, then, with her giving every bird his mate "By evene acord" (line 668) and with their subsequent "blisse and joye" (line 669). Before their departure, "As yer by yer was alwey hir usaunce" (line 674), some are chosen to sing a "roundel" to please and honor Nature by welcoming the returning Summer, and to commemorate Saint Valentine, "that art ful hy on-lofte," whose day this is (lines 673–92). Seen from an overall perspective, Nature's laws of mating and procreation will now, as always, be fulfilled. Cosmic order and the common profit cannot be separated within this natural locus; they are both served, despite the vagaries and conflicts which arise in the love affairs of individual members of the social microcosm.[33]

The temporal and spatial schemes of the *Parliament* work in concert with its figures and images to give the poem its overall atmosphere of unity, integration, and harmony.[34] The spatial focus of the poem is the walled park, within which all of the miracles and cruel ire of worldly love take place. Just as the spatial aspect of the park is symbolic of the entire spectrum of love's experience, so in certain respects is its temporal aspect. At the one extreme we find the ideal of happiness in love manifesting itself eternally, without change, and at the other extreme we find the figurative manifestation of unhappiness in love as death. The creatures who choose to enter this realm, be they human beings or a humanized, allegorical microcosm of birds, do so within the framework of diurnal, annual, and mortal time.

This diurnal, finite aspect of time is the real measurable time within which Nature's creatures live and die. Thus the eternally green portion of the park appears without human inhabitants, as an ideal, while the dead unfortunates depicted on the temple walls are part of an attainable, if undesirable, reality. The miracles and cruel ire of love are not, in this locus, mere abstract notions, though they are first embodied in the allegorical imagery of the inscriptions and the park. They are, rather, the specific instances of the phenomenon the narrator calls "love," as it runs its course in particular individuals. The closest he comes to witnessing miracles in this time-bound context is the joy of the birds whose mating has proved successful "By evene acord" (line 668). Love's ire is reflected in the paintings of the martyrs, who have indeed died as the result of their love affairs. Between these extremes are those whose fates remain in abeyance: the emblematic "two yonge folk" who await Venus's disposition of their case (lines 278–79) and the eagles who must wait out their year.

The birds reveal their consciousness of time's passage and of the inevitability of death, collectively and individually, through their words. The allegorical figures manifest their influence within a temporal, mortal world, but they are not themselves subject to time and change. Cupid and Wille forge arrows to "sle," "wounde," and "kerve" human beings, and the various other personifications likewise play roles in human affairs, yet all appear essentially static, as permanent emblems of what their names say they are. The female dancers who do "here offyce alwey, yer by yeere" (line 236) and their male counterparts who appear perpetually trying to crown Priapus with flowers, as well as Venus' two supplicants, function as timeless emblems of the worship of Venus and Priapus by the collective human race, and so of the perpetual power of these phallic and venereal forces. Venus and Priapus themselves appear virtually immobile, frozen in appropriate attitudes, while the human figures engage in emblematic activity. Descriptive details, however, reveal that Venus is aware of time and functions within it. She awaits nightfall, the time of day propitious for the exercise of her power (line 266). Presumably she does respond to the prayers of her petitioners. She is responsible for the broken bows of the maidens who wasted their time (line 283) in Diana's service, while the martyrs who did not waste their time have reached the end of their time through her agency.

Nature, too, is a perpetual force, "vicaire of the almyghty Lord" (line 379), manifesting her influence through the annual, cyclical gathering of the birds. She bids them take their places, "As they were woned alwey fro yer to yeere" (line 321). The females must agree to the males' choices, for this is Nature's "usage alwey, fro yer to yeere" (line 411). The birds sing their roundel "As yer by yer was alwey hir usaunce" (line 674), and the song itself celebrates Nature's seasonal manifestation. The unchanging yearly cycle governs the species, which is constant within time and subject to Nature's laws. The individual birds are clearly time-bound and conscious of time's passage, and Nature governs them accordingly. She sets forth a temporal scheme for choosing their mates "by ordre" (lines 390–413) and recognizes individual moments therein: "whoso may at this tyme have his grace, / In blisful tyme he cam into this place" (lines 412–13). She tries to end the delay in the mating process (line 619). At the end she must capitulate to the formel's wish for a year's respite. Timeless herself, she rules a world of creatures who are acutely conscious of time's passage.

Certain repeated elements in the *Parliament* connect the temporal, finite realm of earthly love to the cosmos which Scipio envisions. In terms of literal space the park corresponds to the "lytel erthe" (line 57) that Scipio views. The earth is contained within the nine spheres, where somewhere "about th'erthe" (line 80) the spirits of the lawless and lecherous are punished until such time as they will enter the "blysful place," Heaven, which has no physical location. There is no Hell, no place of permanent punishment, in this cosmic landscape. Everything which Scipio sees, at least in Chaucer's version of the Ciceronian vision, is contained within the physical cosmos and is therefore subject to temporal laws. Africanus speaks of Heaven, the final home of man's immortal soul, but Scipio never actually sees it.

As figurative space the park, as it were, opens outward to touch conceptually upon the cosmic landscape of the *Somnium*. The "miraculous" portion of the park, the earthly paradise of love, has its verbal and conceptual links with "hevene"; both are "blysful" places where "joye is that last withouten ende" (lines 48–49; cf. lines 76–77, 83, 127–30, 171–210). In the same way, Cicero's realm of punishment, more a Purgatory than a spiritual Hell in the Christian sense, has its symbolic counterpart in the realm of death-in-love in Venus's temple. Death in the symbolism of the garden is a figurative representation of the worst manifestation of failure in love, with its attendant torments. The landscape of such failure, the conception of it, then, touches upon or mirrors the realm of spiritual torment in Cicero's cosmos.

Diurnal time frames the cosmic vision of the *Somnium*. Scipio and Masinissa talk "til the day gan misse" (line 40), and that night Scipio receives his vision. Upon waking, Scipio will return to his temporal life to earn his place in the eternal hereafter and to tell others what he has learned in his vision. The vision, like that of Chaucer's narrator, is thus firmly linked to the visionary's earthly life both by its temporal framework and by its content. From the cosmic perspective, the span of mortal human life is reduced to insignificance: "oure present worldes lyves space / Nis but a maner deth" (lines 53–54), "ful of torment and of harde grace" (line 65), and in "certeyn yeres space" (line 67) every star will return to its original place and all that mankind has ever done will be forgotten. We cannot be certain that Chaucer associated this conclusion of the great cycle of the mundane year with the Christian millennium, but it seems likely that he would. At any rate, Christian and Platonic views of the temporal world resemble one another: individual endeavor within a single life-span disappears from human memory over the sweep of many centuries, while the centuries themselves are subsumed under the eternity of the soul's immortality.

Still, individual, temporal life remains significant; in Cicero, those who serve the "commune profyt" come swiftly into the blissful realm of eternity, while lawbreakers and lechers arrive there only after "many a world be passed." In the earthly park, too, time circumscribes individual activity, and the brevity of individual life is subsumed by the temporal perpetuity of Nature, Venus, and the other forces which govern or influence humanity. Venus and Nature themselves, one assumes, will ultimately be subsumed, if not extinguished, in the eternity which envelops the finite, temporal world. At any event, until the providential plan is completed in time, whatever the fates of individual petitioners to Venus and of lovelorn birds, the entire complex process revealed in the park will continue, and this continuity within the yearly cycle points toward the eternity beyond it.

The *Somnium* offers service to the "commune profyt" as the surest way for the individual to attain heavenly bliss. In the park of love this ideal receives no explicit emphasis, although it is not rejected. It may well be that the sort of political, public activity which engages Scipio is simply irrelevant in the more private, individual realm of love. However, I think it fair to say that, whatever private motives may impel them, all of the birds wish to serve the public good and in their ways attempt to do so. After all, they want to be joined to their lawful mates, and that alone will serve the common good of the species, whose duty under Nature's law is procreation. The tercelet may seem more rationally public-spirited than the cuckoo, but both wish to expedite the public business for which they have assembled. Chaucer, I would suggest, offers a more complex and "poetic" view of the "commune profyt" and how it is ultimately served than the *Somnium*, in the case of the birds and, by analogy, in the realm of human activity as well.

Finally, the birds choose their mates and sing their roundel. Nature holds the potential chaos of the parliament in check, preserving harmony and order in the microcosm. She governs the Ciceronian macrocosm as well as the park of earthly love; both are Nature's realm. The music of the spheres, source of melody and harmony on earth (lines 59–63), manifests itself in the harmonious sounds of the ideal, Edenic landscape in the park (lines 190–203), but it is not confined to this dream of perfection in love. The encompassing order and harmony of Nature—"That hot, cold, hevy, lyght, moyst, and dreye / Hath knyt by evene noumbres of acord" (lines 380–81)—cannot be subverted by individual squabbles, imperfect motives, and irrationality because it is itself macrocosmic in scope. The birds, mated "By evene acord" (line 668), attain the "commune profyt" in spite of themselves, and their roundel, uniting praise of Nature and Saint Valentine "that art ful hy on-lofte" (line 683), expresses the order which persists in the temporal world and reflects the divine order of the "almyghty Lord." Love's miracles and cruel ire, in all their manifestations, are part of this larger order, and, from the larger perspective, the general good is continually served.

At the end of the poem the noise made by the birds awakens the narrator, and he returns to his books:

> And with the shoutyng, whan the song was do
> That foules maden at here flyght awey,
> I wok, and othere bokes tok me to,
> To reede upon, and yit I rede alwey.
> I hope, ywis, to rede so som day
> That I shal mete some thyng for to fare
> The bet, and thus to rede I nyl nat spare.
> [Lines 693–99]

He does not appear to have benefited from the educative experience of his vision. He returns to the waking state in which he began and resumes his reading, hoping to find something more helpful. His vision has suggested that the kind of love he is interested in is indeed confusing, ambiguous, and not amenable to rational certainty in its individual manifestations, but he still does not realize that this is the normal state of affairs. However, in returning to his reading, he himself enacts the natural, cyclical continuation of activity figured in the birds' yearly mating ritual and in his simile of the "olde feldes" (lines 22–25).[35] Like the male eagles, he has not resolved his dilemma; certainty continues to elude him, and he patiently perseveres "alwey" in the hope that he will someday "fare the bet." The twin possibilities of success or failure remain for him as for them, not, to be sure, in love, but in understanding, and communicating his understanding of, love. In remaining faithful to his calling he is, like Scipio and the eagles, playing his individual part and attempting to serve the common good in the larger order of his world, no matter whether or not he succeeds.

The *Parliament* is a Boethian vision poem by virtue of the relationship of the vision to the visionary's preoccupations, and that relationship is unusual in that it depends upon his confusion and desire for knowledge about a subject, "love," which he approaches as a perpetual outsider. He seeks knowledge for the sake of knowledge. He reads and writes about love to satisfy his curiosity and, perhaps, to enlighten and amuse others; Chaucer deliberately excludes him from direct participation in the experience of his vision. The narrator functions as a seer, a recipient of visionary enlightenment, but not, at least where the primary subject of worldly love is concerned, as a surrogate for others who undergo the experience of love itself. It seems to me a mark of Chaucer's intellectual humility and reticence that he presents a complex philosophical view of one of the more important aspects of human life in the guise of an uncomprehending visionary. This guise enables him to avoid the appearance of speaking as an austere poet-seer, lecturing to an audience of the unenlightened on a subject he is privileged to know better than they. Chaucer's audience must discover for itself, with little or no help from his visionary, the meaning figured forth in the poetic allegory of his vision.

Part Three   Visions of Love, Loss and Fortune

8

PEARL

I n this part we shall examine four Middle English poems in the Boethian vision tradition which I have grouped together as "Visions of Love, Loss and Fortune." All these poems treat questions which arise from the at times problematical relationship between secular sorts of love and the kind of adversity which the suffering Boethius of the *Consolation* attributes to the malevolence of Fortune. *Pearl* employs a Boethian vision to console its narrator for what he initially sees as personal worldly misfortune, the loss of a beloved child. Chaucer's *Book of the Duchess* likewise draws upon the *Consolation* for its structural framework and deals with the problem of personal loss. James I of Scotland's *Kingis Quair* takes the text of the *Consolation* as its starting point and deals centrally with the concepts of love and fortune. Robert Henryson makes no direct reference to Boethius in his *Testament of Cresseid*, but Boethian structure and idea nonetheless figure prominently in his poem.

Recognizing *Pearl* as a Boethian Apocalypse is a first step toward understanding the poem's structure and meaning.[1] Its close resemblance in purpose, overall structure, narrative strategy, and, to a degree, subject matter to other examples of the genre leads Michael Means to call it a "Pure Consolatio."[2] Recognition of *Pearl*'s generic relationships has, however, been at best sporadic. William Henry Schofield in 1904 noted significant parallels between *Pearl* and the visions of Boethius, Alanus, and Lorris.[3] In 1953, John Conley attempted to demonstrate that *Pearl* is a Christian *consolatio*, a literary

151

kind for which Boethius's *Consolation* supplies the prototype.[4] Unfortunately, Conley discusses only certain thematic parallels between the two works and does not establish clearly the characteristics of this genre. Recently, Means, Paul Piehler,[5] and A. C. Spearing[6] have attempted to see the poem as part of a continuing literary tradition.[7] Still, the general lack of appreciation of the extent of *Pearl*'s debt to Boethian tradition can be attributed largely to our imperfect understanding of the tradition, even when its existence is in some vague way recognized. The Boethian characteristics of *Pearl* must be understood in the light of this long tradition, and not simply as random traces of the influence of one or another of its members.

The various controversies surrounding *Pearl* have effectively obscured its place in Boethian tradition. The question of whether the poem is autobiographical has been laid to rest for lack of concrete evidence one way or the other, but that of whether the relationship of the poem's narrator and the pearl-maiden is that of father and daughter continues to arise from time to time. The argument over whether its purpose is elegiac or allegorical-didactic appears to have subsided with the realization that it can be a bit of both. Suspicions that the poet's theological views are less than orthodox have proved unfounded, but the search for his ideological influences continues, as does the discussion of the poem's allegory and symbolism.[8] Neither doctrinal content nor the influence of other kinds of medieval literature has any direct relevance to a discussion of its genre, nor does the fact that it may be elegiac, allegorical, or symbolic. The poet draws upon a broad literary and theological background, but if we are to properly appreciate his achievement, we must begin by recognizing the centrality of the Boethian Apocalypse to *Pearl*'s structure and approach to its subject.

Like Boethius's *Consolation* and its progeny, *Pearl*'s purpose is not mystical or controversial but practical. It treats theological and eschatological matters, but the doctrines included in the poem are limited to those directly pertinent to the problems of a human narrator. The narrator's vision of the pearl-maiden is intended to restore his ability to live in his temporal world. The problem implicitly posed here, as in the *Consolation*, is that of reconciling the narrator to life in a world where events appear often unjust or simply incomprehensible. The experience of a serious personal misfortune (whether autobiographical or fictional is of no importance) triggers the narrator's consciousness of his existential dilemma; grief over an obviously personal loss prevents his reason and his religious training from comforting him and enabling him to accept what has happened:

Pearl

A deuely dele in my hert denned,
Þaȝ resoun sette myseluen saȝt.
I playned my perle þat þer watȝ spenned
Wyth fyrce skylleȝ þat faste faȝt;
Þaȝ kynde of Kryst me comfort kenned,
My wreched wylle in wo ay wraȝte.

[Lines 51-56]

The poem records the narrator's struggle to come to terms with his experience. Though his misfortune is particular and personal, he is, in his reaction to it, a representative of humanity at large. His situation is analyzed and placed in the larger context of human life by the maiden and, finally, by the narrator himself. He emerges with a new perspective upon his particular problem and upon his place in his world. As in the *Consolation*, the information the narrator receives in his vision confirms what he seems already to know but cannot apply to his present situation; he must relearn things about Kryst and Heaven in the light of his own experience, and needs assistance to do so. At the end of the poem nothing in his situation has changed, but he is better able to deal with it. Like the *Consolation*, *Pearl* has a tentative, provisional quality to its ending: the narrator has received no guarantee of a brighter future, but new hope and optimism have replaced his original grief and despair.

The ideological content of *Pearl* coincides at several important points with that of the *Consolation*. Conley sees a basic similarity of theme in the two works: "The theme of *Pearl*, as of the *Consolation*, might be called the sovereign theme of the Christian tradition, as of life itself: the nature of happiness, specifically false and true happiness."[9] Fortune's gifts, appearing in *Pearl* primarily as the transitory aspects of human life, are presented at least implicitly as the source of false happiness, while God is specifically established as the supreme good and so the source of true happiness. Divine Providence may be ultimately beyond human comprehension, but it is nonetheless affirmed as being absolutely just. Piehler calls attention to the transformation of the narrator's idea of Fate to the maiden's idea of Providence in the symbolism of lines 273-76, noting that what is here represented by the transformation of symbols is in the *Consolation* presented through the philosophical dialogue.[10] The course of life recommended by the instructresses in both works is one of virtue in accordance with the divine will, a turning from worldly to eternal values. However, one should never be surprised to find Boethian themes and concepts in any serious work of the period; their presence in *Pearl* cannot in itself be construed as proving direct Boethian influence.

The overall structure, what A. R. Heiserman has called "The Plot of *Pearl*,"[11] gives a more reliable indication of Boethian influence. A medieval reader familiar with poems of this kind would, I think, recognize this "plot" as it begins to unfold; it would influence his expectations about the purpose of the poem and its method of approaching its subject matter. This structure is essentially dramatic, centering upon a dialogue between a troubled narrator-visionary and the authority figure who confronts him in his vision. *Pearl*'s first stanza group, the prologue to the vision (lines 1–60), corresponds to the Boethian "complaint": the narrator is introduced by means of his emotional lament over his present circumstances. It is not immediately clear precisely what these circumstances are, but his helplessness, confusion, and despair are readily apparent. In the *Consolation* the narrator's turbulent emotions prevent him from recognizing where to turn for help; Philosophy's sudden arrival suggests that Boethius has habitually turned to her for comfort in the past. *Pearl*'s authority figure is a human spirit rather than a personification, but the narrator has himself pointed toward the relationship between his authority figure and his vision: ". . . Ofte haf I wayted, wyschande þat wele, / Þat wont watȝ whyle deuoyde my wrange / And heuen my happe and al my hele" (lines 14–16). His "perle" will once again cheer him, but in a more profound and lasting way than he can at this point imagine.

The maiden's arrival, like the arrivals of Philosophy and Nature, is abrupt and dazzling, and the visionary is slow to recognize her (lines 157–252). This initial lack of recognition can here be explained by the maiden's transformed state, but it, together with the narrator's silence before her, carries the same implications as the parallel scene in the *Consolation*: it indicates the seriousness of his mental condition and is a measure of the present distance between them. Despite their estrangement the presence of the authority has a comforting effect on the visionary, until she begins to upbraid him. In severe tones she sets out to disabuse him of his misconceptions about her and about his own condition. In the ensuing dialogue a change is being effected in the narrator's consciousness. As in the *Consolation* the visionary dialogue culminates in the contemplation of the nature of the divinity and in the reconciliation of the narrator to his present life.

The *Consolation* was not the only model available to the *Pearl* poet, although it is the prototype for visionary works of this kind. Cicero's *Somnium Scipionis*, Boethius's closest structural predecessor, bears some striking resemblances to *Pearl*. In the *Somnium* a deceased relative, Africanus, who is the subject of conversation immediately before the dream, serves as the primary authority figure. If one accepts, as I think we must, the identification of the pearl-maiden as the dreamer's daughter,[12] the comparison seems obvious, and we may note that the *Somnium* is much closer in structure to *Pearl* than is Boccaccio's eclogue, *Olympia*, once thought to be its source.[13] Upon the arrival of his dead father, Paulus, Scipio immediately expresses his wish to join Paulus permanently, but Paulus reproves him for his emotional disregard for the divine will and purpose (chap. 3). Similarly, *Pearl*'s narrator expresses his intention to remain reunited with the maiden, and is sternly reminded that he must await God's judgment (lines 277–360). The central conflict in the *Somnium* is between temporal values and eternal ones; the gaze of the visionary must be drawn from the sublunary world upward, to the contemplation of the eternal goal and home ("hanc sedem aeternam domum"; chap. 4–7). This is true, at least by implication, of Boethius as well, but in the *Somnium* this theme is much more explicitly stated, as it is in *Pearl*: "I rede þe forsake þe worlde wode / And porchace þy perle maskelles" (lines 743–44).[14] This moral position in the *Somnium* is subsequently enforced by Scipio's vision of the heavens and by the explicit promise that a life of virtue will earn him a place there (chaps. 7–9). This vision and promise has no direct counterpart in the *Consolation* but corresponds to *Pearl*'s vision of the New Jerusalem (lines 973–1152) and is echoed by the maiden's discourse on salvation.

Various other aspects of *Pearl* have precedents and counterparts in earlier Boethian works. In the "complaint" of the *De planctu* (met. 1), Alanus presents in compressed and sometimes enigmatic form many of the themes and images which he will develop in his vision of Nature. *Pearl*'s prologue resembles Alanus's opening section in the abundance and enigmatic quality of the themes, images, and even single words whose significance will be developed later. The first three stanzas (lines 1–36) present the narrator's loss in a general way: images and themes of beauty, singularity, value, royalty, gems, loss, death, longing, grief, comfort, music, light, vegetation, and regeneration, all of which will reappear, are compressed into a few lines here. The next two stanzas (lines 37–60) describe the narrator's return to the place of his loss and his mental state. References to reason and will, and to Christ, are added to some of the themes and images already introduced. A discussion of the development of the elements present in *Pearl*'s prologue is impossible here, but careful reading of the poem suggests that these first sixty lines are a sort of index to the whole work.[15]

The maiden's use of the biblical parable of the vineyard (lines

493–588) to make an important point about the nature of divine justice and salvation resembles Philosophy's presentation of the personified concept of Fortune, but insofar as it is narrative in form, it is closer to Alanus's fable of Venus's defection. Its purpose is to illuminate the doctrine the maiden wishes to teach the narrator. The final vision of the Heavenly Jerusalem in *Pearl* functions in a slightly different way; it is less a device to teach doctrine than it is a final confirmation of the doctrine that has already been presented. It is similar in practice to the final vision of the *De planctu*; the narrator's role as participant in the visionary dialogue is finally reduced to that of observer. He is privileged to view a scene which embodies a supernal mystery, and which is intended to finally confirm, and securely establish his faith in, that mystery.

The poet's use of the locus of action as an adjunct to meaning in *Pearl* has precedents in earlier Boethian Apocalypses, but it is not precisely analogous to any one of them. In Boethius and Alanus little attention is paid to setting and little importance attached to it. In the *Architrenius* place is more closely and in a more complex way related to meaning; places have specific conceptual functions. Likewise, in *Pearl*, specific places, and the movement from place to place, have conceptual implications for the work as a whole. There are three distinct loci in *Pearl*: the "erber," the place which is associated with the narrator's physical loss and subsequent grief; the marvelous forest in which he finds himself in his vision, a place which is unlike the everyday physical world, and which is separated by an impassable river from the third locus, the realm of eternity where the maiden and the New Jerusalem appear. The narrator begins in the physical world, the "doeldoungoun" (line 1187) to which he returns after he awakens. The realm across the river, which the narrator thinks is "Paradyse" (line 137), and which on account of original sin he cannot enter while living (lines 313–24), is the realm now reserved for the spirits of the blessed dead. It seems likely that, as Kean argues, it is the Earthly paradise,[16] but the poet is never explicit on this point. The visionary landscape in which the narrator stands is likewise never explicitly defined, and it is not important that we know where or what precisely it is. It is a conceptual locus between Heaven and earth, superior in beauty to the latter but inferior to the former.[17] This place reflects the narrator's conceptual "place," his role within the vision. He has spiritual truth directly available to him here, but he remains tied to the material reality and human limitations of earthly life. He is allowed to come this far through God's grace and can go no farther while he lives.

Finally, we must notice what is perhaps too obvious to require any comment at all: the *Pearl* poet thoroughly exploits the emotional potential of the Boethian genre. The narrator has suffered a serious loss, is understandably disconsolate because of it, and must be weaned away from his grief. The doctrine of the vision is directed to this purpose; instruction and emotion are directly and closely related. As Gordon observes:

> The doctrinal theme is, in fact, inseparable from the literary form of the poem and its occasion; for it arises directly from the grief, which imparts deep feeling and urgency to the whole discussion. Without the elegiac basis and the sense of great personal loss which pervades it, *Pearl* would indeed be the mere theological treatise on a special point, which some critics have called it. But without the theological debate the grief would never have risen above the ground.[18]

In *Pearl* as in all other Boethian Apocalypses, the narrator is the central consciousness; it is through him that the reader experiences and learns from the vision. This point about the narrator's centrality was made years ago by Charles Moorman, who, apparently under the influence of Francis Fergusson's study of the *Purgatorio*, compares *Pearl*'s narrator to the heroes of Henry James and to Dante's Pilgrim.[19] No one since has seriously challenged Moorman's view, but many have unwisely ignored it or have simply failed to grasp its importance. It is through the agency of the narrator that we learn about the pearls, symbolic and otherwise, in the poem, and we must keep this fact clearly in mind when reading it; the narrator and the pearls are separate but not separable. A careful examination of the development of the narrator must therefore precede any attempt to deal with the poem's symbolism.

The function of *Pearl*'s first stanza group is that of the opening "complaint" of Boethius: it reflects the confusion and divided sensibility of the dream's protagonist (lines 1–60). He speaks of the loss of his "pryvy perle," but his language and the sheer intensity of his grief point somewhat ambiguously beyond a literal gem, toward a human being, a beloved girl who has died. His grief and desolation are emphasized, though there are vague hints of solace in the "sange" he hears (lines 19–22) and in the suggestions of natural regeneration (lines 25–36). He returns to the place where his pearl went into the ground — a gesture which would make little sense if the pearl were only a literal gem — and is overcome with grief. The nature of his internal strife is clearly defined: "dele" prevents "resoun" from setting his heart at rest, and his "wylle" in "wo" conflicts with the comfort that "kynde of Kryst" offers him (lines 51–52, 55–56).[20] It is clear that he has something more than the loss of a literal gem on his mind. His choice of "perle" as a figure reflects the limitations inherent in his view of his loss before his vision; at this point, he conceives of it almost exclusively as the loss of a material object, albeit an object of rare beauty and value. This does not mean, as Conley suggests, that the "perle" itself is "an imperfect good," one of the mutable things of this world, but only that he sees it as such, that he mourns only that aspect of it which is mutable. It is the narrator's attitude, not the "pearl" itself, that is subject to criticism here. He makes no distinction in his mind between a lost gem and a dead child.[21] He is guilty of the sin of cupidity and of *stultitia*, as Conley says,[22] not because what he loves *is* a material object but because he thinks of it as a material object.

The narrator falls asleep and finds himself transported in spirit to the marvelous landscape of his vision (lines 61–72). The phrase "in Godeȝ grace" (line 63) indicates the real source of his vision but does not, it seems, indicate that he recognizes in any profound way God's influence as yet; a bit later he credits "fortwne" with his conveyance here (lines 97–98, 129–32).[23] He does not know where he is (line 65), and while this landscape for the moment cheers him considerably (lines 85–86, 121–24), the alteration in his mood has no substantial basis. He is simply caught up in the physical appearance of the place, its "adubbement." Pearls form a major part of this "adubbement," but he does not associate them with his own lost "perle" (lines 81–84). He is not even satisfied with what he has now; the land across the river seems "Paradyse" to him, and he almost immediately desires to cross over (lines 133–44). When he finally sees the maiden on the other side, his reaction is a mixture of recognition and confusion. He both does (line 164) and does not know her, and withdraws into silent bewilderment (lines 169–84).

The description of the maiden (lines 181–240) confirms for the reader her identity as the lost "perle." Her beauty, the pearls which adorn her—"A precios pyece in perleȝ pyȝt" (line 192)—and the verbal echoes in lines 189–92 of the first lines of the poem all point toward this identification. The abundance of pearls here reflects ironically upon the narrator's grief over the loss of a single gem and suggests that what he has found is of greater value than what he lost. While he describes her—fearing that she may run off at any moment (lines 186–88)—he cannot himself quite connect this vision with his earlier grief, nor can he begin to understand the significance of the pearl she wears:

Bot a wonder perle wythouten wemme
Inmyddeʒ hyr breste watʒ sette so sure;
A manneʒ dom moʒt dryʒly demme,
Er mynde moʒt malte in hit mesure.
I hope no tong moʒt endure
No sauerly saghe say of þat syʒt,
So watʒ hit clene and cler and pure,
Þat precios perle þer hit watʒ pyʒt.
[Lines 221–28]

His enigmatic allusion to their relationship (lines 233–34) suggests again that he recognizes her but preserves the atmosphere of confusion. The narrator's first words to her,

"O perle," quod I, "in perleʒ pyʒt,
Art þou my perle þat I haf playned,
Regretted by myn one on nyʒte?"
[Lines 241–43]

reveal that he is still uncertain about her identity, even while confirming the reader's suspicion that the lost pearl is in fact a human being. Significantly, the maiden never directly confirms or denies that she is "his" lost pearl. She both is and is not his pearl; she has been transformed from earthly child to heavenly spirit, and so "is" the spirit of the "perle," but is not what he thinks she is. He must be taught to understand and accept this transformation.

The maiden attempts at once to correct some of the narrator's misconceptions. He initially blames her for his suffering (lines 241–52), and she in turn rebukes him, not for his egocentric tone — their reunion cannot, after all, degenerate into a family quarrel — but for thinking her lost. Adopting his metaphor, she observes that he should be glad that his jewel is safe in this new garden "cofer" (lines 257–64). Mourning a lost "gemme" is "a mad porpose," what he lost was in fact only "a rose" which has become "a perle of prys" by virtue of its new "kyste," and he has misjudged his "wyrde" (lines 265–76). Doctrine concerning worldly life and divine providence is highly compressed into a few lines here, and the narrator apparently cannot comprehend it. The "pearl" of which she speaks is clearly not a pearl in the simpler, metaphorical sense in which he has been using the term, but his succeeding remarks, though apologetic, show that her rose-pearl metaphor is lost upon him. In fact, he compounds his original error, and is again rebuked and treated to a more detailed refutation of his views. He has, she says, been faithless and prideful in believing only his senses and in presuming that he can join her now. He must cease his lamentations, pray, and submit himself to God's will (lines 277–360).

Once again he apologizes, revealing increased humility and asserting his belief in divine mercy, but his grief has scarcely abated (lines 361–96). He simply shifts the subject from his emotional state to her "astate" (lines 389–96), as though anxious to leave a sensitive point. She praises his newfound humility as being pleasing to her and to God (lines 397–408) and begins to tell him of her life as a queen of Heaven (line 409–20). Her remarks only confuse him, though; he interrupts, assuming in his literal-minded fashion that, as in earthly kingdoms, there can be but a single queen, Mary, in Heaven. She answers by expounding upon the mystery of divine grace ("cortaysye"); all Christian souls are members of Christ and, as such, are kings and queens in Heaven (lines 421–68). New questions arise at once: he wishes to know the relationship between earthly merit and heavenly reward, arguing that her tender age at the time of her death should make her less deserving of reward than those who served God throughout their adult lives (lines 469–92). He cannot think of grace and eternal reward in other than human terms, and she cannot elucidate such spiritual matters except through parable. The parable of the vineyard is meant to convey to him the mysterious quality of Christ's goodness and so to justify her claim to regal estate in Heaven, and she explicates it insofar as it is possible to explain a mystery (lines 493–588), but he cannot understand. In the face of parabolic mystery he demands a reasonable "tale," citing the Psalter to support his earthbound, legalistic notion of just rewards (lines 589–600). Again, her argument, centering upon the quality of childlike innocence, justifies her presence in Heaven. She speaks of spiritual grace, which is "gret inoghe" whether it is freely given to the baptized innocent or earned by the righteous adult (lines 601–720). This straightforward theological exposition leads her to the symbolic pearl on her breast. It is the pearl of great price of Matthew 13.45–46, and it is explicitly said to represent "þe reme of heuenesse clere" for which all men should forsake worldly values (lines 721–44).

Unfortunately, the narrator is like the members of the multitude to whom Christ speaks in parables, in the same chapter of Matthew where the pearl of great price appears: "Therefore I speak to them in parables: for seeing they see not, and hearing they hear not nor do they understand" (13.13). Again he fails to understand the maiden's words and simply changes the subject from innocence and salvation to her beauty and its Creator (lines 745–56). Though he formulates his question differently, he is really seeking the same information she has just given him: "Breue me, bryȝt, quat kyn offys / Bereȝ þe perle so maskelleȝ?" (lines 755–56). Just as he has failed to understand her "offys" as queen, so now he responds to her allusion to herself as Christ's "make" with earthbound incredulity, assuming that she has displaced all other eligible young ladies in Heaven, as would an earthly wife (lines 757–80). She responds with an account of the New Jerusalem, its nature, and its "brides" (lines 781–900). Here again he does not quite understand her: his tone of extreme humility and deference (lines 901–12) suggests that he has been completely awed by her latest disclosure of her "offys," but he continues to think of her as a living person, asking about the location of the castle in which she must dwell and confusing the New Jerusalem with the Old (lines 913–36). Her explanation of the distinction between the two Jerusalems is scarcely more successful, for he asks to visit her "blysful bor," which is of course impossible (lines 937–72). Still, she has the Lamb's permission to show him the Heavenly City from the outside, which she does in the vision which follows (lines 973–1152).

The vision of Heaven, based upon the Book of Revelation, marks the end of the dialogue and the culmination of the process of enlightenment (if one can call it that). It would not appear that the narrator has earned this vision by his rather questionable intellectual progress; he has not understood the series of distinctions between earthly and heavenly life at all clearly. He has, however, achieved a sort of intuitive recognition of the distance between his situation and hers. Beginning in a state of misery over her physical absence, he has progressed emotionally through self-pity and curiosity to deepening humility and awe before her spiritual presence. His reaction to his vision of Heaven is one of sublime wonder and delight. He can actually see that the City is brighter and purer than sun or moon; the apostle John's description is here confirmed by personal experience. In recognizing that this experience is genuinely visionary, and therefore unavailable to embodied humanity, he appears to have gained a sense of the distance between the earthly and the spiritual:

> I stod as stylle as dased quayle
> For ferly of þat frelich fygure,
> Þat felde I nawþer reste ne trauayle,
> So watȝ I rauyste wyth glymme pure.
> For I dar say wyth conciens sure,
> Hade bodyly burne abiden þat bone,

Boethian Apocalypse

Þaȝ alle clerkeȝ hym hade in cure,
His lyf were loste an-vnder mone.
[Lines 1085–92]

Still, his emotional reactions remain recognizably human. Christ's wounds elicit his naive pity:

Alas, þoȝt I, who did þat spyt?
Ani breste for bale aȝt haf forbrent
Er he þerto hade had delyt.
[Lines 1338–40]

He now recognizes the maiden as a queen, but she remains "my lyttel quene" (line 1147), and at the very apex of his "delyt," "luf-longyng" (for Heaven rather than simply for the maiden, perhaps)[24] causes him to attempt rashly to cross the river separating them (lines 1151–52). Thus to the very end of the vision there remains ambivalence between his earthly and spiritual impulses.

The narrator's entry into the river results in his abrupt awakening. It is madness, though of a very human sort, that drives him to attempt something he should know he cannot achieve — "My maneȝ mynde to maddyng malte" (line 1154) — for the maiden told him as much long before (lines 313–24). Emotion, though of a different quality, has again overcome his reason (lines 1157–60). Yet this time his realization of his error seems almost simultaneous with its commission; he speaks of himself as "mad arayde," "rasch and ronk," acting counter to his "Prynceȝ paye," even as he plunges into the water (lines 1161–68), suggesting that his perspective upon his own actions is somewhat clearer than it was at the beginning of the poem. When he awakens, he immediately acknowledges and accepts the Prince's will in this matter (lines 1174–76). He expresses a sense of loss and sorrow upon waking, but such feelings are now balanced against happiness in knowing that his pearl is "in garlande gay" in Heaven (lines 1177–88). His new mood is one of positive resignation rather than despair: "So wel is me in þys doel-doungoun / Þat þou art to þat Prynseȝ paye" (lines 1187–88).

The narrator recognizes his error in striving against God's will, and he sees the general lesson inherent in his experience. He places his actions in the context of universal human behavior:

Bot ay wolde man of happe more hente
Þen moȝte by riȝt vpon hem clyuen.
Þerfore my ioye watȝ sone toriuen,
And I kaste of kytheȝ þat lasteȝ aye.

162

Pearl

Lorde, mad hit arn þat agayn þe stryune,
Oþer proferen þe oȝt agayn þy paye.
[Lines 1195–1200]

This defect in human nature has been at the heart of his difficulties all through the poem. His vision, as Spearing observes, is an incomplete mystical experience, but not an inconclusive one.[25] His attempt to cross the river is a reflection of ordinary human weakness, and he understands it as such. In the final stanza we learn that the visionary experience has enabled him to recognize and accept the divine will and to be comforted by his faith in the justice of things that he cannot entirely understand. In the last two stanzas a new note of confidence has suggested to a few critics a new narrative voice or a time lapse separating them from the rest of the poem,[26] but nevertheless we must conceive of these stanzas as growing directly out of the vision. The voice is still that of the narrator, but his consciousness has grown as a result of his experience and of his reflection, for an unspecified period of time, upon it. He has found in Christ the means to lay his grief to rest and has committed his pearl to God. And finally, in the Eucharist, the "bred and wyn" which is presented daily to living men, he has found a way to be reunited with his pearl, now a member of Christ's body, as she has pointed out (lines 457–62), while still in this life.[27]

The development of the *Pearl* narrator's consciousness, then, resembles that of Boethius in its centrality, but it does not progress in straightforward fashion and does not end in full understanding. Within his vision the narrator from the beginning desires more than has been or will be given to him. His continual questions reveal both his need for knowledge of the world of the spirit and his inability to comprehend it when it is given. He never fully understands the difference between earthly and heavenly life, though he does finally seem to realize that there is a difference. Like Amant in the *Roman*, he is an ironic figure who errs right to the end of his vision, an object of humor and frustration for the reader who can understand more than he can of his own experience.[28] Unlike Amant, however, as Larry Sklute has observed,[29] he commands not only frustration but also sympathy from the reader. His attempt to cross the river is a human mistake which we must understand as being dictated by recognizably human impulses and must sympathize with, even though we know that he is wrong.

The vision is calculated to evoke an ambivalent response from the reader. The narrator receives new insights into the mysteries of Heaven, but his intense emotions persist, and he remains, as it were,

163

suspended between earth and Heaven. He cannot achieve the clarity and purity of thought of the maiden, but then, no one can in this life. Ultimately the limited success he does achieve occurs after his vision and is the direct result of his failures within the vision. He remains a human being with human limitations, but he has become a better Christian and so better able to live his earthly life. He does not achieve mystical union with God, but neither does his vision fail to achieve its apparent purpose, practical comfort, and enlightenment. The reader is, I think, expected to recognize that he shares a common bond of human limitation with the narrator; the narrator's feelings are like his, in kind if not in degree, and the lesson of faith and resignation which he learns the reader must also learn. The success of *Pearl* as a didactic work depends upon the failures and shortcomings of its narrator.

The pearl-maiden functions in precisely the same way as the earlier Boethian authority figures we have discussed. She guides the suffering visionary from despair and confusion back to psychic and spiritual health. She is not a personification but rather a human spirit. Presumably any of her heavenly sisters could offer the narrator the same doctrinal guidance, since all partake of one and the same divine essence, but she alone is especially suited to the task because of the love she and he bear toward one another. Moreover, through no fault of her own, she is the cause of his initial grief as well as the source of its resolution. By her very presence, as well as her words and the final vision of Heaven, she reveals precisely what has been lost to him and what has not. She may be a fictional spirit, but if she is, she is a brilliantly conceived ficiton, needing no secondary, abstract identity to justify her role in the poem.

Questions concerning the maiden's possibly allegorical or symbolic meaning and her relationship to other pearls in the poem continue to arise, however. Her physical appearance, like those of more obviously abstract Boethian figures, is to a degree emblematic of her identity. The pearls which adorn her clearly suggest great beauty, purity, value, and, in their spherical shape, perfection, while the pearl on her breast is specifically said to signify eternal life, the realm of Heaven. Bishop has shown that her white gown and crown are the symbolic attire of the newly baptised (adults), signifying the lost innocence of Adam restored through the Sacrament, and the crowns are appropriate to souls which become kings and queens in Heaven. Thus her attire symbolizes matters of particular importance in the ensuing dialogue, baptismal innocence, and divine royalty.[30] The loci in which she appears obviously are inseparable from her identity: she is separated from the narrator by the river, which must symbolize death, in a paradisal landscape which may be the Earthly Paradise, and later in the Heavenly City itself. Her initial anger and impatience are perhaps unworthy emotions for a blessed spirit but are comparable to those of figures like Philosophy and Nature. Like her more abstract cousins, she is a self-defining figure; her entire discourse is intended to reveal to the visionary what she has become, and her appearance in the heavenly procession constitutes the final proof of what she has said. Finally, like almost all other authority figures, she is static; her identity is fixed, and her character cannot develop. She has in Heaven achieved her ultimate reality.

What changes in the course of the poem is not the maiden but rather the narrator's (and reader's) understanding of what she is. Before his vision he speaks of her as a lost "pearl," a worldly treasure worthy of a worldly prince. Slowly and with difficulty he is disabused of this initial misconception so that, despite a continuing inability to comprehend the nature of spiritual beings, he can see her in her eternal reality in the procession of the Lamb. She emerges, then, as a member of the heavenly host who has been saved by divine grace after dying in a state of postbaptismal innocence. As an inhabitant of Heaven, she wears the pearl of price, symbolic of the "place" and therefore of the condition, eternal life, which is its essence; she lives in the celestial City; she partakes of the nature of Christ and Mary and is in so doing a "bride" of Christ and "queen" of Heaven. None of these privileges is really separable from the others or from the maiden herself, since all are attributes of the mystical union of the divine part of every blessed human spirit with its Creator. Louis Blenkner accurately states the relationship of the pearl symbol to the maiden:

> The seemingly shifting central pearl symbol can, through enlightened hindsight, be seen to be constant. Like the *margarita pretiosa* of Matthew xiii: 45–6, it symbolizes the precious and eternal perfection of "þe reme of heuenesse clere" (l. 735). As such, it may be applied to the Heavenly City itself or to any object which partakes of its perfection—as, for example, to souls possessing eternal beatitude . . . or in a broader sense to all souls, who may become "precious perleʒ vnto his pay" (l. 1212).[31]

The maiden, because she is united with the divine essence, is everything that is supremely good; once she has been identified as a blessed spirit, she has been defined, and whatever else can be said about her is mere elaboration of this ultimate fact. Her identity and the nature of Heaven are the same thing, and the narrator cannot quite comprehend it because his bonds to the temporal world limit his knowledge of divinity. The maiden cannot finally be defined by narrator or poet because Heaven and God cannot be defined.

The maiden cannot, however, be identified simply as what the narrator thinks he has lost at the beginning of the poem. He thinks his pearl-child is lost to him because he fails to recognize what, in essence, she was or what she has become. Her essential being is not lost at all, and in the last lines of the poem he seems to realize that he can be reunited with her in this life by partaking of the Eucharist. "Pearl" is used throughout the poem as a metaphor for the maiden, a metaphor which deepens in significance as we learn more about her, but only the pearl of price which she and the others "þat riȝtwys were" (line 739) wear is explicitly symbolic in a way that can be easily articulated. The maiden herself is symbolic only insofar as any concrete representation of divinity must necessarily be symbolic, that is, representative of something ineffable and humanly indescribable. Thus many of the specific suggestions about her "meaning" are justifiable, though inadequate. She is a "real," though perhaps fictional, child, a literary device, pure maidenhood, a perfected soul, the Eucharist, innocence, Heaven, eternal life, the pearl of price, and so forth. The symbolic associations of pearls — purity, perfection — are likewise attributes appropriate to her. Her "meaning," like that of the Rose in the *Roman*, shifts as the narrator's and reader's perceptions are illuminated by her different aspects, but the integrity of the figure remains intact. She remains primarily and finally the blessed soul of a specific human being.

Despite its occasional use of symbolism and figurative language, *Pearl* follows the Boethian pattern in presenting its central meaning on the literal level of its narrative. Its subject, the narrator's consciousness, is represented directly to the reader, through what he says and does. This consciousness is influenced by the teaching of the maiden, which is as literal and explicit as human language can make it. Doctrine has been selected and organized for a single purpose, to restore the narrator's faith and the ability to live with his loss. He learns what he needs to know, and the reader learns through his experience. The reader receives some specific information about Heaven and salvation, which he probably knows already, and, more generally, he is brought to a recognition of the necessity and benefit of preserving one's faith despite adversity and human imperfection. He should finally learn about his own human fallibilities and limitations by observing those of the narrator.

Within the framework of the literal narrative, parable, symbol, and apocalyptic vision are employed to clarify the ideas and doctrines being presented. Where possible and necessary, the implications of these figurative devices are made explicit in the text itself. The parable of the vineyard is thus explained by the maiden as being about the goodness of God, with particular application to the gift of salvation she has received, and the parable of the pearl of price is similarly interpreted as referring to Heaven. The vision of the New Jerusalem comes directly from Revelation so that it may be recognizably authoritative, and its details are in no way interpreted within the poem because interpretation is unnecessary. This vision "means" what it says; it is total vision, a symbolic representation of the invisible realm of God. All of these figurative passages retain a degree of ambiguity and mystery, as does the maiden herself. The penny, the pearl of price, and John's City all mean Heaven and eternal life, but they do not really explain what that is. At the heart of the doctrine of *Pearl* is Heaven itself, aspects of which can be described directly or in parable or symbolism, but which in its totality is a mystery which cannot be explained in literal, rational terms. This point is a major element in the meaning of the poem; we are not encouraged to attach simple ideological equivalents to its few genuine symbols. The final vision of Heaven, for example, is "pure" vision, what Bishop calls an "apocalyptic symbol,"[32] in which a spiritual truth is spoken of in physical terms because there is absolutely no other way in which to speak of it.

Despite its occasional use of figurative language and literary devices, *Pearl* has not been proved to be a continuous allegory, in which the primary elements of the literal narrative yield other, more or less concealed meanings.[33] The maiden incorporates numerous associations and aspects into her role as a blessed spirit but otherwise is precisely what she appears to be, and is not the narrator's soul or anything else not apparent in the literal text. The narrator is a specific human being, like Boethius, and as such is only in the most general way an Everyman figure. His particular story can, and no doubt should, lead the reader outside the framework of the narrative to generalizations about proper human behavior and values, but the same can be said for almost any character in any narrative. His typically human portrayal does not make *Pearl* an allegory of the spiritual condition of humanity, even though certain points about that subject are inherent in the poem's overall meaning. No one of the various allegorical interpretations of *Pearl* that have been offered through the years, whether twofold or fourfold, allegory of poets or allegory of theologians, seems to me very convincing.[34] Most often such interpretations either reorganize material present on the literal surface of the poem into the four categories of the biblical exegetes or into other categories and levels, in which case they do not add anything to one's understanding of what the poem actually says, or else they read multiple meanings into images and figures which may contain such meanings elsewhere but cannot be proved to do so in *Pearl*.[35] *Pearl* is conceived as a revelation rather than as allegory. The revelation may at times take the form of direct, literal discourse and at others that of symbolism, but its purpose is always to illuminate what is unknown or obscure. There is no double or multiple meaning here; there is only a single, sophisticated literal narrative, from which the perceptive reader can and should draw various interrelated conclusions about Christian life.

9

THE BOOK OF THE DUCHESS

eoffrey Chaucer's *Book of the Duchess* is the earliest of his longer poems, usually dated in the year 1369.[1] Like the late-fourteenth-century works of Gower and the *Pearl* poet which we have considered, it is a Boethian Apocalypse, but recognition of its generic relationship to Boethius's *Consolation* has been hindered by two critical preoccupations. First, "According to a tradition recorded by John Stow and still accepted by nearly all critics, the poem was written in commemoration of the death of Blanche, duchess of Lancaster and first wife of John of Gaunt."[2] This view has forced critics to deal with its elegiac aspect as a primary factor in its interpretation. Specifically, one must consider the nature of the relationship of the principal figures in the poem, the narrator, the Black Knight, and the dead lady, "goode faire White" (line 948), to the historical Geoffrey Chaucer, John of Gaunt, and Blanche of Lancaster. Second, it has long been recognized that the poem owes a major debt to thirteenth- and fourteenth-century French love-vision poetry, from which Chaucer borrows liberally. This debt has been analyzed in detail by James I. Wimsatt; a glance at his table of "Sources of the Diction of the *Book of the Duchess*" alone should convince one that the poem is a sort of mosaic of bits and pieces borrowed from Chaucer's French predecessors.[3]

Three of the principal French sources for *The Book of the Duchess*, Froissart's *Paradys d'Amours*, Machaut's *Dit de la Fonteinne amoreuse*, and his *Remede de Fortune*, are vision poems written in the

Boethian Apocalypse

Boethian tradition. Wimsatt calls them "poems of complaint and comfort" because they "have the same basic narrative pattern of lover's complaint answered by a comforter."[4] No one of them, however, furnishes a model for the overall structure of *The Book of the Duchess*. Chaucer draws upon the *Paradys* for his dream machinery, the *Fonteinne* for the story of Ceys and Alcyone, and the *Remede* for part of the Black Knight's complaints and story.[5] Any or all of these poems could have influenced Chaucer's structure, since that appears to have evolved out of his familiarity with the Boethian genre in general, along with the more direct influence of the *Consolation* itself.

Only in recent years have critics begun to recognize Chaucer's basic debt in terms of both theme and structure to Boethius. Bernard L. Jefferson observed in 1917 that "the influence of Boethius is only indirect through the *Roman de la Rose* and the *Remede de Fortune*,"[6] but in 1965, D. W. Robertson, Jr., suggested that the situation of the dreamer-narrator and the Black Knight parallels in a general way that of Boethius and Philosophy in the *Consolation* and that this parallel "would hardly have escaped Chaucer's audience."[7] In 1969, I attempted to show that "the dialogue. . . deliberately and closely follows the pattern of the first two books of the *Consolation*."[8] Since then this debt has been recognized by several others,[9] but it remains necessary to see the poem against the background of the whole Boethian tradition to fully appreciate Chaucer's place therein. Structural flexibility is inherent in the tradition, and Chaucer takes advantage of this flexibility to reshape the Boethian structure for his own artistic purposes.

A troubled first-person narrator is central to the Boethian genre. His "complaint" about his condition is the constant element which alerts the reader to the kind of work he is reading. The Boethian visionary is the central consciousness and, in one sense, the subject of the entire work, even though the focus may shift for long periods to other figures. He is not an abstraction but a "real" person. Often his problem is not clearly defined in the opening complaint, which, from the *Consolation* forward, tends to articulate his state of mind rather than its cause. Indeed, the main thrust of the subsequent vision is that of definition and analysis of the true, as opposed to the fancied, nature of the visionary's problem; such analysis should lead to the knowledge which will provide him with a new perspective on himself and his concerns. Chaucer's narrator in *The Book of the Duchess* is such a figure; the first sixteen lines of the poem form the complaint which establishes its genre.

The narrator begins by describing his own distraught state of mind. As Bronson observes, he speaks of his present condition, "into which he must be understood to have lapsed again upon waking" from his dream.[10] He has not been sleeping well, and consequently he suffers from severe depression which renders him indifferent to virtually everything (lines 1–11). He is confused and lacks direction, "a mased thyng / Alway in poynt to falle a-doun" (lines 12–13) who, in his suffering, knows not "what is best to doo" (line 29). He realizes that his mental state is "unnatural"—"agaynes kynde" (line 16)—but obviously cannot effect a cure by himself. Although he is unable to diagnose the eight-year malady which causes his insomnia, he does know that "there is phisicien but oon" (line 39) who can heal him.

The nature of the eight-year sickness and the identity of the unnamed "phisicien" have been the objects of considerable speculation. Both are, in this context, ambiguous. The sickness has been identified as love longing, mourning for the deceased Blanche of Lancaster, or some species of spiritual distemper. The metaphor of the physician might, in Chaucer's time, refer to the object of one's earthly love, or to God or Christ.[11] Indeed, two centuries earlier, Chretien de Troyes had made a special point of the ambiguity of the metaphorical physician, and it seems inconceivable that Chaucer should be unaware of this ambiguity.[12] Had he desired that his audience be sure of his meaning, he would certainly have made it clearer than in fact he has. At this point the audience knows all it needs to know of the cause of the narrator's discomfort. That he knows of a cure and of a "phisicien" who can cure him, and yet apparently does nothing to help himself, further indicates his state of mind; he is confused, ignorant of the proper course of immediate action, and sorely in need of guidance out of his inertia, impotence, and uncertainty. The expectation of a reader of Boethian Apocalypse would be that some sort of visionary experience should illuminate the nature of this malady.

To "drive the night away" (line 49), the narrator says, "this other night" (line 45) picked up a book in which he found the story of Ceyx and Alcyone. The story comes to Chaucer ultimately from Ovid, supplemented by Machaut's *Dit de la Fonteinne amoreuse*, but Chaucer makes various alterations in it.[13] In Chaucer's version Alcyone becomes the central figure; he radically compresses, or else eliminates, all of the material in Ovid preliminary to and inclusive of Ceyx's departure and death, focusing upon Alcyone's state of mind after Ceyx has set sail. Alcyone's anxiety during Ceyx's absence (lines 76–121) has no parallel whatever in Ovid. There she waits patiently and prays that Juno will protect Ceyx from danger (*Met.* 573–82). Nothing suggests that she thinks he might be dead. Chaucer, however, emphasizes her grief and her fear that Ceyx has perished and gives her a prayer to Juno for news of him:

> And but thow wolt this, lady swete,
> Send me grace to slepe, and mete
> In my slep some certeyn sweven
> Wherthourgh that I may knowen even
> Whether my lord be quyk or ded.
>
> [Lines 117–21]

In Ovid, Juno takes pity upon Alcyone and sends a dream unasked. Even more striking is Chaucer's alteration of the message that Alcyone receives in her dream. Ovid's Ceyx specifically requests that his wife mourn his death: "Arise, go, shed tears and put on mourning clothes. Do not send me unwept into the void of Tartarus" (*Met.* 11.669–70). Chaucer's Ceyx offers different advice:

> My swete wyf,
> Awake! let be your sorwful lyf!
> For in your sorwe there lyth no red.
> For, certes, swete, I nam but ded;
>
> .   .   .   .
>
> I praye God youre sorwe lysse.
> To lytle while oure blysse lasteth!
>
> [Lines 201–11]

Chaucer's alterations of Ovid reveal the primary thematic relationship between the narrator and Alcyone. Both are in a state of confusion, of "wonder" (lines 1, 78), which borders on madness. Alcyone's anguish stems from her lack of definite knowledge about Ceyx; like the narrator, she needs guidance in the form of specific information. The narrator's instinctive sympathy for her (lines 95–100) underscores the similarity of their mental states, especially since he presently has "felynge in nothyng" (line 11). Just as the narrator knows "phisicien but oon" (line 39) who can cure him, so Alcyone knows "no reed but oon" (line 105) for her predicament. She prays for sleep and a dream which will help her. The verbal echo, together with the similarity between their two states of mind, suggests that the narrator should follow her example and pray to his own God for a dream to guide him out of his own undefined difficulties. Alcyone's doubts and fears before her dream have been added to emphasize a relationship between her troubled mind, prayer, and dream, and so to link her experience to that of Chaucer's narrator.

Chaucer's Ceyx advises Alcyone against her "sorwful lif" because "there lyth no red" in sorrow over an irrevocable event. Even though the nature of the narrator's malady is unspecified, it could scarcely be more serious than that which Alcyone must endure. Thus he should himself follow Ceyx's advice and at least attempt to rid himself of his melancholy. Ceyx's message should deter him from a life of futile suffering and remind him of the transitory nature of worldly bliss. Chaucer's Alcyone dies of grief because she fails to heed Ceyx's advice. Hers is an unnatural death which recalls the narrator's fear that he will die of his mysterious affliction (lines 23–24). Finally, Ceyx's message carries implications which are essentially, though not exclusively, Christian, and which therefore necessitate Chaucer's elimination of the Ovidian metamorphosis. Ovid's conclusion suggests a kind of afterlife alien to Chaucer's Christianity and would neutralize Ceyx's emphasis upon accepting the inevitability of the end of worldly bliss.

I have been speaking of Chaucer the poet and the first-person narrator of the poem as two distinct persons. Given this distinction, the question may arise whether one is justified in speaking of Chaucer's alterations in Ovid's story rather than the narrator's alterations in his retelling of that story. One must, I think, trust the narrator insofar as he appears as a reporter of the essential facts about the human characters and of the substance of their speeches. There is simply no reason to distrust him. Indeed, when Chaucer represents him as having omitted a portion of what he has read, he makes him say so (lines 215–20), even though his alleged reason and Chaucer's real reason may not be the same.[14] But the narrator does alter and distort the tone of the story, and I shall shortly consider these alterations and distortions, for they are essential to an understanding of him and of the structure of the poem itself.

The insertion at this point in the poem of a narrative which the visionary claims to have read in a book is a new device in the Boethian genre, although precedents certainly exist for interpolated exempla from Alanus on. As Wimsatt observes, Chaucer's use of the Ceyx and Alcyone story resembles Lorris's introduction of the story of Narcissus; both stories are related thematically to the larger works and in a way predict later developments in the main narratives.[15] Further, in both the *Roman* and *The Book of the Duchess*, the interpolated Ovidian tale functions as a warning to the visionary-narrator, who chooses to ignore its implications. The Narcissus story, however, appears, along with several others, within the *Roman*'s vision, not before the vision begins, and it is simply retold rather than read from a book. The device of reading a book, whose content serves as an introduction to the vision, appears to be Chaucer's invention.[16]

Boethian Apocalypse

The prominence of the story of Ceyx and Alcyone indicates its importance to the overall structure of the poem. Alcyone is a literary analogue to the narrator; her state of mind prior to her vision parallels his. Like Narcissus in the *Roman*, she provides a negative example for the visionary; she ignores the practical doctrine offered in her dream and dies as a result, suggesting that Chaucer's visionary should heed the vision he is about to receive. Her prayer and subsequent vision anticipate the prayer and vision of the narrator, just as her grief over the death of her spouse anticipates the grief of the Black Knight. The entire Ceyx and Alcyone narrative provides a thematic link between the narrator and his vision. At the same time it further illuminates his state of mind, in that the reader is able to observe his reaction to this literary exemplum.

The narrator's reaction to the story he has read demands our attention. He begins by observing that he read the story to pass the time away: "For me thoughte it beter play / Then play either at ches or tables" (lines 50–51). As far as he is concerned, reading "fables" (line 52) is merely an amusement. He suggests the reason behind this attitude in the succeeding lines:

> And in this bok were written fables
> That clerkes had in olde tyme,
> And other poets, put in rime
> To rede, and for to be in minde,
> While men loved the lawe of kinde.
> This bok ne spak but of such thinges,
> Of quenes lives, and of kinges,
> And many other thinges smale.
> [Lines 52–59]

His allusion to "olde tyme" when men loved "the lawe of kinde" is not, I think, a positive judgment, as is sometimes assumed, but a negative one. Not that the law of Nature is in any way evil in itself, but after all it is subordinate to, and has been superseded by, the law of God, as we have seen in Alanus, Meun, and Gower. A period in history in which men followed only the law of Nature must certainly have been a period of paganism; the narrator has read a pagan story, and he knows it. Because it is a pagan story, he takes the same attitude toward it that he takes toward all of the "fables" in a book which speaks only of "lives of kings and queens, and many other trivial things."

Thoughtful readers of Chaucer's time did not take the "fables" of such pagan authors as Ovid at all lightly. They read them on the literal level as moral exempla or as allegories or at the very least as sources of

174

moral and philosophical *sententiae*.[17] But this is precisely Chaucer's point: the narrator, probably because of his peculiar mental condition, is being unacceptably obtuse. He takes a foolishly narrow, parochial attitude toward the story of Ceyx and Alcyone and, in consequence, fails to derive from it the kernels of genuine wisdom which it contains. There is a comic tone in the narrator's retelling of the story at the point at which one expects him to treat it with the least respect, that is, when the pagan gods become involved in the action. Chaucer expects his audience to recognize that it is the narrator, not the "clerkes . . . and other poets," who turns the episode of Juno, the messenger, and Morpheus into a burlesque of Ovid.

Because of the narrator's attitude toward pagan literature, he misreads the Ovidian fable and misplaces his interest in it. Sleep is his primary concern, and so he devotes the larger share of his attention to the episode of Juno and Morpheus. He cannot, however, actually believe in a God of Sleep, and so his prayer to Morpheus and "hys goddesse," Juno, is merely a mock prayer uttered, as he says, "in . . . game." His assertion that he knows "god but oon" (line 237) further emphasizes his negative attitude toward the story. He is interested in Alcyone's success at slumber, but he ignores her visionary dream, even though he needs just such a dream to guide him. Similarly, he misses the significance of Ceyx's message, which is in its general implications applicable to himself, even though he knows "god but oon." He should, and in fact does, know where his cure lies — with the "phisicien but oon," at this point identifiable, perhaps, as a deity, "god but oon," rather than a lady — but in taking the entire story merely as a pagan fable, without perceiving the kernel of truth in it, he fails, like Boethius early in the *Consolation*, to make use of his knowledge. He offers a mock prayer to Juno and Morpheus when he should offer a genuine prayer to the Christian God for aid in his spiritual distress.

Fortunately, sleep comes to the narrator in spite of his obtuseness, and with sleep comes the dream which he needs. He does not attribute this dream to Morpheus, but neither does he attribute it to God. He remarks only that he "nyste how" it came (line 272). His further suggestion that he cannot interpret his dream is no surprise in view of his previous failure to comprehend the story he has read. He never indicates that the dream which he is about to relate has any meaning for him. At the outset one suspects that, like Alcyone, the narrator will fail to heed the vision he is about to receive and will be unable to find his way out of his difficulties. This is precisely what happens; at the end of his dream he is no nearer his "cure" than he had been before he picked up his book of "fables." His allusions to Joseph and Macrobius (lines 276–89), however, imply that his dream does indeed mean something and that the audience should attempt to discover that meaning.

A few critics have suggested that, from the very beginning of the dream, a new mood of "joy, relief and happy expectancy" appears in the poem and that this new mood is a result of some alteration in the narrator's state of mind.[18] As Bronson remarks, "He is no longer carrying any of that load of oppressive sorrow under which he fell asleep."[19] He is no longer inert, gloomy, and confused, but active, happy, and enthusiastic about the world in which he finds himself. The "mery," if all but deafening, song of the birds enthralls him (lines 310–11). The paintings on his windows — scenes of love and war from "al the story of Troye" (line 326) and "al the Romaunce of the Rose" (line 334) — give him "gret joye" (line 325). He likewise notices with pleasure the spring weather (lines 335–43). The sound of hunting horns makes him "ryght glad" (line 356), and he hurries to join the hunt (lines 344–86). Undaunted by the failure of the hunt, he attempts to play with a "whelp" (lines 387–96), who leads him through a forest, in which he appears keenly aware of the beauties of Nature around him (397–442).[20]

The narrator, as he appears in his dream, scarcely seems the same person who read the story of Ceyx and Alcyone; he is no longer in an "unnatural" state of mind. Indeed, the "natural" behavior of everything in this prologue to his meeting with the Black Knight underscores his own "natural" behavior. Birds sing; men pursue one of their customary peacetime recreations, the hunt; dogs chase the hart; the hart attempts to elude his pursuers; even the puppy behaves in a puppyish manner. Vegetable nature, accordingly, reacts as it always does to the spring season:

> Hyt had forgete the povertee
> That wynter, thorgh hys colde morwes,
> Had mad hyt suffre, and his sorwes,
> All was forgeten, and that was sene.
> For al the woode was waxen grene;
> Swetnesse of dew had mad hyt waxe.
> [Lines 410–15]

All of this "natural" behavior contrasts sharply with the "unnatural" grief of the Black Knight. The opposition of the "natural" and "unnatural" in the poem is not fortuitous, nor is it without moral implications. One need only consider Alanus's *De planctu naturae*, with which Chaucer was certainly familiar.[21] There moral rectitude and conformity to Nature's laws are virtually synonymous, as are immorality and unnatural behavior. Nature is subordinate to God and ignorant of revealed truth and theology, but clearly a violation of her laws constitutes a violation of the will of God, since she carries out his dictates.[22]

When the narrator comes upon the Black Knight, he immediately assumes that only a man who "ayleth" (line 449) would sit in solitude while a hunt is in progress. His subsequent remarks imply that the Knight's behavior reflects an unhealthy, unnatural state of mind. The narrator, even before he knows anything about the Knight's malady, remarks upon its unnatural quality:

> Hit was gret wonder that Nature
> Myght suffre any creature
> To have such sorwe, and be not ded.
> [Lines 467–69]

After he has heard the Knight's "complaynte," he alludes to the displeasure which the God of Nature must take in such behavior:

> For he had wel nygh lost hys mynde,
> Thogh Pan, that men clepe god of kynde,
> Were for hys sorwes never so wroth.
> [Lines 511–13]

These passages recall the narrator's comments upon his own state of mind at the beginning of the poem—he lives in a manner which is "agaynes kynde" (16ff.)—and that of Alcyone, "nygh wood" (line 104) because of the "sorwe" from which she will ultimately die.[23]

I am suggesting, then, that the primary function of this prologue to the narrator's meeting with the Black Knight is to give the narrator (and the audience) an adequate vision of himself in a healthy state of mind. His dream, like Alcyone's dream, is intended to help its dreamer resolve his dilemma by somehow revealing a cure for his mysterious ailment, and one aspect of this cure is his vision of himself as he should be—active, happy, and eager to participate in the innocent pleasures of life. If he later fails to understand or act upon the advice sent him in his dream, that is not the fault of the dream itself. Throughout his dream the narrator behaves precisely as he should in his waking state; he has full control of his faculties, and consequently he has a proper perspective on human misfortune which the Knight lacks.

As Kittredge observes, the narrator is anything but obtuse in his dream; he knows the cause of the Knight's grief because he has overheard his "complaynte" (lines 475–86).[24] He feigns ignorance in his conversation with the Knight for, it seems, three related reasons. First, he wishes to know as much as possible about the Knight's loss and his grief:

> Anoon ryght I gan fynde a tale
> To hym, to loke wher I myght ought
> Have more knowynge of hys thought.
>
> [Lines 536–38]

Second, he wishes to offer whatever consolation he can: "For, by my trouthe, to make yow hool, / I wol do al my power hool" (lines 553–54). Finally, as Bronson suggests, he must avoid direct reference to the Knight's loss until he has sanction to speak of the lady's death from the mourner's own mouth.[25] It would be presumptuous for an eavesdropper to burst forth with words of sympathy or consolation before the Knight has told his story.

Such tact would be impossible for the obtuse narrator in his waking state, but one sees him at his best in his dream. There is no contradiction between the genuine obtuseness of the narrator in the waking prologue and his acuity within the dream itself; in his dream he is free from his disconcerting malady. Awake, he is still "mased" and understands nothing; in his dream he understands virtually everything. Awake, he sympathizes with Alcyone, who shares his own confused state of mind, and his sympathy makes him feel even more depressed. Asleep, he is capable of disinterested sympathy:

> And whan I herde hym tel thys tale
> Thus pitously, as I yow telle,
> Unnethe myght y lenger dwelle,
> Hyt dyde myn herte so moche woo.
>
> [Lines 710–13]

Such sympathy does not, however, preclude the conclusion that the Knight, like Alcyone, is in error in the extremity of his grief, in the unnatural quality of his suffering.

The appearance of the narrator in a healthy state of mind profoundly alters the basic premises of the Boethian vision. Within the dream the symptoms of his undefined malady — sleeplessness, confusion, and indifference to the world around him — are gone. Consequently, he no longer needs help; the Boethian authority figure has become superfluous. The dreaming visionary sees himself as his own example of how he should approach life; all that is lacking is that the theory behind the practice of his healthy attitude should be somehow articulated. This reversal of the usual visionary situation prepares the way for Chaucer's most striking innovation in the Boethian form: the narrator becomes the authority figure in his own vision, while the role of the Boethian consolee is transferred to the Black Knight, whose state of mind is identical to that of the waking narrator and of Alcyone.[26]

The dialogue between the healthy narrator and the Black Knight closely follows the general pattern of the first two books of Boethius's *Consolation*. It is, then, a Boethian dialogue within the larger Boethian Apocalypse. Chaucer's purpose in following this pattern appears to be twofold. The overt parallels to the *Consolation* should reveal to the reader the generic situation, so that he can follow what is transpiring. In a dialogue in which neither participant is a deity or an abstraction, it is important that the instructor be readily identifiable, especially when the mode of instruction is as subtle as it is here. Further, the doctrine of the *Consolation* is thematically relevant to the Knight and, by analogy, to the narrator. The advice about excessive, futile grief which Alcyone failed to follow after her vision, and which the waking narrator likewise ignored in his reading of the Ovidian story, is in the dream, in more subtle form, offered by the visionary to the Knight. This exchange of roles, with the visionary playing authority figure, necessitates a basic alteration in the usual point of view of the Boethian vision and consequent adjustments in the development of the dialogue.

The Knight's "complaynte" (lines 475–86), parallels the mournful verses with which Boethius begins the *Consolation* (1, m. 1). Boethius calls this lament a "querimoniam lacrimabilem" (1, pr. 1), and Chaucer translates these words as a "weply compleynte."[27] Of course, Boethius reports the verses which he himself writes, while the narrator reports a song which he has overheard, but this slight difference is necessitated by the altered point of view. The narrator is the aggrieved figure in the *Consolation*, while Chaucer's narrator functions as the consoler. At any rate, both Boethius and the Knight give lyric expression to their personal misfortunes, and both wish for Death to end their miseries.

The narrator approaches the Knight and stands "ryght at his fet" (line 502), just as Philosophy approaches and sits at the foot of Boethius's bed ("uppon the uttereste corner of my bed").[28] The Knight fails to notice the narrator and remains silent (lines 503–10); likewise, Boethius remains "stille," his sight "dirked." The narrator's comment that the Knight's grief approaches madness — "For he had wel nygh lost hys mynde" (line 511) — parallels Philosophy's observation that the muses, rather than assuaging sorrow, destroy Reason — "destroyen the corn plentyvous of fruytes of resoun"²⁹ — and her evaluation of Boethius's present state of mind: "now lyth he emptid of lyght of his thoght."³⁰

Philosophy's initial offer of aid — "But tyme is now . . . of medicyne more than of compleynte"³¹ — corresponds in a general way to the narrator's similar offer (lines 536–57), and, although the narrator tactfully refrains from comment, her analysis of Boethius's problems could easily fit the condition of the Knight: ". . . he is fallen into a litargye, which that is a comune seknesse to hertes that been desceyved."³² The words with which the narrator offers consolation to the Knight seem a deliberate paraphrase of Lady Philosophy:

> But certes, sire, yif that yee
> Wolde ought discure me youre woo,
> I wolde, as wys God helpe me soo,
> Amende hyt, yif I can or may.
> [Lines 548–51]

She tells Boethius, "Yif thou abidest after help of thi leche, the byhoveth discovre thy wownde."³³ The physician-patient metaphor which runs all through the *Consolation* is reflected in the Knight's literal-minded remark that no "phisicien" can heal him (line 571), which itself echoes the narrator's earlier "phisicien" allusion (lines 39–40).

The Knight's account of his mistreatment at the hands of Fortune (lines 558–709) parallels Boethius's account of his misfortunes (1, pr. 4). A note of self-pity runs through the Knight's recitation:

> But whooso wol assay hymselve
> Whether his hert kan have pitee
> Of any sorwe, lat him see me.
> [Lines 574–76]

> This ys my peyne wythoute red,
> Alway deynge and be not ded,
> That Cesiphus, that lyeth in helle,
> May not of more sorwe telle,
> And whoso wiste al, by my trouthe,
> My sorwe, but he hadde routhe
> And pitee of my sorwes smerte,
> That man hath a fendly herte;
> For whoso seeth me first on morwe

May seyn he hath met with sorwe,
For y am sorwe, and sorwe ys y.
[Lines 587–97]

This same note appears, though less emphatically, in Boethius's account: "Ne moeveth it nat the to seen the face or manere of this place? . . . Was my face or my chere swych as now whan I soghte with the the secretis of nature . . . ?"[34] The Knight's treatment of Fortune as his enemy likewise parallels Boethius's attitude at the corresponding point in the *Consolation*. Boethius begins his account of his imprisonment: "And nedeth it yit . . . of rehersynge or of ammonicioun? And scheweth it nat ynogh by hymselve the scharpnesse of Fortune, that waxeth wood ayens me?"[35]

Although the Knight rails against Fortune, at the same time he reveals that he knows that her treatment of him is consistent with her nature (lines 630ff.). He even excuses her in the very speech in which he condemns her falsity (lines 670–84). These observations of the Knight correspond to Philosophy's suggestion that Boethius has within his own mind the knowledge of Fortune and God's universe necessary to effect his own cure (1, pr. 5, 6). Since the narrator has not the authority over the Knight that Philosophy has over Boethius, it would be foolish for him to suggest that the Knight has "forgotten what he is" ("thow has left for to knowen thyselve what thou art"),[36] but the Knight suggests much the same thing himself. His assertion that "y am sorwe" (line 597) seems to imply that he has forgotten his nature as a man.

Chaucer does not, of course, follow the pattern of the *Consolation* slavishly, and his omissions and alterations are sometimes instructive. While various references to God are scattered through these early portions of the *Consolation*,[37] Chaucer's two characters seldom mention him.[38] The omission does not reflect upon the narrator's piety, since, after all, he has very little to say in the dialogue, but it does make the Knight's state of mind seem particularly obsessive and desperate. Again, the narrator expresses sympathy for the Knight, while Philosophy remains austere and unmoved by Boethius's lamentations. The reason for this alteration is, clearly, that Philosophy represents pure Reason, an idealized abstraction, while Chaucer presents the narrator as a "real" person.

The narrator attempts to convince the Knight to scorn Fortune (lines 710–44). His pity (lines 710–14) is much less for the Knight's loss than it is for his suicidal state of mind, as his succeeding references to

Socrates, who "ne counted nat thre strees / Of noght that Fortune koude doo" (lines 718–19), and to the "dampned" lovers, who died for love, make clear.[39] His attitude here corresponds to that of Philosophy after hearing Boethius's account of his misfortunes: "So that I seie that the face of this place ne moeveth me noght so mochel as thyn owene face."[40] Philosophy's "easy medicine" at the beginning of book 2 of the *Consolation*, like that of the narrator in this passage, consists of the attempt to persuade the patient to scorn Fortune's blows, although she must first make Boethius recognize the true nature of Fortune, while the Knight has already done so without any prompting. The Knight's reply that his loss is too great to be ignored—"hyt ys nat soo. / Thou wost ful lytel what thou menest; / I have lost more than thou wenest" (lines 742–44)—parallels that of Boethius to Philosophy and implies much the same thing: "Serteynly . . . thise ben faire thynges and enoynted with hony swetnesse of Rethorik and Musike; and oonly whil thei ben herd thei ben delycious, but to wrecches it is a deppere felyng of harm."[41] Chaucer glosses this passage: "This is to seyn, that wrecches felen the harmes that thei suffren more grevously than the remedies or the delites of thise wordes mowen gladen or conforten hem." The "honey-sweetness" of the narrator's quite sensible advice clearly is not sufficient to "gladen or conforten" the bereaved Knight, although it does force him to cease speaking of his lady as a mere piece in Fortune's chess game and to describe her as a human being.

Lady Philosophy counters Boethius's objection:

> "Right so it is. . . . For thise ne ben yit none remedies of thy mala-dye, but they ben a maner norisschynges of thi sorwe, yit rebel ayen thi curacioun. For whan that tyme is, I schal moeve and ajuste swiche thynges that percen hemselve depe. But natheles that thow schalt noght wilne to leten thiself a wrecche, hastow foryeten the nowmbre and the maner of thi welefulnesse?"[42]

Philosophy then reminds Boethius of his former joys, but since the narrator is not an omniscient goddess, the Knight must recall his joys himself (lines 758–1310). The narrator, of course, asks to hear the Knight's story because he desires more information,[43] but the pattern of consolation follows that of Boethius nonetheless. Philosophy further comments that Boethius has been a happy man: "If thow considere the nowmbre and the maner of thy blisses and of thy sorwes, thou mayst noght forsaken that thow n'art yit blisful. For yif thou therfore wenest thiself nat weleful, for thynges that tho semeden joyeful ben passed, ther nys nat why thow sholdest wene thiself a wrecche; for thynges that semen now sory passen also."[44] This statement seems directly applicable to the Knight's tale of requited love. As a youth in love he was a "wrecche," but that passed; for a time he was blissfully happy and that, too, has passed.

The Knight's account of his love affair includes the eulogy to Blanche the Duchess. On the basis of the Knight's description, both the narrator and the audience must admit that his happiness could scarcely have been more perfect or his loss more crushing. We see the lady not only as a paragon of beauty and virtue in herself but also as a beneficent moral influence upon the Knight who loves her. She has been his inspiration and guide in his growth from thoughtless adolescence to maturity. The Knight's early service to the God of Love can scarcely be thought praiseworthy; it is nourished by youth, ignorance, and idleness; lacks a particular object; and appears to be no more than the first sexual stirrings of the average male adolescent (lines 758–804). Likewise, his description of the earliest stage of his attachment to the lady suggests the obsessive, puppylike devotion of a teen-aged boy:

> For certes she was, that swete wif,
> My suffisaunce, my lust, my lyf,
> Myn hap, myn hele, and al my blesse,
> My worldes welfare, and my goddesse,
> And I hooly hires and everydel.
> [Lines 1037–41]

As Robertson and Huppé have pointed out, in Christian terms such devotion to a lady with whom he has never even spoken is idolatry.[45]

The Knight's description of his lady, conventional though it is in its physical details, emphasizes her moral virtues:

> She nas to sobre ne to glad;
> In alle thynges more mesure
> Had never, I trowe, creature.
> [Lines 880–82]

> But goode folk, over al other,
> She loved as man may do hys brother;
> Of which love she was wonder large,
> In skilful places that bere charge.
> [Lines 891–94]

> Therwith she loved so wel ryght,
> She wrong do wolde to no wyght.

183

> No wyght myghte do hir noo shame,
> She loved so wel hir owne name.
> [Lines 1015–18]

The narrator twice interrupts the Knight to comment upon his good fortune (lines 1042–44, 1112–14), and each of these interruptions elicits an affirmation from the Knight himself of his joy and good fortune, even though he had begun his description of his first encounter with the lady by cursing Fortune (lines 811–16). The feigned ignorance of the narrator thus functions as the "easy medicine" of Philosophy, bringing the mourner soothing memories of his former joys.

In view of what the Knight tells the narrator of his youthful ignorance and the lady's character, her initial refusal of his suit seems quite proper (lines 1236–44). At this time he was unworthy of her love. Later, however, he was apparently able to convince her of his maturity and of the virtuous nature of his love, and she accepted him as her servant:

> So hit befel, another yere,
> I thoughte ones I wolde fonde
> To do hir knowe and understonde
> My woo; and she wel understod
> That I ne wilned thyng but god,
> And worship, and to kepe hir name
> Over alle thyng, and drede hir shame,
> And was so besy hyr to serve;
> And pitee were I shulde sterve,
> Syth that I wilned noon harm, ywis.
> So whan my lady knew al this,
> My lady yaf me al hooly
> The noble yifte of hir mercy,
> Savynge hir worship, by al weyes—
> Dredles, I mene noon other weyes.
> [Lines 1258–72]

From the last statement we learn that this was no mere sexual union. The Knight goes on briefly to tell the narrator how his lady undertook to govern him in his youth, and how blissful was their life together (lines 1273–97).

Finally the narrator's questions draw from the Knight the plain statement that the lady is dead (lines 1298–1309). Kittredge and his followers notwithstanding, the Knight does not appear to be consoled at the end of his conversation with the narrator.[46] "Allas, that I was bore!" (line 1301) echoes his remark, shortly after the narrator first offers to help him, "me ys wo that I was born" (line 566), and is virtually the same sentiment to which he gave voice in his "compleynte" (lines 481–86). Moreover, this statement of despair corresponds to that of Boethius after Philosophy has reminded him of his former joys: "O norice of alle vertues, thou seist ful sooth; ne I mai noght forsake the ryght swyfte cours of my prosperite...; but this is a thyng that greetly smerteth me whan it remembreth me. For in alle adversities of fortune the moost unseely kynde of contrarious fortune is to han been weleful."[47]

In the *Consolation* this reassertion of Boethius's unhappiness is preceded by Philosophy's lyric statement concerning the transitory nature of all earthly things (2, m. 3), and followed by her exposition of true and false felicity. Chaucer does not introduce into his poem a passage which corresponds to the former, nor does he go on to the latter, because, after all, he is giving a eulogy of Blanche, and it would be utterly tasteless to turn this eulogy into a sermon on the folly of trusting to Fortune. Moreover, he has, through the Black Knight, praised the Duchess for her virtues, and there is no need to state explicitly the Boethian doctrine which the parallel structure between the dream and the *Consolation* implies. Chaucer's audience should recognize that the only consolation available to the Black Knight is that of Boethius—that virtue emanates from God and, therefore, can never finally perish. The lady was a paragon of virtue, and so her soul must be in Heaven, as the narrator's question, "... where is she now?" (line 1298) seems to suggest. The Knight must, like Boethius, learn to distinguish between the perishable gifts of Fortune and the immortal attributes of the virtuous.[48]

Boethius's *Consolation* continues with Philosophy's discussion of the immortality of the soul and of true happiness (2, pr. 4ff.). By the beginning of book 3, Boethius is ready to receive her "stronger medicine"; he is equal to the attacks of Fortune—"I trowe nat now that I be unparygal to the strokes of Fortune"[49]—and he has cast off his lethargy. The Knight, at the end of the dream, has yet to reach this stage. His only answer to the narrator's question about the lady's whereabouts is the inadequate "She ys ded!" (line 1309). Boethius speaks, in the last three books, of true happiness (and related matters) and concludes with the statement that true happiness will be the gift of those who live virtuously:

> ...and God, byholdere and forwytere of all thingis, duelleth above, and the present eternitie of his sighte renneth alwey with

the diverse qualite of our dedes, dispensynge and ordeynynge medes to gode men and tormentz to wikkide men. Ne in ydel ne in veyn ne ben ther put in God hope and preyeris that ne mowen nat ben unspedful ne withouten effect whan they ben ryghtful.

Withstond thanne and eschue thou vices; worschipe and love thou vertues; areise thi corage to ryghtful hopes; yilde thou humble preieres an heigh.[50]

Thus the narrator's comment, "Be God, hyt ys routhe!" (line 1310), seems the only one appropriate to the situation. It is "a pity" that the Knight has lost his lady, but her death should not cause such immoderate grief as the Knight has revealed.

At this point the "hert-huntyng"—both the literal hunt and the searching of the Knight's "hert"—is over "For that tyme" (lines 1311–13). The hunters return home, and the narrator awakens. The attempt to console the Knight is incomplete and therefore unsuccessful; the direction toward such resolution as his problem will admit has been pointed, but that is all. He has made some progress toward acceptance of his lady's death, just as Boethius has progressed at the corresponding point in the *Consolation*, but he falls short of complete acceptance of his loss. The narrator-visionary upon waking decides to put this "queynt" dream, which he cannot interpret (lines 270–89), into verse (lines 1330–33), but the present tense he uses at the beginning of the poem indicates that he has not been able to apply his visionary experience to his waking condition.

The narrator's dream, like Alcyone's, has been sent to guide him out of his spiritual malady. In his dream he sees himself in a healthy state of mind and sees a knight immersed in a life-denying melancholy much like his own waking condition. The doctrine implied in this vision of spiritual health and disease is essentially the same as that given Alcyone by Ceyx: one must deal with misfortune by resigning himself to it, eschewing grief, and seeking divine aid. Even death itself is "only" death. This is the lesson of Boethius as well. Alcyone dies because she ignores the doctrine sent her, the Knight remains sunk in despair, and the narrator cannot understand his own vision and so returns to his "mased," insomniac state, but their fates in no way invalidate the doctrine they have received. For the narrator, at least, there is still hope when the poem ends.[51]

By making the cause of the narrator's melancholy much vaguer than that of either Alcyone or the Black Knight, Chaucer generalizes the applicability of the doctrine offered through Ceyx's speech and through the truncated Boethian dialogue. The *Consolation*, after all, addresses itself not only to unjustly imprisoned public servants but to all who must live in a confusing, apparently unjust world. The narrator can scarcely have suffered a more severe misfortune than has Alcyone or the Black Knight, and if Ceyx's (and Boethius's) advice offers the only practical consolation for their similarly tragic losses, then it should be equally pertinent to him. The presence in *The Book of the Duchess* of a Boethian visionary suffering from an unspecified misfortune suggests that the doctrine inherent in his vision should help not only those who have lost loved ones to Death but all those who must live under the burden of Fortune's blows.

The Book of the Duchess is a carefully organized, coherent Boethian Apocalypse. The historical, elegiac aspect of the poem adds a new dimension to the genre — which had not been used for elegiac purposes before — but it does not interfere with its philosophical content or its basically practical purpose. The elegiac aspect has, however, deflected attention from the primary emphasis of the visionary fiction; its aesthetic function requires careful evaluation, and the degree of its importance to the structure of the poetic argument must be determined in relationship to the work as a whole. To view the bulk of the poem as an elaborate framework for a eulogy of the deceased Blanche of Lancaster is certainly to distort the poet's purpose in composing his poem.

In view of Chaucer's portrayal of the Black Knight as a mourner unable to master his grief, it would seem unwise to identify him with Chaucer's patron, John of Gaunt.[52] The narrator describes the Knight as being "ryght yong... / Of the age of foure and twenty yer, / Upon hys berd but lytel here" (lines 454–56), while John was twenty-nine when his wife died. Even if the "foure and twenty" is a scribal error,[53] an allusion to John's scanty beard, as Robertson suggests, would hardly be tactful.[54] Chaucer in these lines seems to be emphasizing the Knight's youth as a partial explanation for his lack of moderation in his grief. Chaucer may also intend the details here as a signal to his audience, who would be aware of the occasion for the poem, that the mourning Knight should not be identified with John. I do not know what John of Gaunt looked like in 1369, but I am tempted to guess that he had a very full beard.

Near the end of the poem appears the punning allusion to Lancaster and Richmond, and perhaps to Blanche and John as well: "A long castel with walles white, / Be seynt Johan! on a ryche hil" (lines 1318–19). Coming after the dialogue has abruptly terminated, these lines may well be no more than a veiled identification of the Duchess whom Chaucer is eulogizing and her husband. The placement of the allusion would certainly hinder Chaucer's audience from identifying John of Gaunt very closely with the grieving Knight, whose despair has been revealed in the Boethian dialogue. Furthermore, the narrator does not say that the Black Knight returns to the "castel"; he says that "this kyng" (line 1314) rides homeward thence. Nowhere in the poem does he call the Knight a "king," nor does he ever suggest that he is of royal birth. The most likely candidate in the poem for the epithet "king" is the emperor Octovyen, even though he has not been mentioned for almost a thousand lines (lines 366ff.). An emperor, at least, is royalty, and Octovyen presumably has ridden a horse to the hunt; a knight is not royalty, and the Black Knight appears to be on foot. If anyone in the poem should be identified as John of Gaunt, it should perhaps be Octovyen, in which case Chaucer has presented his patron as having returned from mourning to the familiar pursuits of his social class. Aside from this rather cryptic allusion, however, there is no good evidence for the identification of Octovyen as John, and thus it appears wiser to refrain from identifying either him or the Black Knight as Chaucer's patron.

If the Black Knight is not to be identified as John of Gaunt, then who is he, and what, precisely, is his relationship to Blanche the Duchess? The primary obstacle to an answer to these questions seems to be the tendency to identify the lady "goode faire White" (line 948) too closely with the real Blanche of Lancaster, in spite of Chaucer's highly conventional, idealized portrait.[55] The lady in *The Book of the Duchess* is no more literally Blanche of Lancaster than the narrator "is" Chaucer or the Knight, John. We must think of her as an ideal woman who has died and of the Knight as the unfortunate lover who mourns her to excess. This approach would not, I think, weaken the force of Chaucer's eulogy of the real Blanche. The original audience of the poem would have been aware of its eulogistic purpose in advance and would recognize the tribute which Chaucer offers by inviting a comparison of his fictional lady as being "like" Blanche without making the literal-minded parallel assumption that the Black Knight is "like" John or, for that matter, the "mased" narrator of the story of Ceyx and Alcyone is "like" Geoffrey Chaucer.

In combining the essentially philosophical, educational Boethian genre with a more topical, even personal, eulogy, Chaucer has exploited both the emotional tendencies of the genre and its ironic tendencies. The Black Knight carries the burden of genuine, serious suffering usually borne by the Boethian visionary. Thus he commands the reader's sympathy for his predicament, which is too real and immediate to admit an easy solution. That he is left at the end of the vision still grieving serves the elegiac function of the poem; the subject of the eulogy is worthy of such deeply felt grief, and the impact of her loss upon those who remain to mourn her cannot be easily overcome. There is a certain amount of residual irony in the Knight's inability to come to terms with his grief, even after his dialogue with the sympathetic but sensible narrator, but the lion's share of the irony is directed at the comically obtuse dreamer. Chaucer maintains a delicate balance between reason and emotion here; while both the waking narrator and the knight command both our sympathy and our criticism, the proportions of each are carefully controlled, and only the narrator is ever susceptible to ridicule.

The naïve, obtuse, slightly ridiculous narrator is, with some modification in later poems, Chaucer's usual persona. We have seen similar narrative personae in other Boethian vision poems; the narrator in *Pearl*, for example, at times exhibits ignorance and willful obtuseness comparable to that of the waking narrator in *The Book of the Duchess*. This figure, however, is not finally comic, nor is he treated with unremitting irony. James Wimsatt attributes Chaucer's conception of the comic narrator of *The Book of the Duchess* primarily to the influence of Machaut's individualized, bumbling, comic narrators,[56] and I would agree that Chaucer learned a good deal from Machaut. The primary influence upon Chaucer's portrayal of his narrator, however, must be Amant in the *Roman de la Rose*. From Meun especially, Chaucer appears to have thoroughly absorbed the conception of a central narrative consciousness who consistently makes false judgments and poor choices for himself. So far as I know, *The Book of the Duchess* is the first genuine Boethian Apocalypse in which the visionary experience finally has no beneficent effect upon the visionary, and the *Roman* offers the most likely precedent for irony of this sort. The difference, of course, is that Amant is, at the end of the *Roman*, more reprehensible than pitiable, while the reverse is true of Chaucer's less satirically drawn figure, but they are nonetheless closely related.

What Chaucer appears to have done, then, in *The Book of the Duchess*, is split the Boethian visionary into two figures, an obtuse, comic narrator, for whom he draws heavily upon the ironically drawn Amant, and a genuinely sympathetic, though deluded, sufferer much like those at the center of *Pearl* and the *Consolation* itself. Chaucer's waking narrator thus becomes a largely negative figure, the object of our laughter because of his failure to learn anything. Within his dream, however, he is a positive figure, more closely akin to the Boethian authority figure than to the visionary, a healthy, "normal" man with whom the reader can identify even as he sympathizes with the plight of the mourning Knight. While the reader does not learn with the visionary, whose consciousness cannot be said to develop in the course of the poem, he learns through him, through his visionary experience, as in all other Boethian poems. This narrator-visionary begins and ends as a real person in need of aid; his personal experience precipitates the need which his vision is intended to fulfill, although finally the precise nature of that experience proves less important than his reaction to it, so much so that it is never fully defined. Within his vision he attempts to guide the Black Knight in the manner of a Boethian authority figure. Even here he does not become a mere abstraction, but, like other authority figures, he is a static, self-defining figure — an example of psychic health who knows how one should deal with the misfortunes that are inevitable in this life.

The Black Knight is likewise a real person; he is not an abstraction, nor is he to be identified as the narrator himself, metamorphosed into another body. The dialogue clearly takes place between two distinct human beings; the Knight has his own individual history, which the healthy narrator does not recognize as mirroring his own. His suffering has a specific, clearly articulated cause. He functions as a surrogate for the waking narrator only in that they share a particular, debilitating state of mind and, consequently, have the same "cure" available to them. Insofar as he engages in a dialogue with an authority figure, he is a kind of second visionary figure, and, like the poem's primary visionary, he fails to absorb the doctrine offered him. In relationship to the waking narrator, then, he is a negative example, a vision of what the narrator should not be, if he is ever to defeat the malady which besets him.

The Book of the Duchess cannot, I think, in any valid sense be called an allegory. Chaucer's method of conveying meaning is somewhat complex and indirect, requiring the reader to make connections between the various sections of the poem, but the primary meaning is nonetheless present at the literal level, and there does not appear to be any sort of consistent second level operative. No personifications or deities appear in the vision; even the Knight's chess game with Fortune functions as his quite conscious and fairly transparent metaphor for his unhappy experience. The Ceyx and Alcyone story is an exemplum; its meaning emerges from what happens and what is said within it. The Knight's tale of his love affair could, I suppose, be read as a topical allegory of John of Gaunt's courtship of and marriage to Blanche, but I have seen no evidence of this, and I doubt that a point-by-point comparison would be very convincing.

Incidental images in the poem may carry symbolic overtones, but these do not appear to come together into a consistent allegorical level of meaning. For example, Wimsatt has argued that Chaucer inlays the Knight's long description of his lady with imagery of the Virgin Mary,[57] but such imagery does not make the lady stand for the Virgin. Rather, it serves to underscore her goodness and to suggest the answer to the question "Where is she now?" Such imagery deepens the texture of the poem without changing its apparent implications. Likewise, the traditional associations of dogs with guidance, healing, and rationality presented by John Friedman[58] add significance to the figure of the whelp and help explain his appropriateness as the dreamer's guide, without turning him into a symbol. Again, the narrator's allusion to "hert-huntyng" at the end of the vision (line 1313) seems to refer to the process of searching the Knight's heart, but such wordplay does not mean that the literal hunt described at the beginning of the dream should be interpreted allegorically—there has been a real hunt for a real deer, and that is why the narrator is in the forest in the first place. *The Book of the Duchess* seems to be about how one should deal with worldly misfortune; that is the poem's theme, and that theme emerges from a reading of what is literally said and done within it.

10

THE KINGIS QUAIR

O f all the many vision poems which appear in the century
following Chaucer's death, perhaps the most admired is *The
Kingis Quair*, attributed to King James I of Scotland and so
dated around the year 1435.[1] Since John Preston's key article of 1956,[2]
criticism has emphasized the poem's traditional, literary aspects. The
poet, in his final stanza, acknowledges Chaucer and Gower as his
"maisteris dere" (197:1–7); borrowings and reminiscences from Chaucer's poems are everywhere apparent in the *Quair*, and his profound
influence continues to receive detailed analysis.[3] While unacknowl-
edged by James, his contemporary, John Lydgate, also appears to have
influenced him.[4] Yet despite its extensive borrowings and traditional
influences, the *Quair* remains a remarkable poem, the unique structure of which sets it apart from all other Boethian visions.

At the outset a caveat concerning the "autobiographical" content of
the poem is in order. The information which the poem's narrator
supplies about himself fits well enough the facts as we know them of
King James's imprisonment, release, and subsequent marriage, and
most recent scholars accept its attribution to him. Matthew McDiarmid
insists that it must be considered as a "personal document," "a spiritual
autobiography," to be properly appreciated.[5] I am in partial agreement but would argue that, whatever its apparent fidelity to the
circumstances of the poet's life, one should not lean at all heavily upon
the poem's supposedly autobiographical nature in any discussion of its
genre and its poetic strategy. All writers of Boethian Apocalypse from

Boethian Apocalypse

Boethius himself onward claim to be recounting personal experience; whether they report the circumstances and contents of visions which they actually experienced, in the final analysis, does not matter. Their visionary experiences have been given literary form which makes them coherent and recognizable to an audience familiar with their conventions. Accepting King James (or Chaucer) as the author of a vision poem must not lead one to read unstated information about that author back into the poem to explain it. Whatever the historicity of the personal experience of King James in the *Quair*, that experience has been transformed into an artifact composed primarily of conventional literary elements — of English-speaking birds, mythical goddesses, and ladies seen from tower windows. It is best, therefore, to treat the *Quair* not as a historical record but as a poem — a carefully crafted artifact, intended to reveal what its creator thinks about what he says has happened to him.

The first thirteen stanzas of the *Quair* serve as a prologue to the work; as in Chaucer's vision poems, we are introduced to a narrator who, unable to sleep one night, took up a book to pass the time. The astrological imagery of the opening stanza recalls the opening of Lydgate's *Temple of Glas*.[6] As in the *Temple* and *The House of Fame* the season is winter; James follows Chaucer's lead in correlating the seasonal setting and midnight hour with the age of the narrator-persona who we learn is long past his "tender ʒouth" (10.3). The stars twinkling "Heigh in the hevynnis figure circulere" (1.1–2) will, as McDiarmid observes,[7] ultimately be tied into the destinal theme which emerges later in the poem; however, at this point in the poem and in the narrator's life he is not concerned with the workings of destiny. This narrator is not quite the usual troubled insomniac of Boethian tradition; he had awakened in the middle of the night for no apparent reason (2.1–2). This circumstance, in conjunction with the winter setting, suggests the onset of some sort of enlightenment, the emergence of the narrator from a lethargy, like that of Boethius (*Consolation* 1, pr. 2), in his advancing age. Indeed, the poem which follows is the record of a mature man as he discovers a pattern of meaning behind the key events of his life. At the time of his first waking, however, he does not seem concerned with any particular subject; rather, many diverse things run through his mind in no discernable pattern (2.3–5). He perceives no particular order informing his experience.

To pass the time, he takes up Boethius's *Consolation*, an ostensibly random choice which further signals the *Quair*'s reader about its genre and its thematic content. In his brief description of the *Consolation*

194

(st. 3–7), the narrator emphasizes the value of Philosophy's counsel, of the "moralitee" of this nobly written book, the basis of which he finds in its autobiographical element. Boethius, he says, was cast by Fortune from high estate into impoverished exile; he wrote the *Consolation* to tell how, through the agency of Philosophy, he overcame his worldly "infelicitee." Rejecting "vnsekir warldis appetitis," he made "suffisance" of his "penance" by means of his "vertew" (st. 6). The narrator reads the *Consolation* as the description of an internal process: it is "in him self" that Boethius discovered the cure for his misfortune (5.5–7). Recognizing the metaphorical nature of Philosophy's identity as Boethius's nurse in his youth (1, pr. 3), he understands that the work depicts a process of recollection or relearning; Boethius's "vertew of his ʒouth before" became the "ground" of his later conquest of adversity (6.1–2). Thus the *Consolation* embraces and makes coherent its author's entire life, just as the narrator's own poem will embrace and interpret the events of his life.

Setting the book aside, the narrator next ponders its "matere new," generalizing from it and applying his generalization to his own experience (st. 8–10). He begins with the most basic point of Boethian doctrine, that every human being is subject to the whims of Fortune, adding that the young are especially vulnerable to her "werdes." This latter point is not explicitly made in the *Consolation*; James apparently infers it from the common equation of youth with inexperience, and so with the lack of the wisdom which experience brings. His own experience, as he surveys it in his mind, confirms Boethius's view of Fortune's instability, although its pattern is the obverse of that of the Roman senator: Fortune was first James's foe but later became his friend. Still, the alternation of good and bad "auenture" remains consistent with the Boethian view of life in the world.

The sound of the bell to matins intrudes upon the narrator's musings, and as he rises—as if to go to his morning prayers—he imagines that it speaks to him, saying, "Tell on, man quhat the befell" (st. 11). James has here displaced a common motif of Boethian vision; this bell is the equivalent of the various sounds—the bell in *The Book of the Duchess*, the birds' "roundel" in the *Parliament*, the lovers' "ballade" in *The Temple of Glas*[8]—which awaken visionaries and send them off to record their visions. The narrator, of course, has not yet even intimated that he has already had a vision. More surprisingly, as we learn shortly, his vision will not occur on this sleepless night, but has occurred in the distant past of his youth. The source of the narrator's inspiration to tell his story, and the reason for its belatedness, are at this point in the poem deliberately left vague. Neither he nor the audience knows quite what is happening or why. He himself calls the voice a "fantasye" and an "illusioune" and denies to himself that he has heard a living person (st. 12), but its fantastic quality in itself evokes visionary, otherwordly associations for the impulse which seizes him, while its attribution to the matin bell links his inspiration and the task he is about to undertake with the celebration of the Christian God.

The narrator's response to the voice contains further intimations of divine inspiration and guidance. He sat down, he says, with pen and ink, "maid a croce," and began his book (st. 13). The ambiguity of the cross seems intentional; he perhaps both crosses himself like a man at prayer and inscribes a cross on his paper to indicate the beginning of his story. The gesture indicates his desire for divine aid as he sets forth upon a new task; the scribal mark[9] indicates the start of the poet's "newe thing," the book which is quite explicitly a new departure in his experience as a poet. Indeed, this entire prologue, through its images of awakening and beginning in both the physical and the spiritual senses, suggests much more than just the circumstantial account of how he came to write his story. A personal revelation has begun with his waking from sleep, reading new matter, and setting out to write a new poem. This revelation will clarify itself through his analysis of his past experience, which begins in earnest at the moment when he takes up his pen.

The process of writing down what befell him is a new departure in the narrator's life as a poet, but it is not separate from his past experience; rather, poetic composition brings past experience into the present time of the poem and concludes it as a coherent whole. This prologue is not simply an imitation of Chaucerian poetic practice; it goes beyond introducing Boethian doctrine. Were this not so, the *Quair* would lose little by beginning at the point where the poet makes his scribal cross. The prologue suggests that the poet-narrator is about to do what Boethius did: he will employ his inner resources to make sense of his personal experience and write down this process for the benefit of others. The description of Boethius in the fourth stanza setting his "flourit pen" to work becomes appropriate to James as well. *The Kingis Quair* is both a poem about a visionary experience and a poem about how visionary experience becomes poetry. Making the poem has here become an essential part of understanding the vision which is at its core.

The "newe" poem begins with its own formal prologue and invocation (st. 14–19). Like the openings of Chaucer's *House of Fame*, *Parliament* and *The Legend of Good Women*, the poem's new prologue moves from a series of rhetorical *sententiae* on its general subject, youth, to the particular application of the poet's generalizations, "my self" as a youth. James thus returns to the theme of Fortune and her special power over the young, with a new measure of organization and control over ideas which were formerly just "rolling to and fro" (10.1) in his mind. A youth, he says, is unprepared ("indegest") by nature for life; subject, like unripe fruit, to changing winds; imprisoned, like a bird too young to leave its nest, by its natural needs; ignorant of the pain and travail which the future holds; and therefore prey to both good and ill Fortune (st. 14). His life is filled with insecurity ("vnsekirnesse") because he lacks the "rypenesse of resoune" needed to guide him through the dangers which life brings.[10] His natural contentment ("suffisaunce") is inadequate to govern him when unexpected troubles beset him. Like all other youths, the narrator was like a ship cast adrift upon "the wawis of this warld," without the rudder of Reason to guide him past the "rokkis" that imperil his "viage" (st. 15–16).[11]

James carries the nautical metaphor of the new prologue over into the invocation of stanzas 17 and 18, suddenly shifting the meaning of its terms. It is not until the third line of this invocation that his reference to the "wynter nyght" and his use of the present tense, "I wake" (17.3), reveal that the metaphorical voyage is no longer that of youth. He now is praying to the muses for poetic inspiration and guidance; as he explains in the following stanza, the boat has become the "mater" of his poem, its sail his "wit," which lacks the "wynd" of inspiration to drive it forward. The "rokkis blake" are "the prolixitee / Off doubilnesse that doith my wittis pall," the difficulties he encounters in expressing his thoughts, but more specifically, perhaps, the "double" reference of the nautical metaphor itself, and the double meaning, literal and figurative, of the circumstantial account of his youth, which follows this invocation.[12] The shift in meaning here suggests an analogy between the youth setting out upon his life in the world and the poet's endeavoring to recount his experience. Both need guidance, and both find it in the course of the metaphorical journey itself. The "port, quhare gynneth all my game" (17.6) is literally the port from which the narrator sailed as a youth, the starting point for his experience, and also, figuratively, the beginning of the poetic narrative. The implicit goal of the voyage of youth is maturity, together with the wisdom which brings "sekirnesse" and rest; the goal of the voyage which is the process of recounting experience is much the same, that of making coherent order out of this experience.[13]

James's account of his voyage and subsequent capture (st. 20–25) takes on implicit, figurative meaning from the metaphorical statements of the preceding stanzas. James says that on a spring morning[14] when he was about ten years old he set sail on a voyage, whether "throu hevinly influence / Off goddys will, or othir casualtee" he cannot at this early point in his reminiscence say. Upon the advice of his guardians he left his own country, and, on the "wawis weltering to and fro," through the influence of a malign Fortune, he was captured by enemies and imprisoned in their country for eighteen years. This account recalls the description of "sely ʒouth" in the prologue, suggesting the beginning of moral, rational life which follows "the state of innocence" (22.1). Spring, morning, and departure from the security of port all figure the initiation into conscious, responsible life of one who is as yet unable to guide himself and finds security in the advice of others. The metaphor of one's own country as Heaven (or God's presence) appears in the *Consolation* (1, pr. 5) and is a medieval commonplace. The sea and the enemy country figure the world of "auenture" (22.7), Fortune's realm. Inexperienced youth, lacking the "ripeness of reason," cannot recognize that life in this world is guided by divine influence.

The young James's captivity parallels that of Boethius; like Boethius, he is subject to the torments of Fortune so long as he lacks the knowledge necessary to deal with his physical circumstances. In his prison he complains against Fortune, and the questions he raises echo those of Boethius: "What have I done to deserve such a hard 'auenture'?" "Why should Fortune treat me so?" "If God is responsible for my life of 'thraldome,' what is his purpose?" (st. 26–28). The audience may know the Boethian answers to such questions, but the prisoner can neither resolve them nor recognize the flaws in their formulation. He misconceives of his bondage as a purely physical matter, deprivation of "My fredome in this warld and my plesance" (26.4), while others have "suffisance" of these things. Birds, beasts, and fish by nature enjoy such freedom as he lacks (27.1–3). By questioning God's purposes (st. 28), he effectively reveals his failure to comprehend the idea of a providential order. He needs a visionary figure like Philosophy to guide him.

However, before the vision, which the audience must by now expect, James introduces the new element of earthly, romantic love into his narrative. The precise nature of James's love becomes apparent in the course of his story, but a few preliminary observations here may help clarify its relationship to the Boethian philosophical scheme upon which his developing ideas depend. Boethius deals somewhat tangentially with "amor," placing it in a context more cosmic than human. He dismisses bodily pleasures (*voluptas corporis*), to which beasts devote themselves, as partial goods (3, pr. 7); James will similarly reject mere lust. In two famous verse passages Boethius celebrates the divine love which pervades and governs the cosmos. At the end of book 2 of the *Consolation*, having drawn from her discussion of Fortune the conclusion that only adverse Fortune truly benefits man, Philosophy speaks of the rule of love, *amor*, as the power of order in the universe: Love rules the sea and the heavens; if it should loose its reins, the result would be chaos in the natural world; it establishes a sacred bond between people in marriage and in friendship; "O how happy the human race would be, if that love which rules the heavens ruled also your souls!" (2, m. 8). If this love pervades the soul of man, he will be happy. Much later, after explaining the providential order which governs all things, Philosophy speaks again of the ordering power of divine law, the mutual love (*alternus amor*) controlling the heavens, the elements and the fixed course of the seasons. God keeps the course of all things stable: "This is the common bond of love by which all things seek to be held to the goal of good. Only thus can things endure: drawn by love they turn again to the Cause which gave them being" (4, m. 6). Drawn by this all-pervasive love, all things tend toward the source of their being, God.

In the Boethian scheme, love and God's power are virtually identical; of the sort of love which human beings feel toward each other and toward God, Boethius does not speak. Peter Dronke has traced the background through which these two views of love — the Boethian conception of love as a cosmic force emanating from God and the Aristotelian conception of love as "the aspiration of all things toward an immutable" — are fused in Dante.[15] This background, and the philosophical problems which it entails, need not occupy us here; it must suffice to observe that for James, as for Dante, the fusion of these views is to be assumed. James does not distinguish between the love which is an attribute of God and the love experienced by a human being, and this makes it possible for James's narrator, as Andrew von Hendy observes, to be, like Dante, "led, in a sense from love to Love."[16] James integrates the virtuous human affection which Gower calls "love honeste" into a Christianized Boethian philosophical scheme.

James introduces romantic love into his poem by combining and reworking elements from Chaucer's *Knight's Tale* and, to a lesser extent, from *The Book of the Duchess* and *Troilus and Criseyde*. That each of these poems deals with a love affair and employs thematic elements from Boethius may perhaps have reinforced James's reliance upon Chaucer as his poetic mentor. The pattern of events is clearly based upon part 1 of *The Knight's Tale*: The prisoner, bewailing his unhappy fate, looks from a window in his tower onto a garden below, where he sees a beautiful lady. Uncertain at first whether she is a goddess or a creature of flesh and blood, he nonetheless falls in love with her at first sight and prays to Venus for her aid. James's introduction to the appearance of the lady (st. 29–39), however, is much more elaborate than its counterpart in *The Knight's Tale*. The note of happiness struck in his description of his early rising (st. 29) foreshadows future events and provides a shift away from the gloomy mood of his complaints against Fortune. His awakening suggests a new beginning, a new stage in the consciousness of the young man. Furthermore, the apostrophe to this "happy exercise" (29.5–7), though clearly in the retrospective voice of the mature poet, hints at the working out of a providential sequence of events, in direct contrast to the ignorance of divine purpose expressed by the prisoner in the previous stanza. Although he is in despair because of his separation from the life outside his prison, James takes some slight comfort from looking out at it; significantly, it is nature, the "gardyn faire," which initially offers him solace (st. 30–32).

From his window he hears (and understands) the nightingales singing "ympnis consecrat / Off lufis vse" (33.3–4). They summon lovers to awaken and praise love on this May morning when "of ȝour blisse the kalendis ar begonne" (34.2). The birds' hymn also heralds a beginning which, as a function of the season, is closely tied to the natural world. Although he does not yet know it, their song addresses the prisoner himself (st. 33–35). This welcoming of love raises, ostensibly for the first time, questions in the mind of the prisoner, whose acquaintance with love is wholly at second hand, through books (37.4). He wonders about its nature and power, expressing the skepticism common to nonbelievers (compare *TC* 1.183–210). In attempting to relate what he has read about love's pervasive power to himself, he confuses thralldom to love with his own physical confinement and so assumes (incorrectly) that love could literally release him from prison. He believes that physical freedom is necessary to serve love. His natural interest in love (which, like that of the Black Knight, precedes any attachment to a particular object; *BD* 758–804) conflicts with his perception of his circumstances, and he is unaware of the paradoxes involved in his questions about physical and spiritual freedom (st. 37–39).

The lady's appearance in the garden initiates the prisoner's actual experience of love (st. 40ff.); his vision of this "floure" overcomes him with pleasure despite his incarceration, although he remains conscious of his physical confinement (e.g., 44.3–6). His paradoxical observation that his heart became "hir thrall / For euer of free wyll" (41.5–6) suggests a different sort of thralldom from that he had previously conceived, a voluntary bond which ties the lover to his beloved. His speculation about whether she is "a warldly creature, / Or hevinly thing in liknesse of nature," perhaps "Cupidis owin princesse" or "verray Nature the goddesse" (st. 42–44), is more than a poetic conceit borrowed from Chaucer; he is undergoing a sort of visionary experience, despite its circumstantial, physical reality. By attributing divinity to the lady, he experiences the love which divinity elicits from human beings; by her presence she initiates his consciousness of something beyond the merely physical, of a link between himself and the spiritual world of which he is only dimly aware.

Although still in a state of confusion, bewailing his "infortune" and "chance," the prisoner nonetheless experiences a complete alteration in his consciousness (st. 45). Bound as yet to physical reality, he describes at length the lady's appearance (st. 46–49) before considering finally her more inward attributes (st. 50). Recognizing her to be a "childe" of Nature (50.7), he rejoices and offers a prayer of thanks to Venus for her "grace," acknowledging the divine nature of love (st. 52). While earlier he had questioned the credibility of the nightingale's song, he now encourages the bird to sing (st. 54–59). The rhetoric of his address to the nightingale and of the song he makes to the nightingale's tune (st. 63) continues to employ the largely interrogative mood of his earlier speeches; though gladdened by his love, he is still full of anxious questionings. When the lady departs, he abruptly returns to gloom and suffering; his day turns to night, and he laments her absence (st. 67–72). Still bound to earthly things, he depends upon her physical presence to sustain him. Imagining that Venus alone can remedy his condition (69.6–7), he spends the day in misery, and finally, in the evening, "amaisit verily" (73.5), he falls into a swoon and dreams.

This narrative forms the most elaborate of all the prologues to Boethian visions. Rhetorically, its texture of unanswered questions and conditional, speculative statements reflects the usual confusion of the Boethian protagonist, as does the rapid shifting in mood and sentiment. By combining the original Boethian dilemma of unjust imprisonment and the late-medieval torment of unrequited, apparently unattainable romantic love, James has at least doubled his protagonist's reason for confusion and suffering. Still, he keeps the problem of love qualitatively distinct from that of ill fortune. The imprisonment is presented in wholly negative terms, while the only negative aspect of love here is that it cannot be pursued because of the lover's imprisonment. As in the *Consolation*, imprisonment is to be conceived of as Fortune's withholding of her gifts, but love is not one of those worldly gifts. Love, properly understood, is a divine power which will serve as the means by which Fortune may be transcended, just as Philosophy seems to suggest in the final verses of book 2 of the *Consolation*. The prisoner's love will lead him, in his vision, to the cosmic understanding necessary to endure, and thus to transcend, his physical circumstances.

The prisoner's vision (st. 74–172) answers the questions he has been asking and so provides the guidance which, as a youth lost on the sea of worldly life, he has lacked. The blinding light and disembodied voice promising "confort and hele," which come to him through his chamber window (st. 74), are the earlier, visionary counterpart to the voice of the matin bells; mysterious and unexplained, they suggest divine intervention in the life of the visionary. Within his vision the prisoner finds himself free of his physical constraints, able to pass out of the prison door and at the same time being guided in his ascent through the spheres by an unseen, unnamed power which "araisit" (75.6), "liftit" (77.3) him and "brought" (77.5) him to Venus's chamber (st. 75–77). Divine grace appears to be operating here, although the poet's reticence (and the visionary's youthful ignorance) prevents its explicit recognition.

The first locus on the visionary's hierarchical ascent is the "glade empire" of Venus, which he locates not in the astrological third sphere of the planetary goddess, but in the eighth sphere of "signifere," the zodiac (st. 76).[17] The precise location of Venus's realm may have no special significance here, but perhaps its removal from the planetary sphere to a higher one — at the outer reaches of the natural world — is meant to indicate that this Venus represents more than simply the planetary goddess who governs earthly love. Venus's court is populated by "Loueris that endit had thaire lyfis space / In louis seruice" (78.3–4), arranged in groups ("Eche in his stage"; 79.4) according to the quality of their fortune in love while they lived ("After as lufe thame lykit to auance"; 79.7). Although the four primary groups of lovers are arranged hierarchically in their "stages," residence within the realm, which is love's paradise, appears to be the reward for all of Venus's servants, regardless of the "grete variance" of Fortune in their lives (st. 78–93); unbelievers and apostates from Venus's law are unseen and unmentioned.[18] Corresponding to this scheme, Cupid in this version of Venus's realm has three arrows, which represent graduated degrees in the difficulty with which his human targets attain happiness in love, from "esy cure" through "harder auenture" to "schot without recure" (st. 94–95); among Cupid's victims, presumably, service to love is universal, while success, in the sense of fulfillment in life, is variable.

The visionary appeals to Venus as his only source of help in love, presenting himself as her new but perpetually devoted servant, her "pure man" (st. 99–103). James's Venus is a benevolent, morally positive figure. She lacks the purely sensual qualities of the Venuses of Gower's *Confessio* and Chaucer's *Parliament* and their continental ancestors, and the motifs of punishment and suffering caused by her are minimized. She characterizes her "inspiration" of love in the visionary as an act of "grace" (st. 105). James clearly formulates the distinction between her function and that of Cupid: he furnishes the "stroke," the impulse to love, while she — at the appropriate time — provides the "cure." Like the Venus of Lydgate's *Temple*, she asks little of her petitioner: he must patiently endure the events of his life ("thyne auenture") and let "Gude Hope," belief that things will turn out well, guide him (st. 106).[19] Patience and Hope are necessary because her influence in the world is neither absolute nor autonymous. As she admits, "by ordnance eterne" her (astrological) power has "aspectis," is bound up with other forces such as, in the visionary, the Fortune which deprives his "persone" of "libertee." Thus the complete manifestation of her benevolence must await the end of "certeyne coursis" of events (st. 107–108).[20]

Furthermore, while he awaits the fulfillment of Venus's promise, the visionary must earn his lady's "graice" through "trew seruis" (108.5–7). As Venus explains, he is not yet worthy of the lady, for he is deficient in "wit," "persone," and "myght" to match her "hie birth, estate and beautee" (st. 109–10). He must somehow improve himself in character and understanding, and it is to this end that Venus determines to send him for his "welefare" to Minerva. Venus's special province is the "cure" of his "seknesse," unrequited love, but he needs Minerva to provide the "lore," "hestis," "counsele," in short, the moral instruction which is beyond Venus's ability to supply (st. 111–114.6). In James's formulation, Love-Venus leads the visionary directly to Wisdom-Minerva; the two complement each other. The bond between them is emphasized by Venus's gift of Good Hope to guide him to Minerva; hope, belief in the ultimate benevolence of love's power, brings one to true wisdom and thereafter sustains him in the face of life's uncertainties. Venus agrees in every point with Minerva's "lore"; she says that Minerva's advice will enable him, "by processe and laboure," in time to attain his "floure" (114.1–6).

Finally, Venus charges the visionary to convey her rebuke to those on earth who neglect her laws (st. 115–23). Such unnatural behavior ("vnkyndenesse"; 116.2) causes her to weep; her tears fall to earth as rain, and yet, when her anger ceases, these tears bring forth flowers which, in their "flouris wise," urge men to "Be trewe of lufe and worschip my seruise" (117.6–7). When she weeps, the birds silently mourn, and the lights of Heaven hide from the earth out of compassion. Yet in the spring the birds and flowers join with men in renewing their service to love and repenting their "sleuth." This little myth of Venus's tears expresses poetically the benevolent power of love throughout the universe. Love is natural; it descends from Heaven to men, beasts, and vegetable life and demands only that they, according to their natures, worship by partaking of it. The punishment with which Venus threatens those who neglect her service is that, with Saturn, she will turn her aspect away from them, depriving mankind of "gouernance." This is the divine, Boethian *amor* which governs the universe and brings joy to the souls of men. Venus's punishment parallels the Christian view of damnation as the deprivation of God's presence, the loss of all that is good. Likewise, Venus promises to reward those who repent and worship her with eternal salvation; she is their "hevin" and "paradise," and "here perpetualye / Ressaue I shall ȝour saulis of my grace, / To lyue with me as goddis in this place" (st. 122–23).

The second authority figure is Minerva, who, in the celestial hierarchy of the *Quair*, is superior to Venus in that she supersedes Venus as an instructress and teaches doctrine which has definite bearing upon love but is apparently beyond Venus's province. We may further observe that, in theory, Minerva must be superior to Boethius's Philosophy, whom she closely resembles and whose doctrines she teaches. Philosophy embodies perfect rational thought; Minerva embodies suprarational, divine Wisdom, Sapientia, which here, as in the various other works in which she appears, transcends human Reason in its comprehension of divine mysteries. However, this distinction has virtually no practical application in the *Quair*; unlike the Minerva-Sapience of, for example, *The Court of Sapience*,[21] who can recount the quarrel of the four daughters of God, James's Minerva says nothing which would not be appropriate to Boethius's rational Philosophy.[22]

Good Hope, who, as McDiarmid points out, represents a rational sort of optimism,[23] leads the visionary "by redy wayis ryght" from Venus to Minerva's palace, where the porter Pacience admits them "vnquestionate" (st. 124–25). Hope and patience, as Venus instructed the visionary, lead one from love to wisdom. This second place has no specific location in the cosmos, for the obvious reason that there is no planetary sphere or figure in the zodiac which corresponds to Minerva;

in most allegorical contexts Sapientia dwells with God himself. The visionary presents his case to Minerva (st. 126), who informs him that two courses are open to him, depending upon the grounding of his heart. First, if his love is grounded in "nyse lust," his labor is vain folly which will lead him to pain and repentance; obviously Wisdom does not promote lust. The alternative will earn him "grete worschip and prise"; if he chooses this course, she will give him her "lore and disciplyne." He must base his love upon "vertew" and thereby follow the "gouernance" of God, whose "hye purueyance" controls all (st. 128–31). Minerva deplores lustful men who beguile innocent women, but as long as his heart is firmly set "In goddis law," she will aid him in his "laboure" (st. 132–38). Throughout this colloquy with Minerva, it is clear that virtue in love means the opposite of mere lust; it is rather Gower's "honeste" love—honorable and faithful, with marriage as its goal. James here builds upon Boethian doctrine, employing a somewhat more limited and explicit frame of reference than does Philosophy. In the *Consolation*, books 2 and 3, Fortune's mutability is transcended by eschewing her gifts (including bodily pleasure) in favor of virtue, which, though vaguely defined, leads one to, and is an aspect of, the summum bonum, God himself.[24] Here, with "love" as the frame of reference, worldly lust is to be eschewed in favor of virtuous love, which is likewise associated with God.

The visionary declares his wholehearted, constant, and honorable love for the lady. He admits that "desire" completely encompasses his "wittis," but Minerva accepts desire—presumably a natural adjunct to love—so long as it is "ground and set in Cristin wise," and he assures her that he would never endanger the lady's honor ("worschip"; st. 139–43). Minerva then agrees to help, saying that she will pray to Fortune to cease her opposition to his love, for it is Fortune who governs the "auenturis" of men in the world (st. 144–45).[25] Some clerks argue that human events ("ȝour chance") are predestined and call these events "Fortune," but others argue that man has "in him self the chose and libertee / To cause his awin fortune," that the things that happen are not predestined. Fortune is weak when one has foreknowledge of coming events; God is never subject to Fortune because, as first cause of all things, he has perfect foreknowledge. Therefore, Minerva concludes:

> Fortune is most and strangest euermore
> Quhare leste foreknawing or intelligence
> Is in the man; and, sone, of wit or lore
> Sen thou art wayke and feble, lo, therefore

Boethian Apocalypse

> The more thou art in dangere, and commune
> With hir that clerkis clepen so "Fortune."
> [149.2–7]

As an imperfect human being, ignorant of what the providential order holds in store for him, he must "Pray Fortune help" (150.6). Belief in love's benevolence and wise devotion to virtue will sustain him, but Fortune nonetheless controls the worldly circumstances of his life (st. 146–50).

Here again Minerva's teaching depends upon Boethian arguments. The argument against predestination, barely sketched by Minerva, is fully developed in book 5 of the *Consolation*. Implicit throughout the *Consolation* is the general point that the closer one approaches perfect, divine understanding of the working of this world the freer of Fortune he becomes, that, in other words, the acquisition of Wisdom reduces one's vulnerability to apparently random events which he cannot control. As Boethius learned from Philosophy, so James learns from Minerva not how to change his temporal Fortune but rather how to live in spite of it. The more specific source of Minerva's argument appears to be book 4, prose 6, of the *Consolation*:

> It follows then, that everything which is subject to Fate is also subject to Providence, and that Fate itself is also subject to Providence.
>
> Some things, however, which are subject to Providence are above the force of Fate and ungoverned by it. . . . whatever strays farthest from the divine mind is most entangled in the nets of Fate; conversely, the freer a thing is from Fate, the nearer it approaches the center of all things. And if it adheres firmly to the divine mind, it is free from motion and overcomes the necessity of Fate.

It does no violence to Boethius to read Fortuna for *fata* here; the further one strays from the divine mind, the knowledge of immutable Providence, the more tangled he becomes in the nets of Fortune.

Boethius goes on from here to discuss God's providential order and man's limited ability to understand it. Nothing in the realm of Providence happens by chance. If one recognizes that Providence governs all things, he will realize that even apparently evil things in this world work for a higher good. The argument culminates with the second meter, which celebrates the bond of *amor* which governs all things — and so identifies Boethian *amor* with God and Providence (4, m. 6). While Minerva does not follow this argument to its conclusion, it would seem to be implicit in her teaching. As the young visionary grows in wisdom through the patient practice of virtuous love, he will draw closer to divine *amor*, believe more strongly in a benevolent Providence, and so become less vulnerable to the misfortunes of his temporal life. Minerva's instruction, together with Venus's gift of Good Hope, should be enough to set him on the right path in life, to sustain his belief in his own virtue and its hoped-for rewards. He can transcend Fortune's malevolence through love and so achieve true freedom from temporal instability. Promising to remember Minerva's "doctryne," he takes leave of her and descends to earth ready to reenter the realm of Fortune (st. 151).

Upon his return to earth the visionary finds himself in an idealized landscape (st. 152–58). There is no reason to assume, as McDiarmid does, that this is some sort of earthly paradise;[26] rather, as the catalog of beasts (st. 155–57), together with their diverse attributes, suggests, it appears to be the natural world. Before the vision nature had at times caused the prisoner pain (st. 27), but now, having been made aware of Venus's influence in the natural world, he simply accepts it. He follows a "hye-way," diligently seeking "Fortune the goddesse," as he ponders "From quhenns I come," the realms of Venus and Minerva, and the doctrine he has received there, but by implication perhaps also the *patria* of the *Consolation*, the heavenly home whence all men come (1, pr. 5). Led by his newfound optimism, Good Hope, and encouraged by Minerva's teachings, he is eager to resume his life in the world.

The visionary's encounter with Fortune, with which the vision concludes, figures his full recognition and acceptance of the nature of worldly life and his place in it.[27] The round, walled "place" where he meets Fortune recalls the tower in which he is imprisoned and serves to isolate the realm in which she exercises her power (st. 159). His fear of the pit beneath Fortune's wheel (st. 162) is the normal, appropriate human reaction toward the uncertain future; it does not now deter him from following the course of his life. Virtually the entire world of men appears before him here, taking its chances on the wheel (st. 163–65). Fortune addresses him "in game," almost mockingly; despite her inquiries, she knows who he is (166.2) and what he wants; after all, so long as he lives, the temporal aspect of his life will be under her control. As Minerva advised, he prays to Fortune for her favor. She seems compliant enough, even eager to resume her power over his affairs; since he is too "feble" to climb alone—because of his long suffering at her hands—she helps him onto her wheel, while reminding him of its variable, unpredictable nature. She encourages him, just past the "prime" of the day, and of his life,[28] to get on with the business of living (171.7) and bids him farewell by tweaking his ear so hard that he awakens back in his prison (st. 166–72).

Thus the vision of the *Quair* in a sense extends the pattern of the *Consolation* without contradicting its basic doctrine. Boethius learns to endure Fortune's cruel treatment by transcending it. Since Philosophy demonstrates that freedom and justice operate under a benevolent Providence, there is no need for Boethius to portray his return from the visionary state to his physical prison. Whatever is to happen to Boethius after his vision will have no real importance for him; he knows that he must oppose vice, cultivate virtue, and trust in Providence for his just rewards (5, pr. 6). James's visionary, too, has been prepared to endure whatever Fortune has in store for him, but Minerva's instruction has been less complete theoretically than that of Philosophy, and he is "wayke and feble" (149.5), less capable than Boethius of immediately assimilating the lessons he has learned. His life must continue, and, as a human being, he will remain subject to Fortune's vicissitudes. By living in Fortune's realm, he now has the opportunity to transcend her influences by serving virtuous love and developing his faith in the providential order.

The prisoner's immediate response to his dream, upon waking, reveals little change in his mental state. The poet's apostrophe to the "besy goste" of man, so sorely oppressed by trouble from day to day that it can never rest, marks the return of the young prisoner to consciousness of his confinement (st. 173–74). Indeed, his spirit is more vexed than before by his lack of "sekirnes." The voice of the older poet draws from the suffering of his youthful self a general truth: the spirit of man can never be at rest in this world; only in Heaven, "that place that thou cam fro, / Quhich is thy first and verray proper nest" (173.3–4), is there true respite. Here one remains on Fortune's wheel and so without "sekirnes," security. Still, as the prisoner arises, he wonders about his dream; his final set of questions has to do with its validity, and by asking them he acknowledges the possibility of its truth, of grounds for hope to be found in God's "puruiance" (st. 175–76). Such questions are unusual in Boethian vision poems— validity is ordinarily assumed, by the reader if not by the visionary. The prisoner wavers between doubt and hope, asking for some further sign of grace to confirm what the vision has taught him. It is perhaps because of this seed of hope within him that he receives the sign he desires.

A white "turture" flies in his window, bringing a message of hope which marks the beginning ("kalendis") of his "confort." Like the nightingale whose song first stirred him from his lethargy, this dove is both a real bird and the bringer of otherworldly aid. The message, written upon a real branch "of red jorofflis" which he pins to his bedstead, affirms the providential nature of his "auenture." The dove traditionally symbolizes divine grace, as well as fidelity in love, so that both its sudden presence and its message confirm the hope that Providence will work out the prisoner's "cure." He reads the message with a mixture of hope and fear (180.4); it is not, after all, a detailed prediction of future events but only, as he finally understands, a "First takyn" of help and joy. His "cure" has been "in the hevyn decretit," for which he should rejoice, but the ambiguity of his future, which must be worked out through the agency of Fortune, remains (st. 177–80).

A single stanza (181) brings the narrator forward in time from his prison to the immediate present of the poem. His life improved "day by day" over the period of time during which the providential order of events revealed itself. Love, that which "all my wittis maistrit had tofore," did away with his pains, just as Philosophy's hymn to *amor* suggests it can.[29] Fortune became a positive influence upon the development of his "lore," his wisdom about life, so that now he lives in true freedom ("larges") with his lady. He explains that he writes all this in thanks for the course his life has run (st. 182). "Luffis ordinance," which binds so many "in his goldin cheyne," has brought him to freedom, both spiritual and physical, from "thraldome and peyne." He has attained not the final rest of Heaven but "sufficiance," adequate happiness in this world (st. 183). He prays to Venus for the success of all lovers whose service is acceptable to her and to "resoune," and for those who have yet to begin their apprenticeship and those whose loves have attained fulfillment. Following Venus's injunction, he urges the slothful to amend their lives and "their saulis auance / With thair suete lore" (st. 184–86). Everyone should serve love.

Observing that it would take too long to recount all the circumstances of his recovery, he says that it must suffice the reader to know that through the agency of his "floure" and of the "goddis" all has turned out well. His long pain and true service in love have been rewarded with "perfyte joy" that only death can end (st. 187–88). The lessons of his vision have successfully guided his subsequent life. He therefore offers thanks and praise to the gods, Fortune's wheel, the nightingale, the dove's "gerafloure," the wall of his tower, the saints of March, and the trees of the garden, thus affirming the entire experience of his life. There is no more questioning now; as he brings to its end the account of his life, everything has fallen into its place in the providential order. "By processe," through the conjunction of the gods' "purueyance" and his own virtue in love, he has come into the "presence" of his "floure," into "lufis ȝok that esy is and sure" (st. 189–93).

After a brief envoy (st. 194–95), James concludes his *Quair* by reaffirming the providential nature of the "influence" which has governed the events of his life and recommends his book to the company of the "impnis" of his masters, Chaucer and Gower (st. 196–97). He thus returns to his starting point, the stars "Hich in the hevynnis figure circulere" (196.7), in a sense closing the poem's circular structure. The thought of the poem, however, is not at all circular, since the poet, through the process of writing "quhat the befell," arrives finally at a new understanding of his experience.[30] Only at the end of the *Quair* does he see in the stars his life as the manifestation of a providential plan written by God many years before. Just as God "wrote" his life then, for any who could read it in the stars, so now he has written his life in a different sort of language, discovering for himself, and for the benefit of his reader, that there was a providential order behind its "auentures."

The core of *The Kingis Quair* is its vision, which enables the visionary to understand and deal with life in the temporal world. The influences of Venus—love which emanates from God and manifests itself in human aspiration—Minerva—the divine wisdom which guides men's lives—and Fortune—the inexplicable events through which Providence reveals itself in this world—are intertwined in the visionary's life, and he must understand their roles to achieve what Boethius before him achieved, "sufficiance," temporal happiness. The vision is uniquely embedded in a narrative which spans virtually the entire conscious life of the visionary, revealing its central importance to that life; in other Boethian works the effectuality of such visions can only be assumed by the audience. Vision and waking life here give reciprocal meaning to one another and in so doing lead the visionary-poet to the recognition that divine Providence guides all of life. The *Quair*'s unique chronological structure, its movement from the recent past forward to the point at which the poet begins to write his "newe thing," then back to the more distant past of his youth, and on forward to the poem's immediate present, makes possible the expansion of the Boethian process. This process here includes not only the visionary's initial state of confusion and the vision which comes in response to it but also the life he leads as a response to the vision and, finally, the task of poetic recreation through which he makes a comprehensible whole of it all.

11

THE TESTAMENT OF CRESSEID

obert Henryson's *Testament of Cresseid* regularly receives high critical praise; its editor Denton Fox thinks it "the best poem, English or Scottish, of the fifteenth century."[1] It appears, in part, to be a continuation of Chaucer's *Troilus and Criseyde*, and so critics have dealt with it as a verse romance, while ignoring its formal relationships to the Boethian vision tradition. A. C. Spearing mentions it as "a narrative which includes a dream as an important episode."[2] Among those who discuss the poem at length, only E. Duncan Aswell acknowledges any significant relationship to what he calls "the love-vision conventions."[3] I intend here to approach the *Testament* as a poem in the Boethian tradition, paying particular attention to its formal structure, its narrator, and its use of Boethian doctrine.

In treating the *Testament* as the story of Chaucer's heroine subsequent to her betrayal of Troilus, critics tend to ignore Henryson's narrator and the framework in which he appears and thus focus upon the tale exclusively. Critical controversy has centered upon whether or not Henryson projects an orthodox Christian world view in his poem,[4] upon the relationship of Cresseid to her world,[5] and upon Henryson's attitude toward his heroine. Questions continue to arise about Cresseid's character, her offense, and her punishment. To deal with such questions, adequate weight must be given to the context in which the tale appears; the generic dimension of the *Testament* as a whole must be considered.

Boethian Apocalypse

The opening stanzas of the *Testament* appear to be leading up to the introduction of a vision; the introductory *sententia*, the astrological description of the season, and the description by the narrator of his evening's reading recall the vision poems of Chaucer and his fifteenth-century disciples. The *sententia*, "Ane doolie sessoun to ane cairfull dyte / Suld correspond and be equiualent" (lines 1–2), sets the mood of the poem as a whole. The narrator speaks specifically of the "dyte" of Cresseid, which he thinks of as a "tragedie" (line 4), a tale of the fall of its protagonist from high estate to low through the agency of Fortune. His "writing," it should be noted, occupies the same time frame as the words which we read; for all practical purposes the moment when the narrator begins to write and the opening of the poem are identical, despite his use of the past tense. The season is spring, but the weather is wintry, the appropriate combination for a "tragedy" about love (lines 4–21). As Phoebus descends and "fair Venus, the bewtie of the nicht" (line 11) rises "in oppositioun" (line 13), the sky clears, and the frosts and bitter arctic winds drive the narrator, against his will, from his "oratur." A symbolic relationship between the weather and the narrator's physical and mental condition emerges in the three succeeding stanzas (lines 22–42).

The narrator intends to pray to Venus, "luifis quene, / To quhome sum tyme I hecht obedience, / My fadit hart of lufe scho wald mak grene" (lines 22–24), but because of the cold he retires to his bed-chamber and its fire. Outward heat, he believes, may also revive his chilly heart:

> Thocht lufe be hait, ӡit in ane man of age
> It kendillis nocht sa sone as in ӡoutheid,
> Of quhome the blude is flowing in ane rage;
> And in the auld the curage doif and deid
> Of quhilk the fyre outward is best remeid:
> To help be phisike quhair that nature faillit
> I am expert, for baith I haue assaillit.
> [Lines 29–35]

He is an aged devotee of Venus and, by his own admission, no longer physically suited for her works. He seeks something which Venus cannot possibly grant him, physical rejuvenation, and his devotion wavers comically in the face of his more immediate need for his creature comforts. The weather thus takes on symbolic overtones: spring and the ascendant position of the planet Venus should be propitious for a lover, but the frosty cold and the descent of the sun more appropriately match the narrator's physical state. He needs "phisike" to revive him because "nature faillit"; he hopes that the fire will rekindle his passion and "drink" will induce his "blude" to flow once more (lines 36–38). Warmth and moisture are traditionally the attributes of spring as well as youth, while cold and dryness are associated with autumn and advancing age.[6] Cresseid will pass from the vernal to the autumnal state in the course of the poem, but at this early point it is the contradiction between the narrator's advancing age and his youthful longings of which the reader must be conscious.

Protected from the cold, the narrator takes up a book to shorten the "winter nicht" and summarizes briefly what he reads (lines 39–60). It is the final section of Chaucer's *Troilus and Criseyde*, in which Troilus finally realizes that Criseyde will not return to him. Such an unhappy ending could scarcely comfort an aging servant of Venus who desires another chance at love. His summary speaks only of Troilus's suffering over the loss of Criseyde, whose return he "desyrit maist of eirdly thing" (line 52), but he clearly assumes the reader's familiarity with the whole poem (lines 57–60). He passes over Troilus's posthumous rejection of love, doubtless because he cannot reconcile it with his own attitudes. Nonetheless, the reader must view the narrator's venereal aspirations in the light of Chaucer's "litel . . . tragedye" (*TC* 5.1786) and so recognize that he has surely chosen the wrong love story with which to revive his "faidit hart." He offers only a curtailed summary before setting the book aside in favor of another one.

In the "vther quair" he discovers "the fatall destenie / Of fair Cresseid, that endit wretchitlie" (lines 61–63). The retelling of this story, another "tragedy," occupies most of the poem and corresponds structurally to the Boethian vision which the reader might expect at this point. The story of "fair Cresseid," as the narrator insists upon calling her throughout the poem, can be expected to offer him some sort of information relevant to his present frame of mind, as would a more conventional visionary experience. That he questions the reliability of both Chaucer's story and this new "narratioun" (lines 64–70) ironically confirms in the reader's mind the validity of the poets' "inuentioun," regardless of their historical accuracy. The aging lover resists accepting what he reads about Cresseid and attempts to cast doubt upon these stories because he does not want to believe them.

The "vther quair" begins with Diomede, having sated his desire for Cresseid, repudiating this "fair ladie" in favor of another (lines 71–75). Cresseid, "excludit fra his companie" and "desolait," is set adrift and finally wanders, so it is said, "into the court, commoun," into a life of sexual promiscuity, if not prostitution (lines 76–77).[7] The narrator at once intrudes to express his outrage and amazement that "fair

Cresseid" should have been so "fortunait." Despite his earlier expressions of doubt, he apparently believes what he reads, and his choice of language reveals no sympathy for promiscuity; he speaks of her life as "filth," "with fleschelie lust sa maculait," a "giglotlike" pursuit of "foull plesance" (lines 78–83). Still, he considers her fate a "mischance" and pities her (line 84). Denying Cresseid's personal responsibility, he excuses her "brukkilnes" and places the entire blame upon "Fortoun." He refuses to credit the "wickit langage" of those, including presumably Chaucer, who injure her reputation (lines 85–91). What in Chaucer's narrator seems to be heartfelt compassion for Criseyde (e.g., *TC* 5.1093–99) here has become willful blindness toward her reprehensible conduct.

At some unspecified later time Cresseid returns "Richt priuelie" to the "mansioun" of her father, Calchas. Here she remains, keeping herself apart from "the pepill" out of vanity and shame at having been rejected by Diomede (lines 92–121). The animus of Chaucer's narrator towards Calchas as a traitor to Troy colors Henryson's characterization only slightly. Henryson has made him the priest of Venus and Cupid not, I think, to suggest his disloyalty to Apollo, whom he serves in Chaucer's poem, but rather to create the ironic situation in which he serves the same gods whom his daughter blames for her misfortunes. He appears genuinely solicitous of Cresseid when he welcomes her return:

> . . . Douchter, weip thow not thairfoir;
> Perauenture all cummis for the best.
> Welcum to me; thow art full deir ane gest!
> [Lines 103–105]

His observation that perhaps all happens for the best is, as Fox observes, a "Boethian sentiment," perhaps appropriate to the conclusion of the poem.[8] In the immediate context of Cresseid's fall from Fortune's favor and loss of "fellowschip or refute" (line 94), Calchas's welcome revels him as a true friend, of the sort which, according to Lady Philosophy, ill fortune separates from mere sycophants (*CP* 2, pr. 8). At this point, however, Cresseid cannot appreciate his fidelity to her.

While the populace publicly worships Venus and Cupid, Cresseid, alone in "ane secreit orature," complains against them (lines 120–40). She accuses her gods of breaking their promise that she should be "the flour of luif in Troy," the city she has long since abandoned. Bewailing the lack of a lover to "gyde" and "conuoy" her, she ignores the guidance and protection which Calchas, Venus's own priest, offers her. She places the entire blame for her plight upon the gods:

> O fals Cupide, is nane to wyte bot thow
> And thy mother, of lufe the blind goddes!
> ʒe causit me alwayis vnderstand and trow
> The seid of lufe was sawin in my face,
> And ay grew grene throw ʒour supplie and grace.
> But now, allace, that seid with froist is slane,
> And I fra luifferis left, and all forlane.
>
> [Lines 134–40]

The images of green growth and frost recall the words of the narrator earlier in the poem; just as he believes that Venus can make his faded heart green, so Cresseid suffers from the delusion that Venus might keep her beauty, "the seid of lufe," "ay . . . grene," that somehow the laws of nature could be suspended for her. John MacQueen argues that her allusion to the "seid" now "slane" by frost implies that Cresseid is already conscious of the leprosy which will shortly manifest itself,[9] but there is little evidence of this. Rather, her sense of fading beauty, whether or not justified, seems psychologically appropriate. Though still a relatively young woman, she has used her beauty to attract lovers and has been dependent upon them for her sense of well-being; now finding herself alone, she thinks of herself as having aged and grown unattractive.[10]

Cresseid's angry outburst against "hir wofull desteny" (line 121), taken together with the vision which it precipitates, suggests that the narrator's "vther quair" is itself constructed according to the pattern of Boethian Apocalypse. Her complaint reveals her despair, her misconception about the cause of her unhappiness, and her need for guidance. Furthermore, although she directs her anger against her particular gods, Venus and Cupid, its underlying object is essentially the same as that of the parallel complaints in the *Consolation* and the *Kingis Quair*: Fortune. She protests against the unwelcome change in her circumstances; her statement that "all in cair translatit is my ioy" (line 130) is a commonplace of complaints against Fortune. In the vision we learn that Venus's principal attributes are identical to those traditionally associated with Fortune, instability and variance.[11] Henryson, I think unmistakably, calls the reader's attention to his use of the Boethian form in constructing this poem within his larger poem.

Immediately after uttering her complaint, Cresseid falls into "ane extasie" and receives her vision of Cupid and the seven planetary gods (lines 141–343). This vision cannot, of course, in any sense be called a consolation; it consists of a tribunal called by Cupid for the purpose of punishing the visionary, who remains silent throughout. Still, like Boethian visions, it comes in direct response to the visionary's complaint, presents doctrine which confronts her erroneous assumptions, and ultimately changes the way she views herself and her world. That Cresseid's vision differs from other Boethian visions by delivering its instruction in a wholly negative, punitive manner suggests perhaps that Henryson distinguishes between the benevolent enlightenment offered to medieval Christian visionaries and the sort of confrontation with the other world available to pagans. The authority figures here are scarcely benevolent instructors; they are the planetary gods, depicted with their appropriate, traditional, astrological attributes,[12] and they mean the visionary harm, not help.

Although each planet has its own particular area of influence in the world of men, based upon its ancient mythological associations, taken collectively the planets are conceptually equivalent to Fortune, exercising precisely the same sort of largely unpredictable, unavoidable power over earthly matters as does Boethius's lady with the wheel. Thus they "hes power of all thing generabil, / To reull and steir be thair greit influence / Wedder and wind, and coursis variabill" (lines 148–50). Chaucer explicitly identifies the influence of these gods with Fortune in the *Troilus*:

> But O Fortune, executrice of wyrdes,
> O influences of thise hevenes hye!
> Soth is, that under God ye ben oure hierdes,
> Though to us bestes ben the causes wrie.
> [*TC* 3.617–20]

In the Boethian-Christian view of the cosmos these gods, like Fortune, become figures which embody the unseen powers affecting human affairs. They are the intermediaries between man and an unknowable Providence. In the *Testament*, however, as in the *Troilus*, the pagan characters are ignorant of the divinity which transcends and controls Fortune and their gods. Neither Henryson nor Chaucer suggests the direct intervention of the Christian God in the action of his story, nor does either attempt to spell out the providential purposes behind human events therein. Henryson may believe that human events influenced by the planetary gods are ultimately attributable to an unknowable but benign Providence, that the gods serve God's will, but that belief is irrelevant to the pagan characters of the story. So far as Cresseid knows, these gods are the highest powers that control her earthly circumstances. While she may eventually discover that the suffering they inflict upon her has had a beneficial effect, she can have no idea that this is the consequence of a larger, providential design.

As Aswell demonstrates, the gods are presented in such a way as to make Cresseid "aware that she is subject to change and thus remind her of her mortality, and . . . also exemplify the workings of time and change in the widest cosmic perspective."[13] Their influences may be either benign or malignant or a mixture of both. "Saturn and Jupiter are each pure types, personifications of abstract qualities realized to perfection." Saturn's influence is always malignant; he is "coldness, sterility, cruelty, destructive power." Everything in his appearance suggests lean, cold, gray old age and hostility (lines 151–68). Jupiter "is the complete antithesis of his father—warmth, fertility, kindness, generative power." A benevolent figure, "richt fair and amiabill, / God of the starnis in the firmament / And nureis to all thing generabill" (lines 169–71), he is associated with light, flowers, May, and youth; he has a clear voice, bright eyes, and golden hair and wears green-and-gold clothing (lines 169–82).

The other gods partake "in some measure of the qualities of both Saturn and Jupiter."[14] Mars is fiery like Jupiter but otherwise Saturnine in his hostility and destructiveness (lines 183–96). Phoebus is Jovial, source of light, "Tender nureis," and cause of "lyfe in all eirdlie thing" but dangerous to human sight and variable in his effects upon the world (lines 197–217). Mercury, god of poets and physicians, is nonetheless avaricious and untrustworthy (lines 239–52). Cynthia partakes of the light of her brother, Phoebus, but otherwise resembles Saturn— black and leaden and dressed in a gray cloak with black spots (lines 253–63). Venus occupies "the exact median point" between Saturn and Jupiter and so resembles Fortune, the principle of cosmic mutability and capriciousness, sometimes benevolent, sometimes malevolent (lines 218–38).[15] Her half-green, half-black clothes, the "greit variance" in her expression, and her frequent changes in mood betoken

> . . . that all fleschelie paramour,
> Quhilk Venus hes in reull and gouernance,
> Is sum tyme sweit, sum tyme bitter and sour,
> Richt vnstabill and full of variance,
> Mingit with cairfull ioy and fals plesance,
> Now hait, now cauld, now blyith, now full of wo,
> Now grene as leif, now widderit and ago.
> [Lines 232–38]

Boethian Apocalypse

The influences of these cosmic powers affect Cresseid and the narrator, just as they do all the rest of humanity; like Fortune, they cannot be evaded. The narrator, cold, aged, his life dominated by Saturnian influences, still hopes that Venus will restore him to Jovial "greenness." Cresseid as yet benefits from the Jovial aspects of Venus's power, but Venus's appearance itself betokens the inevitable withering of love's "flowers."

The condemnation of Cresseid by the "parliament" can scarcely be described as a trial (lines 264–343). She is first accused by Cupid, then punished by Saturn and Cynthia. She says nothing in her own defense because the facts of her case, as Cupid presents them, are incontrovertible. He accuses her of blaspheming him and his mother, and therefore of insulting all of the gods (lines 274–94). He has favored her by making her "sum tyme flour of lufe" (lines 279).[16] He denies responsibility for her present unhappiness; that is the result of her own conduct:

> Saying of hir greit infelicitie
> I was the caus, and my mother Venus,
> Ane blind goddes hir cald, and micht not se,
> With sclander and defame iniurious.
> Thus hir leuing vnclene and lecherous
> Scho wald retorte in me and my mother,
> To quhome I schew my grace abone all vther.
>
> [Lines 281–87]

Her gods have favored her with gifts which have made her a most desirable object for lovers, a "flower." If she has misused these gifts and so lost the love she once had, that is not the fault of the gods.

Cupid's indictment of Cresseid constitutes the god's response, on behalf of Venus and himself, to her human irrationality and failure to recognize the nature of the gods she serves. Fortune in the *Consolation* (2, pr. 2) responds similarly to complaints about her gifts, pointing out that she is by nature inconstant and comparing her activities to natural phenomena, day and night, the seasons, and the seas. Venus behaves in precisely the same way; her gift, "fleshelie paramour," is "Richt vnstabill. . . Now grene as leif, now widderit and ago" (lines 235–38). Cresseid's failure to understand this has led to her blasphemy. Beothius goes on to learn that the gifts of Fortune cannot bring true happiness, even to the virtuous (bks. 2, 3), and that vice is the source of its own worldly punishments (4, pr. 2–4). Philosophy's observation concerning "voluptas corporis" seems particularly apt for Cresseid: "What dreadful disease and intolerable sorrow, the fruits of wicked-

218

ness, they bring to the bodies of those who enjoy them!" (3, pr. 7). Cresseid has yet to learn these Boethian lessons, but they are implicit in Cupid's remonstrance, although of course it cannot be Cupid's role to draw moral lessons based upon the nature of his mother. Venus, like Fortune, is a neutral, amoral power; in this context she neither causes nor condones or disapproves of lecherous living; she does not require her servants to emulate her inconstancy or to avoid it; she simply gives and takes away the favors which are within her control.

Cupid argues that divine (but not Christian) "sapience" demands retribution (lines 288–94), not for Cresseid's moral conduct but explicitly for blasphemy against the gods. Her sentence is decided by Saturn and Cynthia, the highest and lowest of the gods, neither of whom is favorable toward her. Saturn, the power of decay and death in the world, favors no one. Cynthia, like Saturn, is by nature cold and gray and as the mythological goddess of chastity could scarcely be sympathetic toward Cresseid. Together they condemn her to suffer from leprosy, "seiknes incurabill, / And to all louers be abhominabill" (lines 307–308); she will be totally and irrevocably deprived of the gift of beauty which Venus and Cupid once lavished upon her. Because leprosy was thought in Henryson's time to be a venereal disease, it is a particularly appropriate form of punishment in physical and moral terms as well. Her sexual promiscuity, physical activity which violates the moral norms of her world, directly causes physical deformity and both physical and mental anguish. In astrological terms the symptoms of leprosy are attributed to the influence of Saturn and Cynthia: her Jovial warmth and moisture changes to cold and dryness (line 318); her lovely eyes, voice and skin are horribly altered (lines 337–40) so that she now resembles Saturn and Cynthia rather than Jupiter and Phoebus.[17]

Cresseid's punishment is best seen in terms of nature, rather than justice. The gods, in MacQueen's phrase, represent "the indifferent laws of the universe."[18] They control generation and decay in the world, and their natural function, like Fortune's, is to give and take away their gifts. They do not control human conduct, although they influence one's inclinations toward, for example, love or war; moral choice belongs to the individual will. Venus's gift to Cresseid has been the beauty which made her a "flour of lufe," but beauty, like a flower, is subject to decay. Cresseid has valued her beauty and the "fleschelie paramour" which it has brought her but failed to recognize its natural mutability. Because her values have been narrow, material, and self-indulgent, she has misspent her life and enslaved herself to Fortune's gifts. When she loses the things she values, her lovers and the material

Boethian Apocalypse

prosperity they bring her, she blames her unhappiness upon her gods and blasphemes them. The gods retaliate by accelerating the process of withdrawing the gifts she values; the beauty which would have faded naturally anyway, leaving her unable to attract new "paramours," is taken in a particularly nasty way, forcefully reminding her of the mutability of earthly things. She has first ignored and then blasphemed what is natural, and nature takes its revenge. The question of whether leprosy is a just punishment for blasphemy is not relevant because the gods do not deal in justice according to a Christian (or Boethian) moral scheme. They simple mete out punishment for disloyalty and insult. Whatever justice there is in Cresseid's leprosy is natural and impersonal; she has lived like a whore and, inevitably, caught the whore's disease.

After Saturn has pronounced his sentence, the narrator intrudes to protest against the god's malice and mercilessness (lines 323–29). He still thinks of Cresseid as "fair" (lines 325, 329), "sweit, gentill and amorous" (line 326), and he begs the god to relent and "be gracious — / As thow was neuer" (lines 327–28). His pity and wish for mercy are humane, but his indignation at Saturn for acting in accordance with his destructive nature — at Fortune for being Fortune — is foolish and pointless. He ignores the inevitability and appropriateness of Cresseid's fate, part out of sympathy for her as a helpless victim of cosmic forces, but part because he has reached the Saturnine stage in his own life and does not want to face its inevitable physical consequences. Venus will not, cannot, make his heart green again; it is himself for whom he mourns.

Cresseid awakens from her "vglye visioun" and, looking into a mirror, discovers that her worst fears have been realized. Her physical decay has become total and irreversible (lines 344–50). However, she cannot at once grasp the full meaning of what has happened to her; she must live a while longer to understand her vision and her life. She recognizes the most literal, physical import of the dream, of course; she has offended "Our craibit goddis" and been punished with the deformity which visibly makes her a living example of their terrible power. The things she values, "All eirdlie ioy and mirth," are lost to her (lines 351–57). She now knows what her gods are like — cruel and implacable.

Calchas, meanwhile, thinks that she is still at prayer, and his cheerful call to supper contains unintentional but painful irony: she should leave off praying, for "The goddis wait all zour intent full weill" (line 364). When he sees her face, "The quhylk befor was quhite as lillie flour," he is overcome with sorrow, for he knows there is "na succour"

220

for her disease. Even Venus's own priest is helpless before the decisions of the gods he serves (lines 358–78). Cresseid, still subject to her vanity and shame, wishes not to be "kend," and goes in secret to the "hospitall" (lines 379–99). She had asked Venus, "Quha sall me gyde? Quha sall me now conuoy?" when she found herself "excludit, as abiect odious," from her former lovers (lines 131–33). Now she is "conuoyit" (line 389) and given "almous" (line 392) by the only man still willing to care for her, Calchas, when all but her fellow lepers shun her. The setting sun and black clouds on the evening of her arrival at the "spittaill hous" symbolize the nadir of her physical and psychological decline; she sits alone, without food or drink, in a dark corner, where, weeping, she laments her fate (lines 400–406).

The "Complaint of Cresseid" (lines 407–69) fully articulates her attitude as she begins her new life as a social outcast, underscoring certain basic changes brought about by her vision. She begins by again lamenting the loss of all her "ioy" and "mirth in eird," which she now rightly attributes to Fortune: "Fell is thy fortoun, wickit is thy weird" (line 412). The gods have turned against her; she wishes herself dead and buried, so that no one in Greece or Troy will know of her degradation. Vanity, a lingering pride in what she has been, is all that she retains of her former life (lines 407–15). Her perception of her loss, however, remains superficial; she still values the temporal gifts of Fortune. Thus she enumerates the items of material prosperity which she no longer possesses, the outward trappings of her "greit royall renoun" (lines 416–24). The noble pastimes of her prosperity, symbolized by the May garden and "fresche flowris," have likewise gone the way of her own "flowering" (lines 425–33). Shifting her focus from past to present, she observes that the "greit triumphand fame and hie honour" for which she was called "of eirdlye wichtis flour" has "decayit"; the "hie estait" by which others judged her and she judged herself has turned to "darknes dour," to the trappings of impoverished obscurity (lines 434–42). The immediate cause of these alterations is physical; her voice is now "hiddeous," her face so "deformit" that no one "lyking hes" to look upon it (lines 443–51).

The two final stanzas of this complaint reflect a subtle but significant shift in Cresseid's outlook, as she projects a future life of sorts for herself (lines 452–69). She calls upon the fair ladies of Greece and Troy to witness her misery. Her secrecy and self-imposed isolation give way to her perception of herself as an example to others of the incomprehensible capriciousness of "friuoll fortoun." The physical decay which she suffers may strike anyone. Beauty, honor, and wealth are transitory, the gifts of fickle Fortune:

221

Boethian Apocalypse

Nocht is ʒour fairnes bot ane faiding flour,
Nocht is ʒour famous laud and hie honour
Bot wind inflat in vther mennis eiris,
ʒour roising reid to rotting sall retour;
Exempill mak of me in ʒour memour
Quhilk of sic thingis wofull witnes beiris.
All welth in eird, away as wind it weiris;
Be war thairfoir, approchis neir ʒour hour;
Fortoun is fikkill quhen scho beginnis and steiris.

[lines 461–69]

The ending of the Complaint thus suggests a first step toward coming to terms with the world outside herself. She has learned the most basic of Boethian lessons: the decisions of the gods, the laws which govern human life, cannot be evaded. However, although she now understands more clearly the essential nature of the temporal world, she continues to ignore a crucial component of Cupid's accusation, and so to evade recognition of her own share of the responsibility for what has happened to her. She knows that Fortune is fickle, but she has yet to learn that individual human conduct, too, affects human happiness.

The commonplace that it is futile to complain against Fortune's blows is obviously appropriate advice for Cresseid at this point in the *Testament*. Her nightlong "chydand with hir drerie destenye" is "all in vane" (lines 470–73). Such lamentation, as the example of Boethius shows, in fact makes a rational understanding of one's proper relationship to the temporal world impossible. Thus the leper lady's advice expresses the sort of stoicism promulgated by Philosophy as the "easy medicine" of books 1 and 2 of the *Consolation*:

. . . Quhy spurnis thow aganis the wall
To sla thy self and mend nathing at all?

Sen thy weiping bot dowbillis thy wo,
I counsall the mak vertew of ane neid;
Go leir to clap they clapper to and fro,
And leif efter the law of lipper leid.

[Lines 475–80]

This, clearly, is the only reasonable course open to Cresseid, and she must follow the lady's advice (lines 481–83); she must accept her life as it is.

The phrase "mak vertew of ane neid" appears in Chaucer's poems, as Henryson certainly knew; two of the contexts in which it appears are particularly relevant to his heroine, and so the reader's recollection must deepen his understanding of Henryson's purposes in using it. At the end of *The Knight's Tale* this same advice forms the conclusion to Theseus's "Firste Moevere" speech (*CT* A 2987–3089). There Theseus is attempting to persuade Palamon and Emelye to end their mourning for Arcite, and he begins by describing the order of the universe, in appropriately pagan, Neoplatonic, philosophical terms derived from the *Consolation* (2 m. 8; 4, pr. 6, m. 6). The first mover established order in the created universe by binding it with a "faire cheyne of love"; within this universe all that is "engendred" is allotted a finite span of life. This universal corruptibility proves the stability and eternity of the creator. It avails "no creature on lyve / Of no degree" to strive against this divine order:

> Thanne is it wysdom, as it thynketh me,
> To maken vertu of necessitee,
> And take it weel that we may nat eschue,
> And namely that to us alle is due.
> [*CT* A 3041–44]

Theseus is speaking specifically of the acceptance of death as an inevitable part of worldly existence, but in more general terms his advice applies to the acceptance of all natural change as part of the corruptibility evident in earthly life. Oaks, he says, live long but are finally "wasted," stones waste away, rivers dry up, cities "wane and wende," and people die at their appointed times. This stoic acceptance of natural, divinely ordained decline and decay is the proper response for Cresseid to her leper's life; sooner or later all things "green" become "withered."

The second Chaucerian context in which this advice appears is even more significant, for it contributes devastating irony to Henryson's passage; Chaucer's Criseyde herself gives this advice to Troilus, just before the end of their last private meeting (*TC* 4.1527–1701). She is attempting to convince Troilus, who wants to flee with her from Troy, that their wisest course lies in accepting their temporary separation. She rightly fears the future consequences of precipitate flight, exhibiting the sort of prudence and foresight which she seems to have lost by the time she reappears in the *Testament*. She swears "on every god celestial / ...and ek on ech goddesse" that she will remain faithful (lines 1534–54). Were he to flee, he would endanger both the city and his reputation; he would lose his honor and be accused of "lust voluptuous" by the people (lines 1555–75). Her own "honeste, / That

floureth yet," would be "spotted" with "filthe" (lines 1576–82). Therefore, she says, he should follow "resoun" and be patient:

> Thus maketh vertu of necessite
> By pacience, and thynk that lord is he
> Of Fortune ay, that naught wole of hire recche;
> And she ne daunteth no wight but a wrecche.
>
> [Lines 1586–89]

A few lines later, after both have again sworn fidelity, she observes that
her love for him is based not upon worldly things like his "estat roial,"
"veyn delyt," or "richesse" but on his "moral vertu, grounded upon
trouthe." Neither time nor "remuable Fortune" can destroy this sort of
love (lines 1667–87). What she says here about her fidelity and reputation, about Fortune, and about the quality of her love, in the light of
her subsequent betrayal hangs over Henryson's poem, undercutting
the pity which we feel for her as a leper forced to "mak vertew of ane
neid." She has compromised, and subsequently lost, the high ideals
with which she departed from Troilus and began her descent into
shame and suffering.

Henryson's oblique evocation of the memory of Troilus effectively
prepares the reader for the emotional climax of the poem, Cresseid's
last encounter with her forgotten lover, who enters the *Testament*
immediately after the leper lady's brief speech (lines 484–574). The
"moral vertu" upon which Chaucer's Criseyde claimed to have based
her love is still apparent in the demeanor of Henryson's "worthie
Troylus," now the chief defender of Troy. He has not allowed his lady's
defection to undermine his devotion to his public duty. Riding back to
Troy from the field "With greit tryumphe and laude victorious," "richt
royallie," he retains the prominence and adulation which Cresseid has
lost (cf. lines 432, 434). He responds to the lepers' prayer for alms out
of "pietie," without knowing that Cresseid is one of them (lines
491–97). Unable to recognize her because of her deformed condition,
he gives alms in memory of the love which he preserves despite the
absence of Cresseid. He has apparently accepted his personal misfortune and remained virtuous in his conduct. The "spark of lufe" which
"kendlit all his bodie in an fyre" has not grown cold as has its object; he
retrieves from his "fantasy" the "idole" of his lost love, but Cresseid
experiences no comparable recollection (lines 498–518). Therefore, he
gives his gold to an unknown leper "For knichtlie pietie and memoriall
/ Of fair Cresseid," without speaking a word; his gesture is a wholly
private one, which he explains to no one despite the pain he feels (lines
519–25).[19]

224

The Testament of Cresseid

The lepers gather around Cresseid, and, seeing Troilus's gold, they recognize that "ʒone lord" for some unknown reason ("How euer it be") favors her more highly than the rest of them (lines 526–32). Cresseid's failure to recognize her former lover has puzzled readers of the poem. On a realistic level, the only plausible explanation is that her leprosy, as Cynthia seems to have suggested (line 337), has impaired her vision.[20] On a figurative level, this failure implies "that Cresseid does not know Troilus," that throughout the poem she has not recognized his true nature and worth.[21] Indeed, in her preoccupation with her own misfortune, she seems to have actually forgotten Troilus; before her vision she mentions his name in conjunction with that of Diomede as one of her lost lovers (line 132) but otherwise gives no thought to him. In his presence she does not conjure up an "idole" of him comparable to the one so deeply "imprentit" in his "fantasy." She does, however, recognize his charitable gesture as "greit humanitie" (lines 533–34). The dramatic effect of the encounter with Troilus and its aftermath depends upon her ignorance of her benefactor until after she has expressed her admiration and gratitude. The intense impact of learning his identity causes her to faint for the second time in the poem (lines 535–39). When she recovers, she realizes the truth, not only about the character of Troilus, but also about herself.

Cresseid's tearful outburst upon waking constitutes a public confession of her guilt for transgressing the laws which govern lovers in her world, and an acknowledgment of the true worth of the lover whom she betrayed (lines 540–74). The refrainlike line, "O fals Cresseid and trew knicht Troylus!" (lines 546, 553, 560), epitomizes her heightened state of consciousness, the final stage in the process of enlightenment initiated by her blasphemy. She had blamed the gods for her unhappiness in love and Fortune for her leprosy; now she blames "Nane but my self" (line 574). She explicitly acknowledges the steadfast virtue of Troilus and her own "wantones" in the pursuit of Fortune's gifts (line 547–53). She has finally realized the justice of Cupid's accusation: while Troilus's "lufe" of her made him virtuous, and therefore admirable, her "fleschelie foull affectioun" led her to "lustis lecherous" (lines 554–60). Again she presents herself as an example to others, but not, as before, an example of Fortune's cruelty. She has become in her own eyes the example of moral failure, of inconstancy and infidelity in love (lines 561–74). Like the narrator of *The Kingis Quair*, she has learned the full meaning of her vision over a subsequent period of time. Her final realization goes beyond Boethian understanding of the essential nature of Fortune and the gods to a partial, secular perception of the Boethian relationship between moral conduct and earthly happiness.

Boethian Apocalypse

Cresseid now knows that her woes originated in her own behavior. Had she remained faithful to Troilus, her beauty would still have faded with age, but true love is not based upon transitory things, and it survives whatever Fortune or the gods might cause to happen. She would not have entered a life of promiscuity, would not have had occasion to lament the loss of her lovers (and of the material prosperity which they brought her), and would not have contracted leprosy. Feeling that she alone is responsible for her unhappiness, she repents her transgressions against the moral laws of her world. There is nothing left before her now but death to free her from her anguish. Her "testament" expresses her final wishes and so reveals how little she has in this world and how ready she is to leave it (lines 575–91). Her body no longer concerns her; she leaves it to the last stage of its corruption, to worms and toads. Her material wealth goes to the lepers who will bury her. The ring given her by Troilus is to be returned to him; by making her death known, she will perhaps free him of his vows of fidelity to her.

Last of all, Cresseid leaves her spirit to "Diane," "To walk with hir in waist woddis and wellis" (line 588). This bequest perhaps reflects her recognition of the value of the chastity (in the sense of fidelity) which she abused in her lifetime. It may also, as Sklute believes, indicate that "Cresseid sees herself as eternally outcast and wandering, never able to find rest, never able to find stability beyond the moon."[22] Certainly it cannot betoken her expectation of Christian salvation. As McNamara points out, for a pagan, even a morally regenerated one like Cresseid, an afterlife in Diana's retinue is the best that she can hope for. Henryson makes no final disposition of her soul because he can neither confirm nor deny its salvation by a Christian God, whose justice transcends human reason.[23] In fact, Henryson appears to be following Chaucer in the noncommittal manner in which he treats the afterlife of his protagonist; the "goost" of Troilus rises "ful blisfully" to the sphere of the moon, whence "Mercurye" sends it to its final home (TC 5.1807–27). Both Chaucer's Troilus and Henryson's Cresseid understand the nature of their world more fully at their deaths, and both derive from this understanding the only sort of comfort their authors can reasonably assign them, that of escape from the tribulations of earthly life.

Cresseid dies thinking of Troilus's "trew lufe," and one of the lepers subsequently informs him of her death (lines 592–609). His reaction to this news might seem somehow inadequate, but it is difficult to imagine what more one might expect of a temperate pagan. The disclosure of her illness and suffering causes him to faint for sorrow.[24]

226

His final words, "I can no moir; / Scho was vntrew and wo is me
thairfoir" (lines 601–602), express his regret that she was unfaithful
(and so suffered the consequences) and his sense of helpless resignation. They constitute a measured response to events which cause him
pain but have always been beyond his control; they do not seem to
suggest moral condemnation. The gray tomb with its golden inscription symbolizes the course of Cresseid's life, from golden youth and
beauty to gray decay and death, while Troilus's epitaph summarizes it
with simple dignity. This epitaph calls the attention of "fair ladyis" to
the fate of one of their number, and so to that of all humanity; once a
"flour," Cresseid is now dead. This is a pagan sort of ending for the
story, suggesting only stoic resignation before the facts of temporal
decline and death.

In the last stanza of the *Testament* the narrator reenters the poem to
offer his final comment upon the "quair" he has just read (lines
610–16). As I have suggested, the placement of this "quair" of Cresseid
in the overall structure of the *Testament* corresponds to that of the
vision in Boethian vision poems. One might therefore expect the
"quair" to offer the narrator some sort of guidance appropriate to his
prior concerns and attitudes. The opening stanzas of the poem reveal a
narrator who is devoted to Venus, a Fortunelike goddess whose powers
and sphere of influence over human life are clearly inappropriate to a
man of his age and its attendant physical condition. The "quair" he
reads has much to tell him about time, change, and human values; it
should provide a critique of, and corrective to, his own misconceptions. The vanity and futility of his devotion to an indifferent Venus,
and so to worldly things in general, should become at least as apparent
to him, given his presumably Christian perspective upon this world
and the next, as they do to the pagan Cresseid at the end of her life.
The doctrine of the epilogue to Chaucer's *Troilus* and that of this
"vther quair" complement one another, and both speak to him of his
own misplaced values.

Still, the narrator's final words do no more than amplify the statement made by Cresseid's epitaph, and in so doing they distort its
implications by oversimplification. He retells this story, he says, to
instruct and admonish "worthie wemen" to be faithful in love, lest
they end their lives as unhappily as "fair Cresseid." Since she is dead,
he will henceforth speak, and presumably think, of her "no moir."
This seems a lame conclusion indeed; he draws the most obvious, and
least profound, possible moral from the book he has read. While not
actually mistaken in seeing a cause-and-effect relationship between
Cresseid's infidelity and her "sore conclusioun," he fails to com-

prehend the deeper and more universal moral implications inherent in Cresseid's discovery of the true nature of her world and herself. That he considers the book a cautionary tale for women in love indicates how narrow and unimaginative a reader he is. Throughout he expresses genuine pity for Cresseid's frailty and the suffering it causes her, but he fails utterly to recognize the inevitability of that suffering or Cresseid's responsibility for it. Therefore, he also fails to perceive any relationship between her misconceptions about life in this world and his own. To him she will always be "fair Cresseid," a "sweit, gentill and amorous" lady unfairly treated by "cruell Saturne." His response to the "quair" is inadequate because he apparently cannot, or will not, understand what it says; it is therefore impossible for him to make significant connections between his reading and his life.

We may think, then, of Henryson's *Testament* as two related poems, the one integrated into the structural fabric of the other. The self-contained poem about Cresseid stands as an independent structural unit within the larger poem, in which the narrator is the only character; indeed, the Cresseid poem can be said to have generated the larger poem, which focuses upon the narrator's reading of and response to it. Both the larger *Testament* and the "quair" of Cresseid depend upon Boethian tradition as it appears in English in Chaucer's vision poems and, perhaps, in the Chaucerian *Kingis Quair*, not simply for their shared thematic concerns but also for their poetic strategy and structure. The narrative "quair" of Cresseid, a third-person Boethian vision poem, resembles *The Kingis Quair* more closely than it does Chaucer's poems in its approach to its visionary core. It consists of a prologue describing the circumstances of the visionary's "complaint," the "complaint" itself, the ensuing vision, and finally an account of the subsequent waking experience through which the ideas presented within the vision manifest themselves and are assimilated into the consciousness of the visionary. The subject matter, characters, and thematic concerns of the "quair" are derived primarily from the *Troilus*, but the thematic elements in Chaucer's romance are at least tinged with Boethian ideas which Henryson could have found in the vision poems of Chaucer and James as well.

As I have said, the "quair" is embedded in the first-person framework provided by the *Testament*'s narrator in such a way that it functions as would the vision in a Boethian poetic structure. The narrator, of course, reads, rather than dreams or otherwise envisions, the story of Cresseid, but nonetheless Henryson's larger structural pattern appears to be modeled upon those of Chaucer's vision poems — particularly *The Book of the Duchess* and the *Parliament* —

and, to a lesser degree, that of *The Kingis Quair*. The *Testament*'s prologue (lines 1–38), like those of Chaucer's visions, introduces the narrator's particular preoccupations. The narrator's reading of the *Troilus* (lines 39–60) corresponds to the uniquely Chaucerian readings of Ceyx and Alcyone, the *Somnium Scipionis* and, in the *Kingis Quair*, the *Consolation*. The "vther quair," then, corresponds to the visions which come in response to their visionaries' preoccupations. Henryson's narrator obviously resembles Chaucer's obtuse visionaries in his advanced age, his interest in love, and his inability to comprehend the literary and visionary experience to which he finds himself exposed, although he seems more obstinately perverse in his attitudes than do his Chaucerian models. His intrusive comments remind the reader that the "quair" of Cresseid is being read by him within the larger poetic structure and so bind the two structures together. These generally wrongheaded comments also correspond to the reactions, questions, and observations of more conventional Boethian visionaries to the instruction which they receive within their visions.

Henryson places his reader in a complex, though readily comprehensible, relationship to the visionary experience of Cresseid and the pseudovisionary, literary experience of the *Testament*'s narrator. The distance maintained between the reader and the two protagonists is unique in the Boethian tradition, and can best be understood in the light of the works which precede the *Testament*. In the prototypical Boethian Apocalypse — the *Consolation* itself, or the *De planctu* — the reader finds himself very close to the experience of the visionary-narrator, who functions as his surrogate. The reader learns what the visionary learns, as the visionary learns it, by vicariously sharing, step by step, his experience. As the genre develops, the element of irony, vaguely suggested in earlier authority figures' occasional scolding of their pupils, grows more prominent, and the distance between the perceptive reader and the somewhat less perceptive visionary widens. In *Pearl*, for example, the visionary is slower to grasp what he is being taught than is the more objective, distanced reader, but the surrogate relationship to a degree persists, so that visionary and reader finally arrive at approximately the same level of understanding. Chaucer, perhaps through the influence of the *Roman de la Rose*, increases the ironic distance between reader and visionary by means of his obtuse, comic personae; the visionaries of *The Book of the Duchess* and the *Parliament* cannot understand and benefit from their visions, and so it is left to the reader to make sense of the visions and their relationships to the visionaries. Thus the reader responds to the visionary experience

229

in a way quite different from, and with insight presumably superior to, that of the visionary.

In the *Testament*, Henryson forces his reader to deal with two separate, though related, visionary experiences. Henryson's fifteenth-century Christian reader would find himself separated from the visionary experience of Cresseid by his perception of the chronological and cultural distance between himself and the pagans of ancient Troy. The use of the third-person narrative voice would, I think, enforce this separation. The reader thus follows from an objective distance as Cresseid experiences and finally understands her vision within the context of her whole life. He can share vicariously in the process of secular enlightenment, derive the moral insight which Cresseid finally attains, and at the same time recognize the limitations inherent in her experience from a later, Christian perspective. That is to say, he can learn from the story of Cresseid the truths which she learns about human life in a secular, pagan context and go beyond these truths to the higher truth of divine Providence.

Needless to say, Henryson's narrator is not the ideal fifteenth-century reader. Not only does he seem unable to place the story he reads in a medieval Christian perspective, but he seems unable to follow its secular moral implications. Thus he functions as a sort of negative surrogate for the reader, who presumably learns from the narrator's failure to comprehend his visionary experience, just as he learns from Cresseid's success. The two visionary experiences are thematically related to one another; both the narrator and Cresseid need to learn the same lessons about the temporal world. From the perspective of the reader the two accounts of visionary experience, one ancient and successful insofar as the visionary emerges from it with new knowledge, the other medieval and a failure, throw light upon one another. Distanced from both the enlightened pagan visionary and the unenlightened contemporary visionary-reader-narrator, Henryson's reader must base his response to the *Testament* upon the interplay between the two poems which the poet has joined into one.

Henryson's poetic strategy, his doubling of the equivalent of visionary experience in a single poem, is unique in the tradition of Boethian Apocalypse, and our continuing admiration of the poem attests to its success. Among the many allegories and vision poems in English which survive from the fifteenth and sixteenth centuries, a handful reveal their poets' continuing interest in, and understanding of, the Boethian type of vision. Of these works, a few deserve our continued critical attention because of their various intellectual and imaginative qualities; in particular, I would single out *The Assembly of Gods*, or

The Testament of Cresseid

The Accord of Reason and Sensuality in the Fear of Death;[25] *The Court of Sapience*;[26] John Skelton's *The Bowge of Courte* and *The Garlande of Laurell*;[27] and Gavin Douglas's *The Palice of Honour*[28] as works which could profitably be studied as late representatives of the Boethian vision tradition. The *Kingis Quair* and the *Testament of Cresseid* distinguish themselves from these other exceptional works, however, as the last truly superior, truly innovative accomplishments of poets working within the tradition of the Boethian genre in the English of the later Middle Ages.

NOTES

1. René Wellek and Austin Warren, *Theory of Literature*, 3d ed., pp. 226–37.
2. Ibid., p. 231.
3. Francis Cairns, *Generic Composition in Greek and Roman Poetry*, p. 6.
4. Wellek and Warren, *Theory of Literature*, pp. 234–35.
5. Ibid., p. 235.
6. Ibid.
7. The most recent and comprehensive study of Boethius's influence is Pierre Courcelle, *La Consolation de Philosophie dans la tradition littéraire: Antécédents et postérité de Boèce*. An earlier survey is Howard R. Patch, *The Tradition of Boethius: A Study of His Importance in Medieval Culture*.
8. Michael H. Means, *The Consolatio Genre in Medieval English Literature*, recognizes Boethius's *Consolation* as the generic prototype for a number of the poems discussed here. As his terminology ("consolatio genre") suggests, however, his conception of the Boethian genre differs in important respects from my own.
9. Fredericus Klingner, *De Boethii Consolatione Philosophiae*, pp. 112–18.
10. See, e.g., Isidore of Seville's definition, which, while correct in its etymology, cites Revelation 1:1 for evidence of its meaning. Isidore of Seville (Isidori Hispalensis Episcopi), *Etymologiarum sive Originum Libri XX*, ed. W. M. Lindsay, 6.2.49.
11. Hermas, *Le pasteur*, ed. Robert Joly, pp. 11–12.
12. E. K. Rand, Review of Klingner, *De consolatione philosophiae*, in *American Journal of Philology* 44 (1923): 87. In *Founders of the Middle Ages*, pp. 161–63, E. K. Rand expands his list of literary types combined by Boethius to include Platonic-Ciceronian dialogue, allegory, apocalypse, consolation, introduction, or incentive (προτεπτιχος) to philosophy, theodicy, and *satura*.
13. F. J. E. Raby, *A History of Christian Latin Poetry from the Beginnings to the Close of the Middle Ages*, pp. 112–13.

1. The following works offer useful discussions of Boethius and the *Consolation* and provide further references: the works by Klingner, Patch, Courcelle, and Rand

Boethian Apocalypse

(pp. 135–80) cited in chap. 1; H. F. Stewart, *Boethius: An Essay*; H. M. Barrett, *Boethius: Some Aspects of His Times and Works*; Margaret Gibson, ed., *Boethius: His Life, Thought and Influence*; Henry Chadwick, *Boethius: The Consolations of Music, Logic, Theology, and Philosophy*.

2. All references are to Boethius (Anicii Manlii Severini Boethii), *Philosophiae Consolatio*, ed. Ludovicus Bieler. All Modern English translations are those of Richard Green, trans., *The Consolation of Philosophy*.

3. Chadwick, *Boethius*, pp. xv, 224.

4. Rand, *Founders*, p. 168. Susan Ford Wiltshire, "Boethius and the *Sumum Bonum*," *CJ* 67 (1972): 216–20, compares the structure of the *Consolation* to that of Classical drama.

5. Courcelle, *La Consolation de philosophie*, pp. 20–28.

6. This point is made by Paul Piehler, *The Visionary Landscape: A Study in Medieval Allegory*, pp. 29–30.

7. Anna Crabbe identifies them with the self-pitying muses of Ovidian elegy; "Literary Design in the *De Consolatione Philosophiae*," in Gibson, ed., *Boethius*, pp. 244–51.

8. Courcelle, *La Consolation de philosophie*, p. 103. For discussions of the figure of Fortuna and her backgrounds see ibid., pp. 103–158; Howard R. Patch, *The Goddess Fortuna in Medieval Literature*.

9. Rand, *Founders*, p. 168. Piehler, *The Visionary Landscape*, pp. 41–42, suggests that the poetic cosmology of some of the meters influences later allegories.

10. W. Schmid, "Boethius and the Claims of Philosophy," *Studia Patristica* (Berlin) 2 (1957): 368.

11. Chadwick, *Boethius*, pp. 131–33 et passim.

12. Ibid., pp. 228–35.

13. Klingner, *De Boethii* Consolatione philosophiae, pp. 112–18.

14. Courcelle, *La Consolation de philosophie*, pp. 17–20; Chadwick, *Boethius*, p. 224.

15. Chadwick, *Boethius*, p. 249.

16. Edmund T. Silk, "Boethius' *Consolatio philosophiae* as a Sequel to Augustine's *Dialogues* and *Soliloquia*," *HTR* 32 (1939): 19–39.

17. Ibid., p. 20.

18. Ibid., p. 21.

19. Ibid., p. 34.

20. Ibid., p. 35.

21. Ibid., p. 38

22. Ibid., p. 36.

23. Crabbe, "Literary Design," pp. 237–74.

24. Ibid., p. 238.

25. Ibid., p. 240.

26. Ibid., p. 256.

27. F. Anne Payne, *Chaucer and Menippean Satire*.

28. Ibid., pp. 3–37; Northrop Frye, *Anatomy of Criticism: Four Essays*, pp. 309–12.

29. Frye, *Anatomy*, p. 309.

30. Payne, *Chaucer*, p. 5.

31. Ibid., p. 6.

32. Ibid., pp. 7–11.

33. Ibid., p. 12.

Notes

34. Ibid., pp. 36–37.
35. Ibid., pp. 57–58.
36. Ibid., p. 59.
37. Ibid., pp. 68–75.
38. Ibid., p. 76.
39. Ibid., p. 84.
40. Ibid., p. 85.
41. Ibid., p. 85.
42. Courcelle, *La Consolation de philosophie*, pp. 29–66, 241–332.
43. This, of course, is not to say that Payne's subsequent readings of Chaucer's works are necessarily invalid. There is no reason why Chaucer could not have employed portions of the *Consolation*'s arguments in fashioning his own "Menippean" poems. But he would not have to read it ironically to do so.
44. The exception is Means, *The Consolatio Genre*, pp. 13–16. On the influence of the *Somnium* and Macrobius's commentary on it see Macrobius, *Commentary on the Dream of Scipio*, trans. William Harris Stahl, pp. 39–55.
45. Courcelle, *La Consolation de philosophie*, pp. 116–24. See also Chadwick, *Boethius*, pp. 7–8.
46. Rand, *Founders*, pp. 158–59.
47. Frank Ernest Rockwood, ed., *Cicero's Tusculan Disputations, I, and Scipio's Dream*, p. viii.
48. Rand, *Founders*, esp. pp. 154–56.
49. Courcelle, *La Consolation de philosophie*, pp. 116–24.
50. References are to Rockford's edition, n. 47 above.
51. Macrobius, *Commentary*, pp. 85–86.
52. Courcelle, *La Consolation de philosophie*, p. 20.
53. "...grauido...pectore"; Fulgentius (Fabii Planciadis Fulgentii V. C.), *Opera*, ed. Rudolfus Helm, p. 8.
54. Leslie George Whitbread, trans., *Fulgentius the Mythographer*, p. 16.

CHAPTER 3, Notes to pp. 39–45

1. For a full-scale theoretical treatment of allegory as a mode of expression see Angus Fletcher, *Allegory: The Theory of a Symbolic Mode*. An interesting attempt to analyze allegory as a specific literary genre is offered by Maureen Quilligan, *The Language of Allegory: Defining the Genre*.
2. A step in this direction is Philip Rollinson, *Classical Theories of Allegory and Christian Culture*.
3. Isidore of Seville, *Etymologiarum* 1.37.22.
4. Fletcher, *Allegory*, pp. 1–2.
5. Cited by Rosamond Tuve, *Allegorical Imagery: Some Mediaeval Books and Their Posterity*, p. 45. Rollinson, *Classical Theories of Allegory*, p. xii, accurately observes that these "levels" "do not refer to four kinds of expression but only two, literal and figurative, with four possible categories of meaning."
6. Robert Worth Frank, Jr., "The Art of Reading Medieval Personification-Allegory," *ELH* 20 (1953): 237–50, 237.
7. Ibid., pp. 244–45.
8. Frye, *Anatomy*, p. 89.
9. Ibid., p. 90.

10. Frank, "Art," pp. 246–47.

11. Courcelle, *La Consolation de philosophie*, pp. 29–66, 241–344.

12. D. W. Robertson, Jr., "The Historical Setting of Chaucer's *Book of the Duchess*," in J. Mahoney and J. E. Keller, eds., *Medieval Studies in Honor of Urban Tigner Holmes, Jr.*, p. 175.

13. Peter Dronke, Review of Courcelle, *La Consolation de philosophie*, *Speculum* 44 (1969): 127.

14. V. L. Dedeck-Héry, ed., "Boethius' *De consolatione* by Jean de Meun," *MS* 14 (1952): 171. According to Roberto Crespo, Meun's preface is a translation of the Latin prologue to William of Aragon's commentary on the *Consolation*; Roberto Crespo, "Il Prologo ala traduzione della *Consolatio philosophiae* di Jean de Meun e il commento di Guglielmo d'Aragonia," in *Romanitas et Christianitas: Studia I. H. Waszink oblata*, ed. W. den Boer et al., pp. 55–70.

15. Tuve, *Allegorical Imagery*, pp. 234, 235.

CHAPTER 4, Notes to pp. 49–71

1. The most important recent critical works dealing at least in part with Alanus and the *De planctu* are G. Raynaud de Lage, *Alain de Lille, poète du XIIᵉ siècle*; Richard Hamilton Green, "Alan of Lille's *De Planctu Naturae*," *Speculum* 31 (1956): 649–74; Paul Piehler, *The Visionary Landscape: A Study in Medieval Allegory*, pp. 46–68; Winthrop Wetherbee, "The Function of Poetry in the *De planctu naturae* of Alain de Lille," *Traditio* 25 (1969): 87–125; Winthrop Wetherbee, *Platonism and Poetry in the Twelfth Century: The Literary Influence of the School of Chartres*, pp. 188–211; George D. Economou, *The Goddess Natura in Medieval Literature*, pp. 72–97; Jane Chance Nitzsche, *The Genius Figure in Antiquity and the Middle Ages*, pp. 88–114.

2. Piehler, *The Visionary Landscape*, p. 46.

3. Marc-René Jung, *Études sur le poème allégorique en France au Moyen Âge*, p. 65.

4. Alanus de Insulis, "*Alan of Lille, 'De planctu naturae,'*" ed. Nikolaus M. Häring, *SMed* 19 (1978): 797–879, 1.3. All references are to this edition, which supersedes that of Thomas Wright, *The Anglo-Latin Satirical Poets and Epigramatists of the Twelfth Century*, 2: 429–522. Wright's edition is translated into English as *The Complaint of Nature* by Douglas M. Moffatt. Häring's edition is translated as *The Plaint of Nature* by James J. Sheridan. I have used Sheridan's translation here.

5. On Alanus's relationship to Macrobius, and on twelfth-century attitudes toward figural expression in general, see Green, "*De planctu*," pp. 656–59; Wetherbee, "The Function of Poetry," pp. 91–99; Wetherbee, *Platonism and Poetry*, pp. 1–73.

6. Macrobius, *Commentary*, p. 87.

7. It should be pointed out, however, that in his later work, the *Anticlaudianus*, Alanus does not appear to be bound by any such restrictions.

8. On the relationship between reason and nature in the *Consolation* see Economou, *The Goddess Natura*, pp. 28–30.

9. Green, "*De planctu*," pp. 652–54.

10. Ibid., p. 670.

11. "Accordingly, when the mirror with these images and visions was withdrawn, I

Notes

awoke from my dream and ecstasy and the previous vision of the mystic apparition left me" (18.164–65).

12. "When I saw this kinswoman of mine close at hand, I fell upon my face and stricken with mental stupor, I fainted; completely buried in the delirium of a trance, with the powers of my senses impeded, I was neither alive nor dead and being neither, was afflicted with a state between the two" (6.4–7).

13. Piehler, *The Visionary Landscape*, pp. 53–54, seems to lean in this direction.

14. This view is articulated by Green, "*De planctu*," passim, and touched upon by Piehler, *The Visionary Landscape*, passim, in their discussions of the work.

15. Piehler, *The Visionary Landscape*, pp. 62–67.

16. Wetherbee, "The Function of Poetry," pp. 101ff.

17. Green, "*De planctu*," passim, notes Alanus's strategy of generalizing from the particular vice to the broader problem.

18. Wetherbee, "The Function of Poetry," pp. 120ff., argues that this resolution is implicit in the work.

19. It should be noted, however, that Nature says only that "many men" ("plerique homines"; 8.165) have caused the rent.

20. Green, "*De planctu*," esp. pp. 658–59, argues to the contrary that the theological extension of Alanus's meaning is required by the text itself.

21. I have drawn slightly on Green's discussion ("*De planctu*," pp. 664–69) of the figurative burden of marriage imagery in the work for what follows.

22. Wetherbee, "The Function of Poetry, pp. 111–12.

23. Ibid., p. 111.

24. On these various interpretations of this figure see C. S. Lewis, "Genius and Genius," *RES* 12 (1936); reprinted in *Studies in Medieval and Renaissance Literature*, pp. 169–71; George D. Economou, "The Character Genius in Alan de Lille, Jean de Meun, and John Gower," *ChauR* 4 (1970): 203–205; George D. Economou, *The Goddess Natura*, pp. 90–95; Green, "*De planctu*," pp. 672–73; Wetherbee, "The Function of Poetry," pp. 112–23; Nitzsche, *The Genius Figure*, passim. See also H. David Bramble, "The Role of Genius in the *De planctu naturae* of Alanus de Insulis," *C&M* 31 (1970): 306–23.

25. See Green, "*De planctu*," p. 674, on the implicit necessity of spiritual regeneration for the salvation of Genius's excommunicants. Wetherbee, "The Function of Poetry," pp. 120–25, attempts to show that Christian resolution is implicit in the *De planctu* itself.

26. Alanus de Insulis, *Anticlaudianus*, ed. R. Bossuat; in Wright, ed., *Anglo-Latin Satirical Poets*, 2:268–428; Alanus, *Anticlaudianus*, trans. James J. Sheridan.

CHAPTER 5, Notes to pp. 73–98

1. Patch, *The Tradition of Boethius*.

2. Courcelle, *La Consolation de philosophie*.

3. *Liber Fortunae*, ed. John L. Grigsby.

4. Johannis de Hauvilla, *Architrenius*, ed. Paul Gerhard Schmidt. All references are to this edition. Recent discussions of this poem appear in Jung, *Études*, pp. 113–21; Piehler, *The Visionary Landscape*, pp. 85–94; Wetherbee, *Platonism and Poetry*, pp. 242–55.

5. Wetherbee, *Platonism and Poetry*, pp. 242–43; Piehler, *The Visionary Landscape*, p. 86; Jung, *Études*, pp. 113, 121n.

6. Jung, *Études*, pp. 120–21. It should be noted, however, that Jung's contrasting of Johannis to Bernardus and Alanus, as a practical moralist to utopian theoreticians, overlooks the practical aspect of the *De planctu*.

7. On Johannis's use of allegorical loci see Piehler, *The Visionary Landscape*, pp. 88–91.

8. C. S. Lewis, *The Allegory of Love*, pp. 78–82, 81.

9. One may note that the encyclopedic tendency is an important aspect of the genre defined by Northrop Frye as "Menippean Satire" or "Anatomy," examples of which include Boethius's *Consolation*; Frye, *Anatomy of Criticism*, pp. 308–12.

10. Wright, ed., *The Anglo-Latin Satirical Poets*, 1:240–392.

11. Ernest Langlois, *Origines et sources du* Roman de la Rose, pp. 93–95, 136–38, 148–50.

12. Lewis, *The Allegory of Love*, p. 157.

13. The most important attempts to deal with the *Roman* as a coherent work of medieval art are the following: Alan M. F. Gunn, *The Mirror of Love: A Reinterpretation of the "Romance of the Rose"*; Lionel J. Friedman, "'Jean de Meung,' Antifeminism, and 'Bourgeois Realism,'" *MP* 57 (1959): 13–23; D. W. Robertson, Jr., *A Preface to Chaucer: Studies in Medieval Perspectives*, pp. 91–104, 195–207; Charles Dahlberg, "Macrobius and the Unity of the *Roman de la Rose*," *SP* 58 (1961): 573–82; Charles Dahlberg, "Love and the *Roman de la Rose*," *Speculum* 44 (1969): 568–84; Rosamond Tuve, *Allegorical Imagery*, pp. 233–84; John V. Fleming, *The "Roman de la Rose": A Study in Allegory and Iconography*; Winthrop Wetherbee, "The Literal and the Allegorical: Jean de Meun and the *De planctu naturae*," *MS* 33 (1971): 264–91.

14. References are to the edition of Lorris and Meun by Félix Lecoy. The standard critical edition of Ernest Langlois has slightly different line numbers. See Charles Dahlberg, trans., *The Romance of the Rose*, appendix, for a table of concordances between line numberings in these editions. The translations used here are Dahlberg's.

15. Patricia J. Eberle, "The Lover's Glass: Nature's Discourse on Optics and the Optical Design of the *Romance of the Rose*," *UTQ* 46 (1977): 241–62, convincingly demonstrates that Meun conceived of his portion of the poem as a "mirror" of and for lovers, in the scientific and moral senses of that term, as "a complex optical instrument designed to reveal to lovers their own nature seen from a multiplicity of perspectives" (p. 255).

16. Gunn, *The Mirror of Love*, pp. 17–45 et passim.

17. Tuve, *Allegorical Imagery*, pp. 252–53. See also Fleming, *The "Roman de la Rose,"* pp. 99–103.

18. Langlois, *Origines et sources*, pp. 1–68.

19. Lewis, *The Allegory of Love*, p. 112.

20. Jung, *Études*, p. 294.

21. Langlois, *Origines et sources*, pp. 93–94.

22. See Friedman, "'Jean de Meung'"; Tuve, *Allegorical Imagery*, passim.

23. Gunn, *The Mirror of Love*, pp. 142–44.

24. Ibid., passim; Tuve, *Allegorical Imagery*, passim.

25. I am not suggesting that the poem is in fact a medieval encyclopedia, only that it tends toward encyclopedism in its comprehensiveness. Gunn, *The Mirror of Love*, pp. 45–51, clarifies this distinction.

26. Langlois, *Origines et sources*, pp. 136–38, 148–50. He does not find them to be sources for Lorris. On the influence of the *Consolation* and its commentaries see also

Notes

Alastair Minnis, "Aspects of the Medieval French and English Traditions of the *De consolatione philosophiae*," in Gibson, ed., *Boethius*, pp. 324–34.

27. Langlois, *Origines et sources*, p. 93.

28. Means, *The Consolatio Genre*, pp. 32–43, 33.

29. Gunn, *The Mirror of Love*, pp. 502–503, recognizes "the lack of immediacy, of concreteness" in Meun's use of the allegorical method of didactic writing.

30. Means, *The Consolatio Genre*, pp. 32–43. Gunn, too, draws attention to what he calls the teacher-student archetype which pervades the *Roman*, carrying out its didactic purpose there as it does in many other medieval works; Alan M. F. Gunn, "Teacher and Student in the *Roman de la Rose*: A Study in Archetypal Figures and Patterns," *ECr* 2 (1962): 126–34. See also Gunn, *The Mirror of Love*, passim.

31. Langlois, *Origines et sources*, p. 94; Robertson, *A Preface to Chaucer*, pp. 198–99.

32. Dedeck-Héry, ed., "Boethius' *De Consolatione* by Jean de Meun," pp. 168–71.

33. This would, of course, give ironic implications to Reson's praise for its future translator in lines 5003–10. See Lorris and Meun, *Roman de la Rose*, ed. Lecoy, 92:282n.

34. Donald Stone, Jr., "Old and New Thoughts on Guillaume de Lorris," *AJFS* 2 (1965): 157–70, argues that Lorris had reached an impasse because of the conflicting demands of the world of love and the world of Reason.

35. See, e.g., lines 4242–46, 4329–30, 4599–613, 5345–403, 5667–94, 6871–912, 7155–98.

36. See Gunn, *The Mirror of Love*, pp. 449–53, for a brief analysis of the poem's psychological "realism."

37. Tuve, *Allegorical Imagery*, pp. 260–61.

38. See Nature's preface to her *descriptio Cupidinis*, *De planctu naturae* 8.269–76: "Either by describing with reliable descriptions or defining with regular definitions, I will demonstrate the indemonstrable, extricate the inextricable, although it is not bound in submission to any nature, does not abide an investigation by reason and thus cannot be stamped with the stamp of any one description. Let the following, then, be set forth as a delimiting of the unlimited, let this emerge as an explanation of a nature that is inexplicable, let this be regarded as knowledge of the unknown, let this be brought forward as a doctrine on the unknowable; let it, however, be refined by the sublimity of the writer's pen."

39. Wetherbee, "The Literal and the Allegorical," pp. 270–74, draws attention to this problem: "What Raison cannot understand, though it is ironically implicit in her speech, is a depravity such as to make man incapable of responding to her love." It should be further noted that Amant's attitude points up his willful refusal to even attempt to pursue a better course of life, whatever the possibility of his succeeding in that pursuit.

40. None of this, it seems to me, denies the validity of Gunn's observation that Meun's reintroduction of Reson "initiates his reinterpretation of the theme of the allegory, and provides the reader with the clue to the meaning and structure of his continuation"; Gunn, *The Mirror of Love*, pp. 144–50. Gunn, after all, is speaking of the Reson episode as it appears in the completed poem, while I am concerned here with the process by which Meun might have been drawn into continuing the poem in the first place.

41. On the ironies and ambiguities which emerge from the narrator's point of view see Paul Strohm, "Guillaume as Narrator and Lover in the *Roman de la Rose*," *RomR*

59 (1968): 3–9; Dahlberg, "Love and the *Roman*," p. 568; Dahlberg, trans., *The Romance of the Rose*, pp. 5–10; Jung, *Études*, pp. 299–302.

42. Langlois, *Origines et sources*, pp. 36–54; Lewis, *The Allegory of Love*, p. 118.

43. Gunn, *The Mirror of Love*, pp. 302–305. See also "Rose" in Gunn's index, p. 575.

44. Tuve, *Allegorical Imagery*, p. 239.

45. Lewis, *The Allegory of Love*, pp. 120–24.

46. See Charles Muscatine, "Locus of Action in Medieval Narrative," *RPh* 17 (1963–64): 115–22, for a provocative discussion of this subject.

47. Lewis, *The Allegory of Love*, p. 119. See Fleming, *The "Roman de la Rose,"* pp. 57–58, for a convincing refutation of this view.

48. Robertson, *A Preface to Chaucer*, pp. 91–93.

49. The figures depicted on the outside of the wall, lines 129–460.

50. Tuve, *Allegorical Imagery*, p. 242.

51. Cf. Robertson, *A Preface to Chaucer*, pp. 99–104; Dahlberg, trans. *The Romance of the Rose*, pp. 20–21; Tuve, *Allegorical Imagery*, pp. 278–79; Fleming, *The "Roman de la Rose,"* pp. 226–37.

52. Fleming, *The "Roman de la Rose,"* p. 52, observes that Meun has reversed the usual course of dream visions like the *Consolation*. The view of Gunn, *The Mirror of Love*, and Gerard Paré, *Les Idées et les lettres au XIIIᵉ siècle: Le Roman de la Rose*, that the end of the poem affirms Amant's experience, depends upon an utter disregard for irony and for the decorum of the views expressed in relationship to the figures who express them, and are amply refuted by Fleming, passim, and Tuve, *Allegorical Imagery*, p. 249n.

53. Tuve, *Allegorical Imagery*, pp. 267–75.

54. Cf. Economou, *The Goddess Natura*, pp. 104–24.

55. On Nature in the *Roman* see also Fleming, *"The Roman de la Rose,"* pp. 189–226.

56. Ibid., pp. 112–41.

57. Tuve, *Allegorical Imagery*, pp. 260–61.

58. The argument offered by Wetherbee, "The Literal and the Allegorical," pp. 285–91, that a higher, providential force can be seen working through the subjective motivations of the participants, and that the conception of a child at the end constitutes the unconscious fulfillment of a divine duty in a fallen world, may be essentially correct but requires some qualification. The passage describing this conception (lines 21689–700) is ambiguous: it is not altogether clear that the mingling of seeds signifies successful insemination or that the enlargement of the bud is anything more than the normal distending of the female genitalia. Even if we assume that a child has been conceived, this conception, as Wetherbee suggests, is an accident; the goal of Nature has been attained in the process of Amant's attaining a quite different goal, pleasure. The immoral quality of Amant's quest is not changed by its results, providential though they may be. All temporal events, good and bad, are ultimately part of divine Providence, but this fact never excuses the sins committed by the participants in these events.

59. Tuve, *Allegorical Imagery*, p. 261.

60. Fleming, *The "Roman de la Rose,"* p. 198.

61. Ibid., pp. 192–97.

62. Wetherbee, "The Literal and the Allegorical," p. 284.

63. Tuve, *Allegorical Imagery*, p. 262.

64. Ibid., passim; Fleming, *The "Roman de la Rose,"* passim.

Notes

65. See, e.g., Langlois, *Origines et sources.*
66. Gunn, *The Mirror of Love*, pp. 61–138.
67. Friedman,, "'Jean de Meung,'" p. 17.
68. Paré, *Les Idées et les lettres*, pp. 31–32.
69. Fleming, *The "Roman de la Rose,"* p. 238. It is a distortion of the passage, however, to claim, as Fleming does (p. 242), that "our youthful Old Man is an authority only on the love of old women."

CHAPTER 6, Notes to pp. 99–118

1. G. C. Macaulay, ed., *The English Works of John Gower*, 1:x. All references are to this edition.
2. Lewis, *The Allegory of Love*, pp. 198–222; Fisher, *John Gower: Moral Philosopher and Friend of Chaucer.*
3. Russell H. Peck, ed., *Confessio Amantis*, pp. xi–xii; Means, *The Consolatio Genre*, pp. 59–65. At about the same time that the substance of this chapter first appeared in print (see Preface), Peck's book-length study of the *Confessio*, greatly expanded from his excellent introduction to his abridged edition of the poem, also appeared in print as *Kingship and Common Profit in Gower's Confessio Amantis*. Among the other valuable works dealing with the poem are J. A. W. Bennett, "Gower's 'Honeste Love,'" in John Lawlor, ed., *Patterns of Love and Courtesy: Essays in Memory of C. S. Lewis*, pp. 107–21; Derek Pearsall, "Gower's Narrative Art," *PMLA* 81 (1966): 475–84; George D. Economou, "The Character Genius in Alain de Lille, Jean de Meun, and John Gower," *ChauR* 4 (1970): 203–10; Donald G. Schueler, "Gower's Characterization of Genius in the *Confessio Amantis*," *MLQ* 33 (1972): 240–56; Patrick J. Gallacher, *Love, the Word, and Mercury: A Reading of John Gower's Confessio Amantis.*
4. Macauley, ed., *The English Works of John Gower*, pp. xxi–xxiii; Fisher, *John Gower*, pp. 116–27.
5. Lewis, *The Allegory of Love*, pp. 198–99.
6. Pearsall, "Gower's Narrative Art," 476.
7. See, e.g., Schueler, "Gower's Characterization of Genius," p. 248.
8. See, e.g., Macaulay, ed., *The English Works of John Gower*, pp. xix–xx.
9. Ibid., p. xix.
10. Peck, ed., *Confessio Amantis*, p. xii
11. Ibid., pp. xviii–xix; on Gower's role as poet see esp. George R. Coffman, "John Gower in His Most Significant Role," in *Elizabethan Studies and Other Essays in Honor of George F. Reynolds*, pp. 52–61; George R. Coffman, "John Gower, Mentor for Royalty: Richard II," *PMLA* 69 (1954): 953–64.
12. Peck, ed., *Confessio Amantis*, pp. xix–xxii.
13. See also Pearsall, "Gower's Narrative Art," pp. 475–76. On the relationship of society and the individual in Gower's thought see Fisher, *John Gower*, pp. 163–203; Peck, *Kingship and Common Profit*, pp. xix–xxv, 1–23, et passim.
14. Cf. Means, *The Consolatio Genre*, pp. 61–62; Schueler, "The Age of the Lover in Gower's *Confessio Amantis*," *MÆ* 36 (1967): 152–58.
15. See Bennett, "Gower's 'Honeste Love.'"
16. Peck, ed., *Confessio Amantis*, p. xiii.
17. Gower never really deals with the place of religious ascetics in the scheme of things.

Boethian Apocalypse

18. Macaulay, ed., *The English Works of John Gower*, p. 493n.172.
19. See, e.g., Economou, "The Character Genius," pp. 208–209.
20. Ibid., p. 206.
21. Ibid., p. 207.
22. Ibid., p. 208.
23. Ibid.
24. Ibid., p. 209. Schueler, "Gower's Characterization of Genius," argues for a similar relationship between these figures.
25. Macaulay, ed., *The English Works of John Gower*, p. xix.
26. Nitzsche, *The Genius Figure*, amply documents them; see also the earlier studies of E. C. Knowlton, "The Allegorical Figure Genius," *Classical Philology* 15 (1920): 380–84; E. C. Knowlton, "Genius as an Allegorical Figure," *MLN* 39 (1924): 89–95.
27. Gallacher, *Love, the Word, and Mercury*, it should be noted, presents a highly detailed, complex, and at times convincing symbolic reading of the poem.
28. Cf. Pearsall, "Gower's Narrative Art," p. 478n.10.
29. Lewis, *The Allegory of Love*, p. 200.
30. Peck, ed., *Confessio Amantis*, p. xxviii.
31. Lewis, *The Allegory of Love*, p. 214.
32. Peck, ed., *Confessio Amantis*, pp. xxv–xxvi. Peck's argument, pp. xxii–xxv, that incest is to be associated with "self-love and singular profit" and so with cupidinous love in general is unconvincing because the text nowhere makes this connection. His argument in *Kingship and Common Profit*, pp. 163–69, is somewhat more persuasive.
33. Peck, ed. *Confessio Amantis*, p. xix.
34. We must, I think, take "gentil love," as Venus uses the term here (8.2344), to mean love free of the "sondri vice" (line 2340) which offends Nature.
35. Schueler, "The Age of the Lover"; Gower's contemporary audience would probably have been much more aware of Amans-Gower's age than were later readers.
36. Bennett, "Gower's 'Honeste Love,'" p. 119, observes that "Only Gower would make his Venus...speak the language of reason."
37. This seems to be the position taken by Lewis, *The Allegory of Love*, pp. 218–20; and by Schueler, "Gower's Characterization of Genius," p. 246.
38. Cf. Coffman, "John Gower in His Most Significant Role"; Fisher, *John Gower*, pp. 154–203.

CHAPTER 7, Notes to pp. 119–147

1. F. N. Robinson, ed., *The Works of Geoffrey Chaucer*, 2d ed., pp. 309–10, 791–92; D. S. Brewer, ed., *The Parlement of Foulys*, pp. 2–3. All references are to Robinson's text except as noted.
2. Robert Worth Frank, Jr., "Structure and Meaning in the *Parlement of Foules*," *PMLA* 71 (1956): 534.
3. See Wolfgang Clemen, *Chaucer's Early Poetry*, p. 136n.2. Bertrand H. Bronson, *In Appreciation of Chaucer's Parlement of Foules*, p. 198, takes this line to mean that he is "in search of explicit information—perhaps on this same subject [i.e., love]—which he could turn to immediate account." A. J. Gilbert, "The Influence of Boethius on the *Parlement of Foulys*," *MÆ* 47 (1978): 293, suggests that the phrase

Notes

"may have a strong philosophical sense" and devotes a long footnote in support of his contention.

4. Brewer, ed., *The Parlement of Foulys*, p. 18.

5. References are to Frank Ernest Rockwood, ed., *Cicero's Tusculan Disputations, I, and Scipio's Dream*.

6. Clemen, *Chaucer's Early Poetry*, p. 134.

7. Brewer, *The Parlement of Foulys*, note to lines 57–58, suggests that Boethius, *Consolation* 2, pr. 7, "was probably in Chaucer's thought," in his description of the "lytel erthe" here.

8. See, e.g., Clemen, *Chaucer's Early Poetry*, p. 133. Brewer, ed., *The Parlement of Foulys*, reads "And disseyuable, & ful of harde grace," attributing Boethian influence to the line in his note.

9. Cf. Macrobius, *Commentary*, 2.11; Brewer, ed., *The Parlement of Foulys*, note to lines 67–68.

10. Cf. Robinson, ed. *Works*, note to line 80; J. A. W. Bennett, *The Parlement of Foules: An Interpretation*, pp. 41–44.

11. "Heaven, Hell and Earth" in lines 32–33 perhaps means simply "the cosmos"; in *The House of Fame* the narrator says that Scipio saw "Helle and erthe and paradys" (line 918).

12. A. C. Cawley, "Chaucer's Valentine: The *Parlement of Foules*," in A. C. Cawley, ed., *Chaucer's Mind and Art*, pp. 134–35.

13. Brewer, ed., *The Parlement of Foulys*, pp. 30–32, and note to line 113; Bennett, *The Parlement of Foules*, p. 56; Economou, *The Goddess Natura*, pp. 128–29, 137–39.

14. Robert W. Uphaus, "Chaucer's *Parlement of Foules*: Aesthetic Order and Individual Experience," *TSLL* 10 (1968): 349–58, makes this point very convincingly, drawing upon Suzanne Langer's distinction between "nondiscursive" form in art and "discursive projection."

15. Chaucer's principal source for the entire description, lines 169–294, is Boccaccio's *Teseida* 7, st. 50–66, which Brewer translates, *The Parlement of Foulys*, pp. 138–40. Echos of the *Roman* and Dante's *Commedia* are also present. See Robinson's notes, Brewer's introduction and notes, and Bennett, *The Parlement of Foules*, pp. 62–106, for more detailed commentary on the sources.

16. Cf. Economou, *The Goddess Natura*, p. 132.

17. Ibid., p. 134.

18. Brewer, ed. *The Parlement of Foulys*, note to line 214.

19. Cf. Economou, *The Goddess Natura*, p. 134.

20. Brewer, ed., *The Parlement of Foulys*, note to line 237.

21. Ibid., note to line 243.

22. On Priapus see especially Emerson Brown, Jr., "Priapus and the *Parlement of Foulys*," *SP* 72 (1975): 258–74.

23. Brewer, ed., *The Parlement of Foulys*, p. 30.

24. See ibid., notes to lines 283–94.

25. Dorothy Bethurum Loomis, "The Venus of Alanus de Insulis and the Venus of Chaucer," in James L. Rosier, ed., *Philological Essays: Studies in Old and Middle English Language and Literature in Honour of Herbert Dean Meritt*, pp. 192–93.

26. J. A. Kearney, "*The Parliament of Fowls*: The Narrator, the 'Certeyn Thyng' and the 'Commune Profyt,'" *Theoria* 45 (1975): 55–71, 61.

27. Cf. Clemen, *Chaucer's Early Poetry*, pp. 146–47.

28. Bennett, *The Parlement of Foules*, pp. 115–16.

29. Cf. Economou, *The Goddess Natura*, pp. 142–44. Economou's assertion that "those who seek sensuality for its own sake have been relegated to the temple and are excluded from the 'grene mede,'" as should become clear, distorts the relationship between the temple and the rest of the visionary locus.

30. See, e.g., Bronson, *In Appreciation*, pp. 212–14.

31. It seems fruitless and probably wrongheaded to attempt to identify the worm-, seed-, and waterfowl with particular social classes. The obvious social distinction here is that between the two secular estates, nobles and commons.

32. Frank, "Structure and Meaning," p. 538.

33. For similar views of the ultimate fulfillment of the common profit see, e.g., Economou, *The Goddess Natura*, pp. 148–50; Kearney, "*The Parliament of Fowls*," pp. 68–69.

34. On various aspects of time and harmony in the poem see especially Cawley, "Chaucer's Valentine"; John P. McCall, "The Harmony of Chaucer's *Parliament*," *ChauR* 5 (1970): 22–31; David Chamberlain, "The Music of the Spheres and *The Parlement of Foules*," *ChauR* 5 (1970): 32–56; Robert L. Entzminger, "The Pattern of Time in *The Parlement of Foules*," *JMRS* 5 (1975): 1–11.

35. For a similar view see Entzminger, "The Pattern of Time."

CHAPTER 8, Notes to pp. 151–168

1. *Pearl*, ed. E. V. Gordon. All references are to this edition. The poem cannot be dated with much confidence; Gordon, p. xliv, places it late in the period, ca. 1360–95, to which the entire group of poems by the anonymous poet is usually assigned.

2. Means, *The Consolatio Genre*, pp. 49–59. Means's criterion for "pure examples of the genre" is simply "poems in which the narrator is educated and consoled by a single instructor" (p. 49).

3. William Henry Schofield, "The Nature and Fabric of *The Pearl*," *PMLA* 19 (1904): 175–81.

4. John Conley, "*Pearl* and a Lost Tradition," *JEGP* 54 (1953): 332–47; reprinted in John Conley, ed., *The Middle English* Pearl: *Critical Essays*, pp. 50–72.

5. Piehler, *The Visionary Landscape*, pp. 144–62.

6. A. C. Spearing, *Medieval Dream-Poetry*, pp. 111–29. Barbara Nolan, *The Gothic Visionary Perspective*, pp. 124–204, acknowledges Boethius's influence upon a visionary tradition of the later Middle Ages which includes *Pearl* and *Piers Plowman*, but she places primary influence upon this tradition with twelfth-century spirituality.

7. The observations of Robert W. Ackerman, "The Pearl-Maiden and the Penny," *RPh* 17 (1964): 615–23; reprinted in Conley, ed., *The Middle English* Pearl, pp. 150–56, on *Pearl* and Guillaume Deguilleville's *Pèlerinage de vie humaine*, reveal a more profound sense of Boethian tradition than is usually found in interpretative studies of *Pearl*.

8. For summaries of earlier views on these subjects see *Pearl*, ed. Gordon, pp. xi–xxxvi; René Wellek, "The *Pearl*: An Interpretation of the Middle English Poem," *Studies in English by Members of the English Seminar of Charles University* (Prague) 4 (1933): 5–33; reprinted in Robert J. Blanch, ed., Sir Gawain *and* Pearl: *Critical Essays*, pp. 3–36.

9. Conley, "*Pearl* and a Lost Tradition," in Conley, ed., *The Middle English* Pearl, p. 63.

10. Piehler, *The Visionary Landscape*, p. 150.

Notes

11. A. R. Heiserman, "The Plot of *Pearl*," *PMLA* 80 (1965): 164–71.

12. The evidence is frequently rehearsed: imagery of and direct references to death pervade the poem; the narrator identifies the maiden as his lost pearl; his intense grief indicates paternal affection, as does his language in speaking of her and in addressing her; she was closely related to him (line 233); she was very young when she died (lines 411–12, 483–85); Norman Davis, "A Note on Pearl," *RES*, n.s. 17 (1966): 403–405; reprinted in Conley, ed., *The Middle English* Pearl, with additional material, demonstrates that line 1208 employs a formula used in medieval letters exclusively by a parent addressing a child.

13. Schofield, "The Nature and Fabric of *The Pearl*," devotes an appendix to *Olympia* as *Pearl*'s source. His argument is rejected by G. G. Coulton, "In Defence of 'Pearl,'" *MLR* 2 (1907): 39–43. See also *Pearl*, ed. Gordon, p. xxxv.

14. For a discussion of this theme, "an emphasis upon a ubiquitous sense of contrast between the nature of Heaven and the nature of Earth, the revelation of which seems. . . to be the poem's main purpose," see Wendell Stacy Johnson, "The Imagery and Diction of *The Pearl*: Toward an Interpretation," *ELH* 20 (1953): 161–80; reprinted in Conley, ed., *The Middle English* Pearl, pp. 27–49, 29.

15. On the imagery and symbolism of these lines and their development see especially Johnson, "Imagery and Diction"; Piehler, *The Visionary Landscape*, pp. 144–54; Stanton Hoffman, "The *Pearl*: Notes for an Interpretation," *MP* 58 (1960): 73–80; reprinted in Conley, ed., *The Middle English* Pearl, pp. 86–102; A. C. Spearing, "Symbolic and Dramatic Development in *Pearl*," *MP* 60 (1962): 1–12, reprinted in Conley, ed., *The Middle English* Pearl, p. 122–48; Blanch, ed., Sir Gawain *and* Pearl, pp. 98–119; Edward Vasta, "*Pearl*: Immortal Flowers and the Pearl's Decay," *JEGP* 66 (1967): 519–31, reprinted in Conley, ed., *The Middle English* Pearl, pp. 185–202; P. M. Kean, *The Pearl: An Interpretation*, pp. 3–88; Louis Blenkner, O.S.B., "The Pattern of Traditional Images in *Pearl*," *SP* 68 (1971): 26–49; Nolan, *The Gothic Visionary Perspective*, pp. 158–76.

16. Kean, *The Pearl*, pp. 89–113.

17. Cf. Charles Moorman, "The Role of the Narrator in *Pearl*," *MP* 53 (1955): 73–81; reprinted in Conley, ed., *The Middle English* Pearl, *Essays*, pp. 103–21. Moorman identifies it as the earthly paradise but gives little evidence to support this assertion. On the poem's loci see also John Finlayson, "*Pearl*: Vision and Landscape," *SP* 71 (1974): 314–43.

18. *Pearl*, ed. Gordon, pp. xviii–xix.

19. Moorman, "The Role of the Narrator in *Pearl*," pp. 104–105. Moorman does not mention Fergusson in this article but does so in his later *The Pearl-Poet*, pp. 41–42. At about the time that Moorman's article appeared, Fergusson's influence was also acknowledged by Marie Padgett Hamilton, "The Meaning of the Middle English *Pearl*," *PMLA* 70 (1955): 805–24; reprinted in Blanch, Sir Gawain *and* Pearl, pp. 37–59, 43–44.

20. Kean, *The Pearl*, p. 41, suggests that "kynde of Kryst" should be translated "Nature, through Christ," rather than "the nature of Christ." Another possibility is to read the entire line (55) "though Nature taught me comfort of Christ" (i.e., the comfort he offers). Either of these alternate readings would suggest that "kynde" refers back to the regeneration imagery of lines 25–36.

21. Conley, "*Pearl* and a Lost Tradition," pp. 63–71; Ian Bishop, Pearl *in Its Setting: A Critical Study of the Structure and Meaning of the Middle English Poem*, pp. 93–95, clarifies this distinction.

22. See also Sister Mary Vincent Hillman, "Some Debatable Words in *Pearl* and Its

Theme," *MLN* 60 (1945): 241–48; reprinted in Conley, ed., *The Middle English* Pearl, pp. 9–17, 9–11.

23. The use of the present-perfect tense (lines 63–64) in the midst of sentences cast in the past tense is supicious and perhaps indicates that we are hearing the voice of the narrator after he has experienced the entire vision.

24. As Louis Blenkner argues in "The Theological Structure of *Pearl*," *Traditio* 24 (1968): 43–75; reprinted in Conley, ed., *The Middle English* Pearl, pp. 220–71, 259–61.

25. Spearing, "Symbolic and Dramatic Development," in Conley, ed., *The Middle English* Pearl, pp. 145–48.

26. Milton R. Stern, "An Approach to the *Pearl*," *JEGP* 54 (1955): 684–92; reprinted in Conley, ed., *The Middle English* Pearl, pp. 73–85, 83–84n; Kean, *The Pearl*, pp. 227–37; Larry M. Sklute, "Expectation and Fulfillment in *Pearl*," *PQ* 52 (1973): 678–79.

27. Cf. Johnson, "Imagery and Diction," in Conley, ed., *The Middle English* Pearl, pp. 47–48; Piehler, *The Visionary Landscape*, pp. 152–53. Is it fanciful to recognize an intentional ambiguity in the syntax of lines 1207–10, with the antecedent of "þat" (line 1209) being both "Krysteʒ dere blessyng" (line 1208) and "hit" (i.e., the pearl; line 1207)?

28. Nolan, *The Gothic Visionary Perspective*, pp. 140–41, recognizes Lorris's importance in the development of the fallible narrator.

29. Sklute, "Expectation and Fulfillment in *Pearl*." See also Spearing, "Symbolic and Dramatic Development," and *The Gawain-Poet: A Critical Study*, pp. 96–170.

30. Bishop, Pearl *in Its Setting*, pp. 113–21. For a very full discussion of pearl symbolism, see Kean, *The Pearl*, pp. 138–72.

31. Blenkner, "The Pattern of Traditional Images in *Pearl*," pp. 48–49.

32. Bishop, Pearl *in Its Setting*, pp. 68–71.

33. For cogent arguments against *Pearl* as a total allegory see, e.g., Hoffman, "*The Pearl*: Notes for an Interpretation"; Spearing, "Symbolic and Dramatic Development," and *The Gawain-Poet*, pp. 128–37; Kean, *The Pearl*, passim; Bishop, Pearl *in Its Setting*, passim.

34. See, e.g., Sister Mary Madeleva, *Pearl: A Study in Spiritual Dryness*; D. W. Robertson, Jr., "The Pearl as Symbol," *MLN* 65 (1950): 155–61; reprinted in Conley, ed., *The Middle English* Pearl, pp. 18–26; Milton R. Stern, "An Approach to *Pearl*"; Marie Padget Hamilton, "The Meaning of the Middle English *Pearl*"; Louis Blenkner, O.S.B., "The Theological Structure of *Pearl*."

35. Blenkner, "The Theological Structure of *Pearl*," in Conley, ed., *The Middle English* Pearl, argues, rather more persuasively than most allegorists, that *Pearl's* narrative follows the pattern of the *Itinerarium mentis ad Deum* (*Journey of the Mind Toward God*) of Saint Bonaventura and other mystical theologians. Though he sees this pattern as the tropological level of the poem, it does not seem to me that *Pearl* thus becomes an allegory of an *Itinerarium*. The pattern is present, if at all, as a framework which helps to organize the literal narrative, and in fact the literal progress does not quite match the pattern. The narrator's repeated failures to understand what he hears and sees create an unresolved tension between the abstract pattern of the *Itinerarium* and his own experience, proving, perhaps, that one need not be a textbook mystic to achieve Christian faith.

CHAPTER 9, Notes to pp. 169–191

1. Robinson, ed., *Works*, p. 266.

Notes

2. Ibid.

3. James I. Wimsatt, *Chaucer and the French Love Poets: The Literary Background of the Book of the Duchess*, pp. 155–62. For references to earlier source studies see Wimsatt's notes and Robinson, ed., *Works*, p. 773.

4. Wimsatt, *Chaucer and the French Love Poets*, p. 103.

5. Ibid.; these poems are discussed in detail on pp. 103–26.

6. Bernard L. Jefferson, *Chaucer and the Consolation of Philosophy of Boethius*, p. 133.

7. D. W. Robertson, Jr., "The Historical Setting of Chaucer's *Book of the Duchess*," in John Esten Keller and John Mahoney, eds., *Mediaeval Studies in Honor of Urban Tigner Holmes, Jr.*, pp. 188–89. See also Gareth W. Dunleavy, "The Wound and the Comforter: The Consolations of Geoffrey Chaucer," *PLL* 3 (1967): 14–27.

8. Michael D. Cherniss, "The Boethian Dialogue in Chaucer's *Book of the Duchess*," *JEGP* 68 (1969): 655.

9. Especially John B. Friedman, "The Dreamer, the Whelp, and Consolation in the *Book of the Duchess*," *ChauR* 3 (1969): 145–62; Russell A. Peck, "Theme and Number in Chaucer's *Book of the Duchess*," in Alastair Fowler, ed., *Silent Poetry: Essays in Numerological Analysis*, pp. 73–115; Charles P. R. Tisdale, "Boethian 'Hert-Huntyng': The Elegiac Pattern of *The Book of the Duchess*," *ABR* 24 (1973): 365–80.

10. Bertrand H. Bronson, "The Book of the Duchess Reopened," *PMLA* 67 (1952): 863–81; reprinted in Edward Wagenknecht, ed., Chaucer: *Modern Essays in Criticism*, p. 278.

11. James M. Hill," *The Book of the Duchess*, Melancholy, and That Eight-Year Sickness," *ChauR* 9 (1974): 35–50, argues plausibly that the illness is a species of head melancholy, known in medieval medical lore, and that the physician is sleep itself.

12. Chrétien de Troyes, *Cligés*, ed. Alexandre Micha, lines 5627–46. Fenice is feigning illness, and her husband has summoned a doctor: "The emperor can wonder when she says that she will have only that doctor who knows how to restore her health easily whenever he wishes. . . . They think she speaks of God but they misunderstand badly, for she means no one but Cligés: he is her god, who can look after her or can cause her to die" (lines 5634–46). See also lines 638–49 for the lover-as-physician metaphor.

13. References are to Ovid, *Les Metamorphoses*, ed. Georges Lafaye, vol. 3, pp. 15–26. See Robinson, ed., *Works*, p. 773, for the reference to Machaut. James Wimsatt analyzes these and other sources in "The Sources of Chaucer's 'Seys and Alcyone,'" *MÆ* 36 (1967): 231–41, and *Chaucer and the French Love Poets*, pp. 113, 115–16.

14. The narrator does not suggest that he has done away with the metamorphosis — that is Chaucer's work. He merely indicates that he has abridged the words of Alcyone "in that swow" (line 215).

15. Wimsatt, *Chaucer and the French Love Poets*, pp. 24–26.

16. Marshall W. Stearns, "Chaucer Mentions a Book," *MLN* 57 (1942): 28–31. See also Wimsatt, *Chaucer and the French Love Poets*, pp. 84–85.

17. On the survival of classical literature and mythology in the Middle Ages see, e.g., E. R. Curtius, *European Literature and the Latin Middle Ages*, trans. Willard R. Trask; and Jean Seznec, *The Survival of the Pagan Gods*, trans. Barbara F. Sessions, pp. 11–147.

18. Clemen, *Chaucer's Early Poetry*, p. 39.

19. Bronson, "*The Book of the Duchess* Reopened," p. 281.

20. Friedman, "The Dreamer, the Whelp, and Consolation," ably discusses the

medieval traditions of dogs as guides, associated with the art of healing and possessed of special reasoning ability.

21. See, e.g., *PF* 316.

22. Nature's limitations in the realm of Christian theology explain, I think, why Chaucer can equate "unnatural" with "immoral" and at the same time speak of a period in history when men followed the "lawe of kinde" as a pagan era. Behavior according to the dictates of Nature is part, but only part, of a Christian way of life. This point, as we have seen, is at least implicit in Meun and Gower, but its corollary, that some "natural" behavior violates Christian morality, does not appear relevant to *The Book of the Duchess*.

23. R. M. Lumiansky, "The Bereaved Narrator in Chaucer's *The Book of the Duchess*," *TSE* 9 (1959): 14–21, comments upon the opposition between Nature's law and the Knight's grief. Robertson, "The Historical Setting," pp. 179–88, treats the Knight's grief as *tristitia*, the sin of worldly sorrow.

24. George Lyman Kittredge, *Chaucer and His Poetry*, pp. 51ff. Dissenting views are offered by W. H. French, "The Man in Black's Lyric," *JEGP* 56 (1957): 231–41; and John Lawlor, "The Pattern of Consolation in *The Book of the Duchess*," *Speculum* 31 (1956): 626–48.

25. Bronson, "*The Book of the Duchess* Reopened," p. 283.

26. Spearing, *Medieval Dream-Poetry*, p. 51, observes that "it would be highly abnormal in a medieval dream-poem for the dreamer and not an authority he meets in his dream to be the source of doctrine."

27. Citations from Chaucer's translation are to Robinson's edition, pp. 320–84.

28. "In extrema lectuli mei" (1, pr. 1).

29. "Uberum fructibus rationis segetem necant" (1, pr. 1).

30. "Nunc iacet effeto lumine mentis" (1, m. 2).

31. "Sed medicinae . . . tempus est quam querelae" (1, pr. 2).

32. "Lethargum patitur, communem illusarum mentium morbum" (1, pr. 2).

33. "Si operam medicantis exspectas, oportet uulnus detegas" (1, pr. 4).

34. "Nihilne te ipsa loci facies movet? . . . Talis habitus talisque uultus erat, cum tecum naturae secreta rimarer . . .?" (1, pr. 4).

35. "Anne adhuc eget ammonitione nec per se satis eminet fortunae in nos saeuientis asperitas?" (1, pr. 4). See also 1, m. 5.

36. "Quid ipse sis nosse desisti" (1, pr. 6).

37. See especially 1, pr. 5.

38. The narrator's remark that the Knight would be damned were he to commit suicide (lines 723ff.) of course implies the existence of a God who distributes rewards and punishments.

39. The narrator's references to these lovers further indicate that he recognizes the cause of the Knight's grief.

40. "Itaque non tam me loci huius quam tua facies mouet" (1, pr. 5).

41. "Speciosa quidem ista sunt, . . . oblitaque rhetoricae ac musicae melle dulcedinis tum tantum cum audiuntur oblectant, sed miseris malorum altior sensus est" (2, pr. 3).

42. "Ita est . . . haec enim nondum morbi tui remedia, sed adhuc contumacis aduersum curationem doloris fomenta quaedam sunt; nam quae in profundum sese penetrent cum tempestiuum fuerit ammouebo. Verumtamen ne te existimari miserum velis; an numerum modumque tuae felicitatis oblitus es?" (2, pr. 3).

43. See lines 536–38, cited above.

44. "Si numerum modumque laetorum tristiumue consideres, adhuc te felicem

Notes

negare non possis. Quodsi idcirco te fortunatum esse non aestimas, quoniam quae tunc laeta uidebantur abierunt, non est quod te miserum putes, quoniam quae nunc creduntur maesta praetereunt" (2, pr. 3).

45. D. W. Robertson, Jr., and Bernard F. Huppé, *Fruyt and Chaf: Studies in Chaucer's Allegories*, p. 83.

46. Kittredge, *Chaucer and His Poetry*, pp. 52–53; Bronson, "*The Book of the Duchess* Reopened," pp. 287–89; James R. Kreuzer, "The Dreamer in the *Book of the Duchess*," *PMLA* 66 (1951): 543–47. Clemen, *Chaucer's Early Poetry*, pp. 44–47, and Lawlor, "The Pattern of Consolation," p. 647, suggest that he is only partly consoled. D. W. Robertson, Jr., *A Preface to Chaucer*, p. 464, says that he "recognizes the providential order" at the end of the dream, but in "The Historical Setting," p. 186, he suggests that he is not consoled.

47. "Vera, . . . commemoras, o uirtutum omnium nutrix, nec infitiari possum prosperitatis meae uelocissimum cursum. Sed hod est quod recolentem uehementius coquit; nam in omni aduersitate fortunae infelicissimum est genus infortunii fuisse felicem" (2, pr. 4).

48. "What is surprising is that the Black Knight fails to see the wider implications of what he has said. He has been lamenting the loss of Blanche as a physical being, a gift of Fortune. But the virtues he has described have nothing to do with Fortune and cannot be destroyed by anything Fortune may do. This fact could hardly have escaped Chaucer's audience, and did not escape the Black Knight's interrogator, who remarked, 'Hardely, your love was well beset; / I not how ye myghte have do bet.' A lady of such virtue is truly loveable" (Robertson, "The Historical Setting," pp. 187–88).

49. "Adeo ut iam me posthac imparem fortunae ictibus esse non arbitrer" (3, pr. 1).

50. "Manet etiam spectator desuper cunctorum praescius deus uisionisque eius praesens semper aeternitas cum nostrorum actuum futura qualitate concurrit bonis praemia malis supplicia dispensans. Nec frustra sunt in deo positae spes precesque, quae cum rectae sunt inefficaces esse non possunt. Auersamini igitur uitia, colite uirtutes, ad rectas spes animum subleuate, humiles preces in excelsa porrigite" (5, pr. 6).

51. The Knight has no future since his existence ends with the dream. The narrator returns to "real," though fictional, life.

52. Kittredge, *Chaucer and His Poetry*, p. 39, and French, "The Man in Black's Lyric," pp. 231–41, speak of the Knight as if he were literally John of Gaunt. J. S. P. Tatlock, *The Mind and Art of Chaucer*, pp. 28–29; Kemp Malone, *Chapters on Chaucer*, p. 37; Bronson, "*The Book of the Duchess* Reopened," pp. 273–77; and Clemen, *Chaucer's Early Poetry*, p. 45, take him to be a conventional, idealized figure who stands for John. Lumiansky, "The Bereaved Narrator," pp. 16–17, denies that he represents John but does not identify him. Robertson, "The Historical Setting," pp. 178–86, argues that he represents all those people who mourned Blanche immoderately.

53. Robinson, ed., *Works*, p. 775.

54. Robertson, *A Preface to Chaucer*, p. 463.

55. On Chaucer's portrait of the lady see esp. Bronson, "*The Book of the Duchess* Reopened," pp. 273–77; Clemen, *Chaucer's Early Poetry*, pp. 54–57; Robertson, "The Historical Setting," pp. 186–88; Stephen Manning, "Chaucer's Good Fair White: Woman and Symbol," *CL* 10 (1958): 97–105.

56. Wimsatt, *Chaucer and the French Love Poets*, pp. 97–102.

57. James I. Wimsatt, "The Apotheosis of Blanche in *The Book of the Duchess*," *JEGP* 66 (1967): 26–44.

58. Friedman, "The Dreamer, the Whelp, and Consolation."

CHAPTER 10, Notes to pp. 193–210

1. The most recent editions of *The Kingis Quair* are those of John Norton-Smith and Matthew McDiarmid (see Bibliography, under James I of Scotland). Both contain discussions of the poem's authorship and date. The discussion here is based upon McDiarmid's text.

2. John Preston, "Fortunys Exiltree: A Study of *The Kingis Quair*," *RES*, n.s., 7 (1956): 239–47.

3. The most provocative of these analyses are Walter Scheps, "Chaucerian Synthesis: The Art of *The Kingis Quair*," *SSL* 8 (1971): 143–65; and Lois A. Ebin, "Boethius, Chaucer and *The Kingis Quair*," *PQ* 53 (1974): 321–41.

4. See James I of Scotland, *The Kingis Quair*, ed. Norton-Smith, pp. xi–xvii and notes; James I of Scotland, *The Kingis Quair of James Stewart*, ed. McDiarmid, pp. 36–38 and notes; and John MacQueen, "Tradition and Interpretation of the *Kingis Quair*," *RES*, n.s., 12 (1961): 117–31, especially pp. 125–30.

5. James I of Scotland, *The Kingis Quair of James Stewart*, ed. McDiarmid, pp. 48–50.

6. James I of Scotland, *The Kingis Quair*, ed. Norton-Smith, notes to lines 1–7.

7. James I of Scotland, *The Kingis Quair of James Stewart*, ed. McDiarmid, p. 50.

8. Lines 1334–66 in John Lydgate, *Poems*, ed. John Norton-Smith, pp. 67–112. All references are to this edition.

9. James I of Scotland, *The Kingis Quair*, ed. Norton-Smith, note to line 91.

10. Youth is conceived of as the period from seven to fifteen years of age. See McDiarmid's note to stanza 15.

11. Preston, "Fortunys Exiltree," p. 342, suggests that the nautical language here recalls *Consolation* 1, m. 2, lines 1–7.

12. McDiarmid in his glossary renders "prolixitee of doubilnesse" as "prolixity of complexity (or deceitfulness)." Norton-Smith offers "deceitful prolixity" in his note to lines 120–21. MacQueen, "Tradition and Interpretation," p. 124, takes it to mean "the extended allegorical narrative upon which the author feels that he is embarking." Perhaps "burden of complexity" might better suggest the meaning of this troublesome phrase.

13. Mary Rhorburger, "*The Kingis Quair*: An Evaluation," *TSLL* 2 (1960): 292–302, and Lois A. Ebin, "Boethius, Chaucer and *The Kingis Quair*," especially pp. 337–41, discuss the importance of the process of writing in the overall structure of the poem.

14. James I of Scotland, *The Kingis Quair of James Stewart*, ed. McDiarmid, note to stanzas 20–21.

15. Peter Dronke, "L'amor che move il sole e l'altre stelle," *SMed* 6, no. 1 (1965): 389–422. On the philosophical background of this dichotomy see also Arthur O. Lovejoy, *The Great Chain of Being*, chaps. 2, 3.

16. Andrew von Hendy, "The Free Thrall: A Study of *The Kingis Quair*," *SSL* 2 (1965): 142.

17. See James I of Scotland, *The Kingis Quair*, ed. Norton-Smith and McDiarmid, notes.

Notes

18. Von Hendy, "The Free Thrall," pp. 145–46, correctly observes that these "groups represent the abstract possibilities of fortune in love," but his analogy to Heaven, Hell, and Purgatory is not convincing. There are, after all, four groups; he places the first two (st. 83–85, 86–87) in "Heaven," the third (st. 88–89) in "Purgatory," and the fourth, least fortunate, in "Hell" (st. 90–93).

19. Cf. *The Temple of Glas* 1194–97, 1201–1204: "But tyme shal come þou shalt for þi sufferaunce / Be wele apaide and take for þi mede / Thi liues ioy and al þi suffisaunce, / So þat goode hope alway þi bridel lede.... / Eche houre and tyme, weke, dai and ȝere, / Be iliche feithful and varie not for lite. / Abide awhile, and þan of þi desire / The time neigheth þat shal þe most delite."

20. Venus's inability to control the worldly circumstances of lovers appears to be derived from Lydgate, *The Temple of Glas*, especially lines 1040–1361.

21. *The Court of Sapience*, ed. E. Ruth Harvey.

22. Ebin, "Boethius, Chaucer, and *The Kingis Quair*," pp. 332–37, draws attention to this distinction between Minerva and Philosophy. It should be noted, however, that this distinction might have been lost upon James and his audience, since commentators upon the *Consolation* from Alcuin on had frequently identified Philosophy as Divine Wisdom, Sapientia. See Courcelle, *La Consolation de philosophie*, pp. 29–66.

23. James I of Scotland, *The Kingis Quair of James Stewart*, ed. McDiarmid, pp. 58–59.

24. E.g.: "We can, therefore, safely conclude that the essence of God is to be found in the good, and nowhere else" (3, pr. 10). "'Well then,' she continued, 'the highest good is proposed equally to good and bad men. Good men seek it by the natural means of the virtues; evil men, however, try to achieve the same goal by a variety of concupiscences, and that is surely an unnatural way of seeking the good'" (4, pr. 2).

25. It seems a bit odd that Divine Wisdom should have to appeal to mere worldly Fortune for help; apparently what James wishes to suggest here is that, since worldly events (*auenturis*) are unpredictable, the wisest course available to one whose worldly happiness depends upon the favorable outcome of such events is to hope for good fortune.

26. Note to st. 152.

27. MacQueen, "Tradition and Interpretation," pp. 121–24, calls attention to the close relationship of Fortune and Nature in this context.

28. James I of Scotland, *The Kingis Quair of James Stewart*, ed. McDiarmid, note to st. 171.

29. "O how happy the human race would be, if that love which rules the heavens ruled also your souls" (*Consolation* 2, m. 8, lines 28–30).

30. On the circularity of the poem's structure see MacQueen, "Tradition and Interpretation," pp. 127–28.

CHAPTER 11, Notes to pp. 211–231

1. Robert Henryson, *Testament of Cresseid*, ed. Denton Fox, p. 1. All references are to this edition. See pp. 16–20 for a discussion of authorship and date.

2. Spearing, *Medieval Dream-Poetry*, p. 182 .

3. E. Duncan Aswell, "The Role of Fortune in *The Testament of Cresseid*," *PQ* 46 (1967): 485.

Boethian Apocalypse

4. E. M. W. Tillyard, *Five Poems: 1470–1870*, pp. 5–29; Marshall W. Stearns, *Robert Henryson*; John MacQueen, *Robert Henryson: A Study of the Major Narrative Poems*, pp. 45–93; Henryson, *Testament of Cresseid*, ed Fox, pp. 20–58; Aswell, "The Role of Fortune"; Dolores L. Noll, "*The Testament of Cresseid*: Are Christian Interpretations Valid?" *SSL* 9 (1971): 16–25; Larry M. Sklute, "Phoebus Descending: Rhetoric and Moral Vision in Henryson's *Testament of Cresseid*," *ELH* 44 (1977): 189–204; C. David Benson, "Troilus and Cresseid in Henryson's *Testament*," *ChauR* 13 (1979): 263–71.

5. E.g., Douglas Duncan, "Henryson's *Testament of Cresseid*," *EIC* 11 (1961): 128–35; A. C. Spearing, "Conciseness and *The Testament of Cresseid*," in *Criticism and Medieval Poetry*, pp. 118–44; Lee W. Patterson, "Christian and Pagan in *The Testament of Cresseid*," *PQ* 52 (1973): 696–714; John McNamara, "Divine Justice in Henryson's *Testament of Cresseid*," *SSL* 11 (1973): 99–107.

6. Henryson, *Testament of Cresseid*, ed. Fox, pp. 50–51.

7. Sklute, "Phoebus Descending," pp. 200–201, argues that the narrator is here accepting mere gossip about Cresseid, but certainly the gossip is confirmed by her dream and her leprosy. The phrase "sum men sayis" (line 77), if it is not simply metrical filler, may be meant to express the narrator's reluctance to believe that Cresseid would descend to such behavior.

8. Note to line 104.

9. MacQueen, *Robert Henryson*, p. 61.

10. We cannot know precisely how old Cresseid is in Henryson's poem; both he and Chaucer are deliberately vague on the subject. But certainly she is well past the prime of her youth.

11. On the conflation of these two figures, see Patch, *The Goddess Fortuna*, pp. 90–98.

12. Stearns, *Robert Henryson*, pp. 70–96.

13. Aswell, "The Role of Fortune," pp. 474–82, 475.

14. Ibid., p. 476.

15. Ibid., p. 478.

16. That Cupid here takes credit for Cresseid's success in love, coupled with the description of Venus as the goddess of "fleschelie paramour," perhaps indicates that he represents a more complex sort of love, which grows out of the basically sexual desire represented by his mother.

17. Henryson, *Testament of Cresseid*, ed. Fox, pp. 23–37, provides a full discussion of Cresseid's leprosy and its various implications.

18. MacQueen, *Robert Henryson*, p. 70.

19. C. David Benson's argument that Henryson's portrayal of Troilus is ironic, that he "exemplifies a system of worldly values" which the Christian reader—and finally Cresseid—rejects, while persuasive in part, seems to me finally unconvincing. The poem, after all, focuses upon Cresseid, not Troilus, whose character is implied rather than analyzed here. Benson, "Troilus and Cresseid in Henryson's *Testament*."

20. See Henryson, *Testament of Cresseid*, ed., Fox, pp. 25–26; MacQueen, *Robert Henryson*, p. 91.

21. Henryson, *Testament of Cresseid*, ed. Fox, pp. 47–48.

22. Sklute, "Phoebus Descending," p. 197.

23. McNamara, "Divine Justice." McNamara offers an excellent discussion of the necessary distinction between the poem's Christian audience and its pagan characters.

24. I think we may assume that, despite Cresseid's belief that Diomede still has the

Notes

"broche and belt," Deiphebe has already recovered them in battle, and so Troilus knows of her infidelity. *TC* 5.1646–66.

25. *The Assembly of Gods*, ed. Oscar Lovell Triggs, EETS, e.s., vol. 69.

26. See chap. 10, n. 21.

27. John Skelton, *Complete Poems*, ed. John Scattergood, pp. 46–61, 312–58.

28. Gavin Douglas, *The Shorter Poems of Gavin Douglas*, ed. Priscilla Bawcutt, STS, vol. 4, no. 3, pp. 1–133.

BIBLIOGRAPHY

Ackerman, Robert W. "The Pearl-Maiden and the Penny." *RPh* 17 (1964): 615–23. Reprinted in John Conley, ed. *The Middle English* Pearl: *Critical Essays*, pp. 149–62.

Alanus de Insulis. *Anticlaudianus*. Edited by R. Bossuat. Paris: Vrin, 1955. Translated by James J. Sheridan. Toronto: Pontifical Institute of Mediaeval Studies, 1973.

————. "*De planctu naturae*." Edited by Nikolaus M. Häring. *SMed* 19 (1978): 797–879. Translated (*The Plaint of Nature*) by James J. Sheridan. Toronto: Pontifical Institute of Mediaeval Studies, 1980.

————. *De planctu naturae, The Complaint of Nature*. Translated from the edition of Thomas Wright by Douglas M. Moffatt. Yale Studies in English, vol. 36. New York: Henry Holt, 1908

The Assembly of Gods. Edited by Oscar Lovell Triggs. EETS, e.s., vol. 69. London: Kegan Paul, Trench, Trubner, 1896.

Aswell, E. Duncan. "The Role of Fortune in *The Testament of Cresseid*." *PQ* 46 (1967): 471–87.

Barrett, H. M. *Boethius: Some Aspects of His Times and Works*. Cambridge: Cambridge University Press, 1940.

Bennett, J. A. W. "Gower's 'Honeste Love.'" In John Lawlor, ed. *Patterns of Love and Courtesy: Essays in Memory of C. S. Lewis*. London: Edward Arnold, 1966, pp. 107–21.

————. *The Parlement of Foules: An Interpretation*. Oxford: Clarendon Press, 1957.

Benson, C. David. "Troilus and Cresseid in Henryson's *Testament*." *ChauR* 13 (1979): 263–71.

Bishop, Ian. Pearl *in Its Setting: A Critical Study of the Structure and Meaning of the Middle English Poem*. New York: Barnes and Noble, 1968.

Blanch, Robert J., ed. Sir Gawain *and* Pearl*: Critical Essays*. Bloomington: Indiana University Press, 1966.

Blenkner, Louis, O.S.B. "The Pattern of Traditional Images in *Pearl*." *SP* 68 (1971): 26–49.

———. "The Theological Structure of *Pearl*." *Traditio* 24 (1968): 43–75. Reprinted in John Conley, ed. *The Middle English* Pearl*: Critical Essays*, pp. 220–71.

Boethius. *The Consolation of Philosophy*. Translated by Richard H. Green. Indianapolis: Bobbs-Merrill, 1962.

———. *Philosophiae Consolatio*. Edited by Ludovicus Bieler. Corpus Christianorum, ser. lat., vol. 94. Turnholti: Typographi Brepols Editores Pontificii, 1957.

Bramble, H. David. "The Role of Genius in the *De planctu naturae* of Alanus de Insulis." *C&M* 31 (1970): 306–23.

Brewer, D. S. *The Parlement of Foulys*. New York: Barnes and Noble, 1972.

Bronson, Bertrand H. "*The Book of the Duchess* Reopened." *PMLA* 67 (1952): 863–81. Reprinted in Edward Wagenknecht, ed. *Chaucer: Modern Essays in Criticism*. New York: Oxford University Press, 1959, pp. 271–94.

———. "In Appreciation of Chaucer's *Parlement of Foules*." *University of California Publications in English* 3, no. 5 (1935): 193–223. Berkeley: University of California Press.

Brown, Emerson, Jr. "Priapus and the *Parlement of Foulys*." *SP* 72 (1975): 258–74.

Cawley, A. C. "Chaucer's Valentine: The *Parlement of Foules*." In A. C. Cawley, ed. *Chaucer's Mind and Art*. Edinburgh: Oliver & Boyd, 1969, pp. 125–39.

Cairns, Francis. *Generic Composition in Greek and Roman Poetry*. Edinburgh: Edinburgh University Press, 1972.

Chadwick, Henry. *Boethius: The Consolations of Music, Logic, Theology, and Philosophy*. Oxford: Clarendon Press, 1981.

Chamberlain, David. "The Music of the Spheres and *The Parlement of Foules*." *ChauR* 5 (1970): 32–56.

Chaucer, Geoffrey. *The Works of Geoffrey Chaucer*. 2d ed. Edited by F. N. Robinson. Boston: Houghton Mifflin, 1957.

———. *The Parlement of Foulys*. Edited by D. S. Brewer. New York: Barnes and Noble, 1972.

Cherniss, Michael D. "The Boethian Dialogue in Chaucer's *Book of the Duchess*." *JEGP* 68 (1969): 655–65.

Chrétien de Troyes. *Cligés*. Edited by Alexandre Micha. Les Classiques Français du Moyen Âge. Paris: H. Champion, 1957.

Bibliography

Cicero. *Cicero's Tusculan Disputations, I, and Scipio's Dream*. 1903. Reprint, Norman: University of Oklahoma Press, 1966.

Clemen, Wolfgang. *Chaucer's Early Poetry*. London: Methuen, 1963.

Coffman, George R. "John Gower, Mentor for Royalty: Richard II." *PMLA* 69 (1954): 953–64.

———. "John Gower in His Most Significant Role." In *Elizabethan Studies and Other Essays in Honor of George F. Reynolds*. University of Colorado Studies, series B, vol. 2. Boulder: University of Colorado Press, 1945, pp. 52–61.

Conley, John, ed. *The Middle English* Pearl: *Critical Essays*. Notre Dame, Ind.: University of Notre Dame Press, 1970.

———. "Pearl and a Lost Tradition." *JEGP* 54 (1953): 332–47. Reprinted in John Conley, ed. *The Middle English* Pearl: *Critical Essays*, pp. 50–72.

Coulton, G. G. "In Defence of 'Pearl.'" *MLR* 2 (1907): 39–43.

Courcelle, Pierre. *La Consolation de philosophie dans la tradition littéraire: Antécédents et posterité de Boèce*. Paris: Études Augustiniennes, 1967.

The Court of Sapience. Edited by E. Ruth Harvey. Toronto: University of Toronto Press, 1984.

Crabbe, Anna. "Literary Design in the *De consolatione philosophiae*." In Margaret Gibson, ed. *Boethius: His Life, Thought and Influence*, pp. 244–51.

Crespo, Roberto. "Il Prologo a la traduzione della *Consolatio philosophiae* di Jean de Meun e il commento di Guglielmo d'Aragonia." In W. den Boer et al, eds. *Romanitas et Christianitas: Studia I. H. Waszink oblata*. Amsterdam: North-Holland, 1973.

Curtius, Ernst Robert. *European Literature and the Latin Middle Ages*. Translated by Willard R. Trask. New York: Harper and Row, 1953.

Dahlberg, Charles. "Love and the Roman de la Rose." *Speculum* 44 (1969): 568–84.

———. "Macrobius and the Unity of the *Roman de la Rose*." *SP* 58 (1961): 573–82.

———, trans. *The Romance of the Rose*. Princeton, N.J.: Princeton University Press, 1971.

Dante Alighieri. *La divina commedia*, ed. C. H. Grandgent. Rev. Charles S. Singleton. Cambridge, Mass: Harvard University Press, 1972.

Davis, Norman. "A Note on Pearl." *RES*, n.s., 17 (1966): 403–405. Reprinted in John Conley, ed. *The Middle English* Pearl: *Critical Essays*, pp. 325–34.

Dedeck-Hery, V. L., ed. "Boethius' *De consolatione* by Jean de Meun." *MS* 14 (1952): 168–71.

Douglas, Gavin. *The Shorter Poems of Gavin Douglas*. Edited by Priscilla Bawcutt. STS, vol. 4, no. 3. Edinburgh: William Blackwood, 1967.

Dronke, Peter. "L'amor che move il sole e l'altre stelle." *SMed* 6, no. 1 (1965): 389–422.

———. Review of Pierre Courcelle. *La Consolation de philosophie*. *Speculum* 44 (1969): 123–28.

Duncan, Douglas. "Henryson's *Testament of Cresseid*." *EIC* 11 (1961): 128–35.

Dunleavy, Gareth W. "The Wound and the Comforter: The Consolations of Geoffrey Chaucer." *PLL* 3 (1967): 14–27.

Eberle, Patricia J. "The Lover's Glass: Nature's Discourse on Optics and the Optical Design of the *Romance of the Rose*." *UTQ* 46 (1977): 241–62.

Ebin, Lois A. "Boethius, Chaucer, and *The Kingis Quair*." *PQ* 53 (1974): 321–41.

Economou, George D. "The Character Genius in Alain de Lille, Jean de Meun, and John Gower." *ChauR* 4 (1970): 203–10.

———. *The Goddess Natura in Medieval Literature*. Cambridge, Mass.: Harvard University Press, 1972.

Entzminger, Robert L. "The Pattern of Time in *The Parlement of Foules*." *JMRS* 5 (1975): 1–11.

Finlayson, John. "*Pearl*: Vision and Landscape." *SP* 71 (1974): 314–43.

Fisher, John. *John Gower: Moral Philosopher and Friend of Chaucer*. New York: New York University Press, 1964.

Fleming, John V. *The* Roman de la Rose: *A Study in Allegory and Iconography*. Princeton, N.J.: Princeton University Press, 1969.

Fletcher, Angus. *Allegory: The Theory of a Symbolic Mode*. Ithaca, N.Y.: Cornell University Press, 1964.

Frank, Robert Worth, Jr. "The Art of Reading Medieval Personification-Allegory." *ELH* 20 (1953): 237–50.

———. "Structure and Meaning in the *Parlement of Foules*." *PMLA* 71 (1956): 530–39.

French, W. H. "The Man in Black's Lyric." *JEGP* 56 (1957): 231–41.

Friedman, John B. "The Dreamer, the Whelp, and Consolation in the *Book of the Duchess*." *ChauR* 3 (1969): 145–62.

Friedman, Lionel J. "'Jean de Meung,' Antifeminism, and 'Bourgeois Realism.'" *MP* 57 (1959): 13–23.

Frye, Northrop. *Anatomy of Criticism: Four Essays*. Princeton, N.J.: Princeton University Press, 1957.

Fulgentius (Fabius Planciadis Fulgentii V.C.). *Opera*. Edited by Rudolfus Helm. Leipzig: B. G. Teubner, 1898.

Gallacher, Patrick J. *Love, the Word, and Mercury: A Reading of John*

Bibliography

Gower's Confessio Amantis. Albuquerque: University of New Mexico Press, 1975.

Gibson, Margaret, ed. *Boethius: His Life, Thought and Influence*. Oxford: Basil Blackwell, 1981.

Gilbert, A. J. "The Influence of Boethius on the *Parlement of Foulys*." *MÆ* 47 (1978): 292–303.

Gower, John. See under Macaulay, G. C., ed.; Peck, Russell A., ed.

Green, Richard Hamilton. "Alan of Lille's *De planctu naturae*." *Speculum* 31 (1956): 649–74.

Gunn, Alan M. F. *The Mirror of Love: A Reinterpretation of the "Romance of the Rose."* Lubbock, Tex.: Texas Tech Press, 1952.

———. "Teacher and Student in the *Roman de la Rose*: A Study in Archetypal Figures and Patterns." *ECr* 2 (1962): 126–34.

Hamilton, Marie Padgett. "The Meaning of the Middle English *Pearl*." *PMLA* 70 (1955): 805–24. Reprinted in Robert J. Blanch, ed. Sir Gawain *and* Pearl: *Critical Essays*, pp. 37–59.

Heiserman, A. R. "The Plot of *Pearl*." *PMLA* 80 (1965): 164–71.

Hendy, Andrew von. "The Free Thrall: A Study of *The Kingis Quair*." *SSL* 2 (1965): 141–51.

Henryson, Robert. *Testament of Cresseid*. Edited by Denton Fox. London: Thomas Nelson and Sons, 1968.

Hermas, *Le pasteur*. Edited by Robert Joly. Sources Chrétiens, vol. 53. Paris: Les Editions du Cerf, 1958.

Hill, James M. "The *Book of the Duchess*, Melancholy, and That Eight-Year Sickness." *ChauR* 9 (1974): 35–50.

Hillman, Sister Mary Vincent. "Some Debatable Words in *Pearl* and Its Theme." *MLN* 60 (1945): 241–48. Reprinted in John Conley, ed. *The Middle English* Pearl: *Critical Essays*, pp. 9–17.

Hoffman, Stanton. "The *Pearl*: Notes for an Interpretation." *MP* 58 (1960): 73–80. Reprinted in John Conley, ed. *The Middle English* Pearl: *Critical Essays*, pp. 86–102.

Isidore of Seville (Isidori Hispalensis Episcopi). *Etymologiarum sive Originum Libri XX*. Edited by W. M. Lindsay. Oxford: Clarendon Press, 1911.

James I of Scotland. *The Kingis Quair of James Stewart*. Edited by Matthew McDiarmid. Totowa, N.J.: Rowman and Littlefield, 1973.

———. *The Kingis Quair*. Edited by John Norton-Smith. Oxford: Clarendon Press, 1971.

Jefferson, Bernard L. *Chaucer and the Consolation of Philosophy of Boethius*. Princeton, N.J.: Princeton University Press, 1917.

Johannes de Hauvilla. *Architrenius*. Edited by Paul Gerhard Schmidt. Munich: Wilhelm Fink, 1974.

———. *Architrenius*. In Thomas Wright, ed. *The Anglo-Latin Satirical Poets of the Twelfth Century*. Rolls Series, vol. 59, no. 1. London: Longman, 1872. Vol. 1, pp. 240–392.

Johnson, Wendell Stacy. "The Imagery and Diction of *The Pearl*: Toward an Interpretation." *ELH* 20 (1953): 161–80. Reprinted in John Conley, ed. *The Middle English* Pearl: *Critical Essays*, pp. 27–49.

Jung, Marc-René. *Études sur le poème allégorique en France au Moyen Âge*. Romanica Helvetica, vol. 82. Berne: Francke, 1971.

Kean, P. M. *The Pearl: An Interpretation*. London: Routledge & Kegan Paul, 1967.

Kearney, J. A. "*The Parliament of Fowls*: The Narrator, the 'Certeyn Thyng' and the 'Commune Profyt.'" *Theoria* 45 (1975): 55–71.

Kittredge, George Lyman. *Chaucer and His Poetry*. Cambridge, Mass.: Harvard University Press, 1915.

Klingner, Fredericus. *De Boethii Consolatione Philosophiae*. Philolgische Untersuchungen, edited by A. Kiessling and U. v. Wilamowitz-Moellendorff, vol. 27. Berlin: Weidmannsche Buchhandlung, 1921.

Knowlton, E. C. "The Allegorical Figure Genius." *Classical Philology* 15 (1920): 380–84.

———. "Genius as an Allegorical Figure." *MLN* 39 (1924): 89–95.

Kreuzer, James R. "The Dreamer in the *Book of the Duchess*." *PMLA* 66 (1951): 543–47.

Lage, G. Raynaud de. *Alain de Lille, poète du XIIᵉ siècle*. Université de Montréal Publications de l'Institut d'Études Mediévales, vol. 12. Montreal, 1951.

Langlois, Ernest. *Origines et sources du* Roman de la Rose. Paris: E. Thorin, 1891.

———, ed. *Roman de la Rose*. See under Guillaume de Lorris and Jean de Meun.

Lawlor, John. "The Pattern of Consolation in *The Book of the Duchess*." *Speculum* 31 (1956): 626–48.

Lewis, C. S. *The Allegory of Love*. 1936. Reprint, New York: Oxford University Press, 1958.

———. "Genius and Genius." *RES* (1936). Reprinted in C. S. Lewis. *Studies in Medieval and Renaissance Literature*. Cambridge: Cambridge University Press, 1966, pp. 169–74.

Liber Fortunae. Edited by John L. Grigsby. University of California Publications in Modern Philology, vol. 81. Berkeley and Los Angeles: University of California Press, 1967.

Loomis, Dorothy Bethurum. "The Venus of Alanus de Insulis and the Venus

Bibliography

of Chaucer." In James L. Rosier, ed. *Philological Essays: Studies in Old and Middle English Language and Literature in Honour of Herbert Dean Meritt*. The Hague: Mouton, 1970, pp. 182–95.

Lorris, Guillaume de, and Jean de Meun. *Le Roman de la Rose*. Edited by Ernest Langlois. 5 vols. SATF, no. 63. Paris: Didot, Champion, 1914–24.

——. *Le Roman de la Rose*. Edited by Félix Lecoy. Les Classiques Français du Moyen Âge, vols. 92, 95, 98. Paris: Librairie Honoré Champion, 1965–70.

Lovejoy, Arthur O. *The Great Chain of Being*. Cambridge, Mass.: Harvard University Press, 1936.

Lumiansky, R. M. "The Bereaved Narrator in Chaucer's *The Book of the Duchess*." *TSE* 9 (1959): 14–21.

Lydgate, John. *Poems*. Edited by John Norton-Smith. Oxford: Clarendon Press, 1966.

McCall, John P. "The Harmony of Chaucer's *Parliament*." *ChauR* 5 (1970): 22–31.

Macaulay, G. C., ed. *The English Works of John Gower*. 2 vols. EETS, e.s., vols. 81, 82. London: Kegan Paul, Trench, Trübner, 1900.

McNamara, John. "Divine Justice in Henryson's *Testament of Cresseid*." *SSL* 11 (1973): 99–107.

MacQueen, John. *Robert Henryson: A Study of the Major Narrative Poems*. Oxford: Clarendon Press, 1967.

——. "Tradition and Interpretation of the *Kingis Quair*." *RES*, n.s., vol. 12 (1961): 117–31.

Macrobius. *Commentary on the Dream of Scipio*. Translated by William Harris Stahl. New York: Columbia University Press, 1952.

Madeleva, Sister Mary. *Pearl: A Study in Spiritual Dryness*. New York: D. Appleton, 1925.

Malone, Kemp. *Chapters in Chaucer*. Baltimore, Md.: Johns Hopkins Press, 1951.

Manning, Stephen. "Chaucer's Good Fair White: Woman and Symbol." *CL* 10 (1958): 97–105.

Means, Michael H. *The Consolatio Genre in Medieval English Literature*. Gainesville: University of Florida Press, 1972.

Minnis, Alastair. "Aspects of the Medieval French and English Traditions of the *De consolatione philosophiae*." In Margaret Gibson, ed. *Boethius*, pp. 324–34.

Moorman, Charles. *The Pearl-Poet*. New York: Twayne Publishers, 1968.

——. "The Role of the Narrator in *Pearl*." *MP* 53 (1955): 73–81. Reprinted in John Conley, ed. *The Middle English* Pearl: *Critical Essays*, pp. 103–21.

Muscatine, Charles. "Locus of Action in Medieval Narrative." *RPh* 17 (1963–64): 115–22.

Nitzsche, Jane Chance. *The Genius Figure in Antiquity and the Middle Ages.* New York: Columbia University Press, 1975.

Nolan, Barbara. *The Gothic Visionary Perspective.* Princeton, N.J.: Princeton University Press, 1977.

Noll, Dolores L. "*The Testament of Cresseid*: Are Christian Interpretations Valid?" *SSL* 9 (1971): 16–25.

Ovid, *Les Metamorphoses.* Edited by George Lafaye. Paris: Les Belles Lettres, 1930.

Paré, Gerard. *Les Idées et les lettres au XIIIe siècle: Le Roman de la Rose.* Montreal: Université de Montreal, 1947.

Patch, Howard R. *The Goddess Fortuna in Medieval Literature.* Cambridge, Mass.: Harvard University Press, 1927.

———. *The Tradition of Boethius: A Study of His Importance in Medieval Culture.* New York: Oxford University Press, 1935.

Patterson, Lee W. "Christian and Pagan in *The Testament of Cresseid*." *PQ* 52 (1973): 696–714.

Payne, F. Anne. *Chaucer and Menippean Satire.* Madison: University of Wisconsin Press, 1981.

Pearl. Edited by E. V. Gordon. Oxford: Oxford University Press, 1953.

Pearsall, Derek. "Gower's Narrative Art." *PMLA* 81 (1966): 475–84.

Peck, Russell A. *Kingship and Common Profit in Gower's* Confessio Amantis. Carbondale: Southern Illinois University Press, 1978.

———. "Theme and Number in Chaucer's *Book of the Duchess*." In Alastair Fowler, ed. *Essays in Numerological Analysis.* London: Routledge and Kegan Paul, 1970, pp. 73–115.

———, ed. *Confessio Amantis.* New York: Holt, Rinehart and Winston, 1968.

Piehler, Paul. *The Visionary Landscape: A Study in Medieval Allegory.* London: Edward Arnold, 1971.

Preston, John. "Fortunys Exiltree: A Study of *The Kingis Quair*." *RES*, n.s., 7 (1956): 239–47.

Quilligan, Maureen. *The Language of Allegory: Defining the Genre.* Ithaca, N.Y.: Cornell University Press, 1979.

Raby, F. J. E. *A History of Christian Latin Poetry from the Beginnings to the Close of the Middle Ages.* Oxford: Oxford University Press, 1927.

Rand, E. K. *Founders of the Middle Ages.* Cambridge, Mass.: Harvard University Press, 1927.

———. Review of Fredericus by Klingner. *De Boethii Consolatione Philosophiae. AJP* 44 (1923): 86–87.

Bibliography

Rhorburger, Mary. "*The Kingis Quair*: An Evaluation." *TSLL* 2 (1960): 292–302.

Robertson, D. W., Jr. "The Historical Setting of Chaucer's *Book of the Duchess*." In John Esten Keller and John Mahoney, eds. *Medieval Studies in Honor of Urban Tigner Holmes, Jr.* Chapel Hill: University of North Carolina Press, 1965, pp. 169–95.

———. "The Pearl as Symbol." *MLN* 65 (1950): 155–61. Reprinted in John Conley, ed. *The Middle English* Pearl: *Critical Essays*, pp. 18–26.

———. *A Preface to Chaucer: Studies in Medieval Perspectives.* Princeton, N.J.: Princeton University Press, 1963.

———, and Bernard F. Huppé. *Fruyt and Chaf: Studies in Chaucer's Allegories.* Princeton, N.J.: Princeton University Press, 1963.

Robinson, F. N., ed. *The Works of Geoffrey Chaucer.* 2d ed. Boston: Houghton Mifflin, 1957.

Rockwood, Frank Ernest, ed. *Cicero's Tusculan Disputations, I, and Scipio's Dream.* 1903. Reprint, Norman: University of Oklahoma Press, 1966.

Rollinson, Philip. *Classical Theories of Allegory and Christian Culture.* Pittsburgh: Duquesne University Press, 1981.

Scheps, Walter. "Chaucerian Synthesis: The Art of *The Kingis Quair*." *SSL* 8 (1971): 143–65.

Schmid, W. "Boethius and the Claims of Philosophy." *Studia Patristica* (Berlin) 2 (1957): 368–75.

Schofield, William Henry. "The Nature and Fabric of *The Pearl*." *PMLA* 19 (1904): 154–215.

Schueler, Donald G. "The Age of the Lover in Gower's *Confessio Amantis*." *MÆ* 36 (1967): 152–58.

———. "Gower's Characterization of Genius in the *Confessio Amantis*." *MLQ* 33 (1972): 240–56.

Seznec, Jean. *The Survival of the Pagan Gods.* Translated by Barbara M. Sessions. New York: Harper & Row, 1953.

Silk, Edmund T. "Boethius' *Consolatio Philosophiae* as a Sequel to Augustine's *Dialogues* and *Soliloquia*." *Harvard Theological Review* 32 (1939): 19–39.

Skelton, John. *Complete Poems.* Edited by John Scattergood. New Haven, Conn.: Yale University Press, 1983.

Sklute, Larry M. "Expectations and Fulfillment in *Pearl*." *PQ* 52 (1973): 663–79.

———. "Phoebus Descending: Rhetoric and Moral Vision in Henryson's *Testament of Cresseid*." *ELH* 44 (1977): 189–204.

Spearing, A. C. "Conciseness and *The Testament of Cresseid*." In *Criticism and Medieval Poetry.* London: Edward Arnold, 1964.

———. *The Gawain-Poet: A Critical Study*. Cambridge: Cambridge University Press, 1970.

———. *Medieval Dream-Poetry*. Cambridge: Cambridge University Press, 1976.

———. "Symbolic and Dramatic Development in *Pearl*." *MP* 60 (1962): 1–12. Reprinted in John Conley, ed. *The Middle English* Pearl: *Critical Essays*, pp. 122–48; and in Robert J. Blanch, ed. Sir Gawain *and* Pearl: *Critical Essays*, pp. 98–119.

Stearns, Marshall W. "Chaucer Mentions a Book." *MLN* 57 (1942): 28–31.

———. *Robert Henryson*. New York: Columbia University Press, 1949.

Stern, Milton R. "An Approach to the *Pearl*." *JEGP* 54 (1955): 684–92. Reprinted in John Conley, ed. *The Middle English* Pearl: *Critical Essays*, pp. 73–85.

Stewart H. F. *Boethius: An Essay*. Edinburgh: W. Blackwood & Sons, 1891.

Stone, Donald Jr. "Old and New Thoughts on Guillaume de Lorris. *AJFS* 2 (1965): 157–70.

Strohm, Paul. "Guillaume as Narrator and Lover in the *Roman de la Rose*." *RomR* 59 (1968): 3–9.

Tatlock, J. S. P. *The Mind and Art of Chaucer*. Syracuse, N.Y.: Syracuse University Press, 1950.

Tillyard, W. M. W. *Five Poems: 1470–1870*. London: Chatto and Windus, 1948.

Tisdale, Charles P. R. "Boethian 'Hert-Huntyng': The Elegiac Pattern of *The Book of the Duchess*." *ABR* 24 (1973): 365–80.

Tuve, Rosamond. *Allegorical Imagery: Some Mediaeval Books and Their Posterity*. Princeton, N.J.: Princeton University Press, 1966.

Uphaus, Robert W. "Chaucer's *Parlement of Foules*: Aesthetic Order and Individual Experience." *TSLL* 10 (1968): 349–58.

Vasta, Edward. "*Pearl*: Immortal Flowers and the Pearl's Decay." *JEGP* 66 (1967): 519–31. Reprinted in John Conley, ed. *The Middle English* Pearl: *Critical Essays*, pp. 185–202.

Wellek, René. "The *Pearl*: An Interpretation of the Middle English Poem." *Studies in English by Members of the English Seminar of Charles University* (Prague) 4 (1933): 5–33. Reprinted in Robert J. Blanch, ed. Sir Gawain *and* Pearl: *Critical Essays*, pp. 3–36.

———, and Austin Warren. *Theory of Literature*. 3d ed. New York: Harcourt Brace Jovanovich, 1977. First published 1942.

Wetherbee, Winthrop. "The Function of Poetry in the *De planctu naturae* of Alain de Lille." *Traditio* 25 (1969): 87–125.

———. "The Literal and the Allegorical: Jean de Meun and the *De planctu naturae*." *MS* 33 (1971): 264–91.

———. *Platonism and Poetry in the Twelfth Century: The Literary Influence*

Bibliography

of the School of Chartres. Princeton, N.J.: Princeton University Press, 1972.

Whitbread, Leslie George, trans. *Fulgentius the Mythographer.* Columbus: Ohio State University Press, 1971.

Wiltshire, Susan Ford. "Boethius and the *Summum Bonum.*" *CJ* 67 (1972): 216–20.

Wimsatt, James I. "The Apotheosis of Blanche in *The Book of the Duchess.*" *JEGP* 66 (1967): 26–44.

————. *Chaucer and the French Love Poets: The Literary Background of the Book of the Duchess.* Chapel Hill: University of North Carolina Press, 1968.

————. "The Sources of Chaucer's 'Seys and Alcyone.'" *MÆ* 36 (1967): 231–41.

Wright, Thomas, ed. *The Anglo-Latin Satirical Poets and Epigrammatists of the Twelfth Century.* Rolls Series, vol. 59, no. 2. London: Longman, 1872.

INDEX

267

Index

Index